IT'S
ALL NEWS
TO ME

Jeremy Vine

**SIMON &
SCHUSTER**

London · New York · Sydney · Toronto · New Delhi

A CBS COMPANY

First published in Great Britain by Simon & Schuster UK Ltd, 2012
A CBS COMPANY

Simon & Schuster UK Ltd
1st Floor
222 Gray's Inn Road
London
WC1X 8HB

www.simonandschuster.co.uk

Simon & Schuster Australia, Sydney
Simon & Schuster India, New Delhi

A CIP catalogue record for this book is available
from the British Library

ISBN: 978-1-84983-776-7

Typeset by M Rules
Printed and bound by CPI Group (UK) Ltd, Croydon, CR0 4YY

For Rachel

CONTENTS

'No. It is in the control of four families.'

Spokeswoman for Naples police, 1994, responding to my question:
'Is crime in this city completely out of control?'

Chapter One

THAT BIGOTED WOMAN

A loaf of bread. A pensioner in Rochdale. A stressed-out assistant to an equally stressed-out prime minister. Random voters. A local MP. A presenter. A studio. A camera. A radio show . . .

How do you put all those items together to make an election car crash?

It is something that has often crossed my mind since the moment Gordon Brown put his head in his hands on my show and seemed – to those who saw it – to signal the defining low as Labour crashed from power after thirteen years. It was also a defining moment for my Radio 2 programme, although it remains slightly vexing that the most memorable few seconds in the recent history of my radio show are only remembered because they went out on television.

But what force is it that puts together all those items? As a broadcaster you wonder about this the whole time. What is the difference between all the interviews you forget, and the one nobody *ever* forgets?

A special kind of jeopardy attaches itself to people in politics and broadcasting. Good luck, for sure – but an abrasive brand of bad luck, too. That morning, as I prepared my show with the producers,

I had no idea it would hinge on the realization by a pensioner in Rochdale that she was out of bread. Gillian Duffy and I would meet in person, several months down the line; what a gem she turned out to be. But for now Mrs Duffy was just an ordinary voter on a mission. The mission was not anything as dramatic as humbling a prime minister. The mission was to buy that sliced white loaf.

It is very rare for anything out of the ordinary to happen in interviews these days. As broadcasters have improved their skills with the rapier, politicians have started lugging huge shields into the arena. They are massively on guard. Their career can end with literally one word – quite a thought. They behave as if you are trying to help them end it, whereas in fact the interviewer just wants enough of the guard down to allow some of the truth out.

But when it goes wrong for them it can be catastrophic. Some say the 2010 general election turned on that single moment involving Gordon Brown and Gillian Duffy.

The sequence of events was like an episode of *24*, where every new development had a camera trained on it. Brown had a conversation in Rochdale with Mrs Duffy. During one of his walkabouts she had confronted him firmly but politely, among other things raising her complaint about immigration – Eastern Europeans were 'flocking' here, she insisted.

On the surface the Prime Minister was extremely nice to the pensioner, saying 'Good woman, good family', but apparently he misheard the word 'flocking' and thought she had said a quite different word beginning with 'F'. So when he climbed into his car, the PM's attitude changed completely. He told an aide she was 'a sort of bigoted woman' and blamed an assistant called Sue for the 'disaster'. Unknown to Brown, he was still wearing a Sky microphone in the car and their camera captured the exchange.

What is interesting, looking back, is that if you watch the original encounter between Brown and Duffy there was nothing in it to justify him thinking it was disastrous. Even with the wrong F-word, it still would not have been that bad. Duffy is the type of salt-of-the-earth voter who will give as good as she gets while remaining courteous, and most politicians enjoy themselves in that kind of encounter.

Not Gordon Brown. Although I have always found him likeable when spending time with him, he does not laugh easily. If you try to picture Brown watching, say, a Michael McIntyre DVD and roaring with laughter, you will find it impossible to do. His brainpower is immense, but somehow the simple act of smiling has become too complicated to master. Gillian Duffy had inflated one of the big black rainclouds in his head.

I have to add a rider. I am the patron of a charity called Hope HIV, which helps African orphans. The organizers asked once if I could enquire about holding a reception in Downing Street. I contacted Sarah Brown, whom I knew a little, and she was more than willing. Brown was Chancellor at the time, and I did not expect him even to know about the event. Yet he turned up, spent time talking individually to us all and even made a speech. When I pointed out a photo of the site of one of the projects, which was essentially just an arid field, he said: 'Isn't that Malawi? It looks like Malawi.' It wasn't – it could have been anywhere – but he had the wide-eyed interest of a child when it came to Africa. All this impartial journalist can tell you is that it was a side of him that looked much more real and much more human too.

So, back to the car and the Sky microphone.

It records him saying that Gillian Duffy is a bigot, and all hell breaks loose.

The Sky people take the tape to their van and play it to Duffy. Her reaction – where she gasps, and her jaw drops below her hemline – reflects even more badly on Brown. He has been rude about a sweet pensioner who said nothing unpleasant to him (it really was 'flocking') and, this being an election, the story will go stratospheric because that is what every story does in an election.

By sheer coincidence, that day I was due to interview Brown.

A week earlier we had been told by Labour that he would be in our Manchester studio, with me in London. I was not terribly happy about this, because interviewing is a contact sport. Doing it down the line is like fencing by telephone. I had asked if we could 'at least put a webcam in the Manchester studio' – just so I could see him and he could see me?

No, Labour said, absolutely no cameras.

Which made what followed utterly puzzling to me.

As Radio 2's big election interview with the PM began, I did not know anything about the Duffy business. I'm in London, he's in Manchester. Our agenda is the banks. Why were they allowed to get in a position where they almost took the country off the cliff with them? Who, by the way, had been Chancellor at the time?

As I go through our pages of carefully prepared questions, my editor Phil Jones says to me in my headphones, 'He's been rude to a pensioner in Rochdale. I'll get the details.'

We forge ahead with the economy, the banks, the uselessness of the Financial Services Authority. Then the editor says, in my head-phones, 'Her name is Gillian Duffy. He called her a bigot.' He brings in a single line of copy from a news agency.

At this point we are twenty minutes into an interview about the financial crisis, not that anyone remembers that. I say to the PM, 'Can I ask you about something that happened earlier? You were speaking to a pensioner in Rochdale. Apparently a microphone picked you up saying, "That was a very bigoted woman." Is that what you said?'

His reply hints at the confusion he is still in over the use of the word flocking:

> *Brown:* I apologize if I've said anything like that. What I think she was raising with me was an issue about immigration and saying there were too many, er, um, er, people from eastern Europe in the country. And I do apologize if I've said anything that has been hurtful and I will apologize to her personally.

It was the evasion of a one-legged scrum half, the kind of lumpen sidestep that signals to an interviewer that it is worth pressing on.

At that very moment on a computer screen in front of me, up pops a new bit of audio labelled 'Duffy Bigot Clip'.

I had no idea we were anywhere near getting the clip, and one expects the BBC process involved in clearing a piece of effectively surreptitiously recorded audio to take months rather than minutes, so credit to the two executives who moved it across their desks faster than a greased ice cube. I was probably as shocked as Brown when I said: 'Someone has just handed me the tape, let's play it and see if we can hear it.'

We both listen to the PM recorded in the back of his car by a Sky microphone:

Brown: *You should never have put me with that woman. Whose idea was that?*

Aide: *I don't know, I didn't see.*

Brown: *That's Sue I think. It's just ridiculous.*

Aide: *I'm not sure they'll go with that one.*

Brown: *They will go with it.*

Aide: *What did she say?*

Brown: *Everything! She's just a sort of bigoted woman. Said she used to be Labour. It's just ridiculous . . .*

At that moment the transmitter in the microphone moved out of range of the camera and static broke across the conversation. The tape ended and, now that both Brown and I had heard it for the first time, I had to ask a question into the silence. This was the exchange that followed.

Vine: That is what you said. Is she not allowed to express her opinion to you, or what?

Brown: Of course she's allowed to express her opinion and I was saying that! The problem was that I was dealing with a question she raised about immigration and I wasn't given a chance to answer it because we had a whole melee of press around her, but of course I apologize if I have said anything that is . . . that has been offensive, and I would never want to put myself in a position where I want to say anything like that about a woman I met. It was a question about immigration, that really I think was annoying.

Vine: And you're blaming a member of your staff there. Sue, is it, or—

Brown: No, I'm blaming myself! I blame myself for what is done. But you've got to remember, this was me being helpful to the broadcasters, with my microphone on. Rushing into the car because I had to get to another appointment. And they have chosen to play my private conversation with the person who was in the car with me. Er, I know these things can happen, I apologize to the lady concerned, I don't think she is . . . that. I think it was just the view that she expressed that I was worried about, that I couldn't respond to.

He is winded, I can hear that. We end on a point about hung parliaments. I say goodbye and play a record.

Then I go out to the control room on the other side of the glass, where all the technical equipment and the producers are. I say, 'God, that was all a bit unusual.'

Phil Jones is looking up, dazed, at the TV screen in the corner. 'You'll never guess what. That whole thing just went out on TV.'

'Eh?' My eyes widen.

He explains, 'Yeah, as he hears the tape, he sort of slumps back in his chair and then falls forwards with his head in his hands.'

It turned out to be the image of the general election. It was even picked up by *The Daily Show* in America where the host Jon Stewart said, 'You can actually see the moment a man's political career leaves his body – booooosh.' The clip got 500,000 hits online on the first day.

But the funny thing is, I could not find out how it happened. Someone put a camera in the control room at Manchester. The Labour aides who rushed into the room were possibly too distracted and too late to see it (I even heard there had been two cameras – they were cross about one, had it removed, and failed to see the other). Not only was the camera turned on, which is an achievement in an organization where anything that can go wrong usually does, but it was plugged into the wall. So the pictures could be patched live into any television coverage. They duly were. Across all channels.

As it happens, I never have the televisions on in my radio studio. It is too distracting. There is one in the control room next door – when people on work experience sit in, I can tell if they really want a job on the radio by whether they spend the whole time gazing up at the television. So I did not see the live broadcast.

It was hard not to feel sorry for Brown. Many listeners did. If the microphone had been switched on when he used the loo, would Sky and the Beeb have broadcast that too? Obviously not, but where is the line? Vince Cable was recorded in his constituency surgery by two reporters from the *Daily Telegraph* posing as giggly mums – he told them he had the 'nuclear option' of resigning and had 'declared war' on Rupert Murdoch. Did he have the right to expect the words would not go outside the room, or does he lose that right when his words become politically significant? Brown was rude about a pensioner he had pretended to like. Is *that* politically significant, because it makes him look two-faced? Or is it only significant because it is a general election campaign and even a speck of soup on a party leader's tie has meaning? Okay, but then do you replay those noises from the lavatory?

Any logic that ends up with a 'yes' to that last question clearly needs rethinking.

But the best question of the lot is – *What about the camera?* Where on earth had it come from? Peter Mandelson had reportedly texted Brown during the interview with the message 'YOU'RE ON TV'. So how had it happened? Why had Labour's veto not applied to that camera?

The following week, just before general election day, I had a kind of answer to my questions. I met a fellow in the election night studio, where I was trying out the swingometer ready for the results programme with David Dimbleby. The colleague's title was something like BBC Deputy Head of Premises Operations Facilities Management. I asked him, 'Were we allowed to have that camera in there?'

Confidently he said, 'Oh yeah, filming on BBC premises, that's completely allowed.'

I said, 'How long has that been a rule?'

He replied, 'About eight days.'

*

More than a year after the event I finally discovered that a producer in Manchester called Claire Gibson was the person on the scene who had insisted that Brown's people should allow the camera in: she will go far. Meanwhile, I can't imagine a chain of events that better demonstrates what broadcasting is about. You can be as professional as you like, but in the end most of it comes down to chance. Good luck and bad luck are the two things no one can plan for. Thousands of students pour out of media studies courses every year, and I bet nobody told them the most important fact of all – you have to be lucky. And sometimes you will do everything by the book, and bad luck will wipe it all out in a second.

Did anyone ever tell Mr Brown that?

No one told me, that's for sure.

Chapter Two

THE IMPORTANCE OF HUMILIATION

I am clocking up the quarter century. That's why I am writing this book. The new Radio 2 staff kettle moaned and I realized. I was staring at that kettle – a shade of distressed green with a lime-encrusted spout – thinking it was taking an improbably long time to show any signs of getting hotter.

'I'd settle for a hint of steam,' I joked to a colleague who walked in. 'Is this the only organization in the world that can source a kettle that doesn't work? I think I first hit the "on" button the day I joined the BBC.'

Displaying the uncommon ability of journalists to miss the point, he asked: 'When was that?'

And so I told him. Way back. The day was so auspicious it even had a name: Black Monday, 1987. Using the famous trick with the word 'after' that news writers have employed for a hundred years, I always make it sound more exciting than it really was. 'Yeah, stock markets suffered the biggest one-day fall in history after I walked into Broadcasting House for the first time.' (The classic example of the genre, which I am still sure I heard: 'The Russians invaded Afghanistan after Daley Thompson won a gold at the Moscow Olympics.')

I need not tell you the events were unrelated. It was sheer chance that my broadcasting career started on 19 October, the same day as the stock market crash.

After beginning my apprenticeship on the *Coventry Evening Telegraph* in 1986 I had been appointed a BBC news trainee, one of a dozen supposedly elite entrants picked from twelve thousand. The dozen were split into two groups, one starting in October and one the following April. We were the mysterious-sounding October Group. The door of the room we assembled in had a big sign on it which said *JOURNALISTS TRAINING,* and I used to look at that sign, certain there was an apostrophe missing but never sufficiently confident to say so. The October Group were all given to understand we would be promoted rapidly to director-general.

Surfacing at Oxford Circus tube in London each day, I approached the majestic outline of Broadcasting House. It looks like an ocean liner that has taken a wrong turning and run aground in pavement. Aged twenty-two, I walked stoically, self-consciously, burdened with a sense of history, piercingly aware that I should be in a state of battle-readiness for the Big Career. I had a head full of ideas. Or maybe just a full head of hair.

And my new employer sprang wonderful surprises.

One morning the new trainees arrived to find a strip of plastic crime scene tape stretched across the front of the building. Some kind of police cordon had been thrown up.

It turned out an enraged woman had entered Broadcasting House with a grudge. She believed that transmissions from the mast on top of the building were interfering with her brain (she was a Radio 4 listener, so she was probably right). She began running in circles around the art deco reception area and screaming. The commissionaires were burly lifers with staff numbers and final salary pensions in those days, so they would have taken their time to close in on her, just to be sure her capture was of the highest possible quality.

Unfortunately she was not only bearing a grudge. She also had a pistol in her bag. Pulling out the gun, she fired. Early reports said the shot hit a commissionaire in the hand, but luckily she had only discharged blanks.

So that morning, the front of the building was taped off by investigating officers.

Years later, reporting from Moscow, I was told a famous Russian joke by an earnest translator called Sasha which brought the commissionaire incident to mind:

> A Swedish tourist falls into a hole in the street. Local Russians pull him out. When he emerges he asks them, 'Why were there no red flags around this hole to warn people of the danger?'
>
> 'You saw the red flags at the airport,' say the Russians. 'They are for the whole country.'

I saw the crime scene tape across the front of Broadcasting House. I should have known: it was for the whole organization.

*

So. I am writing this book because I have now spent more than half my life inside those buildings. They're your buildings really, so you ought to know what goes on in them. You might even want to know what goes on inside the heads of the people inside the buildings. Blimey – now I think about it, someone reading this might be twenty-two and starting out on their own broadcasting career. So if I give you an exhaustive list of all my mistakes, you can ensure you make more interesting ones. I gather I am the youngest person ever to present the *Today* programme, but also the only journalist to have worn a cowboy hat on an election programme. I have been shot at, robbed, stalked, threatened with a bombing, mortared, mortified,

screamed at by the Prime Minister's press secretary, been in a car
that skidded off the road and sailed over an embankment in Croatia,
got bitten by Sudanese mosquitoes, attacked with a plank of wood
by a neo-Nazi shopkeeper and also had chewing gum placed on my
chair by one of Robert Mugabe's aides. Peter Mandelson once told
me, just outside the doors to the House of Commons, 'You are the
only person in Britain who wants to be on television more than I do.'
Unhappily, I worked so hard for the first part of my career that I lost
a girlfriend I was in love with and a wife who couldn't quite get me
to grasp that life included some stuff that happened outside broadcast studios. I joined the BBC at twenty-two and am now
forty-seven. Although you and I might surmise that this means I am
at the halfway point in my career, I have to tell you that is not how
broadcasting works. It is an inherently unstable and dangerous profession, only slightly more predictable than lion-taming, as random
as bull-fighting and less fair than whaling.

A BBC career involves heightened peril on all fronts because of
the way the corporation's private parts are permanently stretched
across a public guillotine. I have seen the blade drop many times and
felt the whoosh of razor-sharp metal just miss me. Does it have to be
that way? It doesn't matter. It just is.

*

As with any profession, there are rules. In fact we should make sure
we emphasize their importance with a capital letter: there are Rules.
There are Rules for broadcasting and there are Rules for the BBC in
particular. Occasionally we will stumble on one as we go through
the book together, and I will italicize it as a lesson learnt. But if you
boil down all the Rules to one simple sentence it would read like
this:

*No matter how important you think you are, you are not very
important.*

The deranged woman with the pistol was not the most alarming feature of my first weeks at the BBC.

For all six trainees the most alarming thing was this: we did not matter at all. We mattered less than the fluff on the floor. This thought was far more threatening than a person in reception with a gun. None of us was worth a cent. We mattered so little we anti-mattered. If our group had not shown up for a year the BBC would quite possibly not have noticed or cared, unless there was a large bloodstain. Joining the world's greatest broadcaster was like arriving in space. All that happened was that we became conscious of our microscopic smallness in the universe; no one would even have heard us scream. We had rolled up in an organization the size of a small country in the expectation that we would be fed with royal jelly and marched straight to the suite of offices marked 'DG' to choose a new shade of leather, but as it turned out we were less significant than a discarded fragment of croissant in the sixth floor canteen.

Yet this lesson was to be the most important we would learn on the entire traineeship.

The legendary John Sergeant, who worked as a political journalist before embarking on the more serious part of his career as a ballroom dancer, understood the principle completely. He was my superior when I worked as a lobby correspondent in the Westminster unit, and was the closest the building had to a celebrity after a famous broadcast outside the Paris Embassy as Mrs Thatcher was toppled in 1990. Sergeant was speaking to the camera; Thatcher appeared over his shoulder to announce she would go on fighting to keep her job; the newscaster in London called, 'She's behind you, John!' and millions watched the veteran Sergeant barge into the melee of younger reporters with the immortal line, '*This* is the microphone, Mrs Thatcher, *this* is the microphone.'

So when Sergeant spoke, we all paid careful attention. One day he took me on one side to indicate that he felt his immediate boss, the political editor Robin Oakley, might be sacked without warning.

Very quietly he told me, 'The people at the top of the BBC don't have very much power, so when they act, it tends to be very violent.'

As he said the word 'violent' he covered his mouth with his hand, presumably to ensure colleagues in other parts of the building could not lip-read him. The effect was of such *Godfather*-esque menace that the hairs stood up all the way down my back. Ten months later, the political editor – whose main duty, remember, is to assess the threat to other people's jobs – was indeed bounced out of his post without warning and replaced by Andrew Marr, after being summoned for a meeting in the bedroom of an exclusive hotel where Robin presumably imagined the praise heaped on him by his line managers would simply be repeated in a more unusual setting.

(Note to self: if, at any point in the future, a manager asks you to attend a meeting in a hotel room, accept the invitation but do not go. The more exclusive the hotel the more risky it is to attend the meeting. Only go if it is a Premier Inn.)

I saved gems from John Sergeant. Actually wrote them down. For example, I did once immodestly point out to him that I was the youngest person ever to present *Today* on Radio 4 – have I mentioned this yet? – albeit because the sudden illness of one of the presenters caught the rota manager short. Sergeant's reply could have gone into a picture frame on any office wall: 'You don't want to be the youngest, Jeremy. You want to be the oldest.'

In a way, Robin Oakley's defenestration was symbolic of all broadcasting: it always ends with broken glass. For Robin the updraft from being BBC political editor – one of the great offices of state, after all – was disrupted by constant turbulence. In a notorious moment at Westminster, Oakley found himself totally lost for words during a live TV interview with the newscaster Michael Buerk. This has happened to me and I swear it is a more terrifying experience than being savaged by a Japanese Tosa. Buerk did not step in to help for a full five seconds. Time on air is measured differently – five seconds of silence on live television is equivalent to two months in the world outside. A shattered Oakley set off back from College Green, opposite Parliament, to be met by Sergeant, who was coming from the office.

Wearing an expression that suggested he was suffering terrible pain over the incident himself, Sergeant told Oakley: 'Don't worry, Robin. We've all *nearly* done that.'

The remark, overheard by a third party and immediately recognized as a classic of the support-sabotage variety, went round the entire BBC in half a day.

Mind you, I was occasionally a victim of the same craftsmanship. An editor warned me to watch out because Sergeant had been heard praising my television packages, and my suspicions were confirmed when I pinned the colleague down on John's exact wording: 'Jeremy's scripts are so good, sometimes you wonder if the story even matters.'

Another time I learnt he had observed, 'Vine is excellent; *his sense of judgement will come.*' Only the second half counted, obviously.

After a mistake in one of my television reports on a weekend bulletin triggered an angry fusillade from the Liberal Democrat leader Paddy Ashdown, Sergeant helpfully rang the other correspondents to brief them. 'You need to know – there's been a row. Paddy's gone into full SAS mode. Yes,' he told them wearily, 'I'm afraid it's Jeremy again.'

Eventually John Sergeant – known fondly to all of us as Sargie – left to become political editor at ITN. His farewell party at the Reform Club was one of the BBC's most uproarious. A character of truly Shakespearian proportions whose appearances on *Strictly Come Dancing* confirmed comic genius as yet another weapon in his armoury, he outlived, outsmarted and eventually outranked all of his enemies. I tried to learn everything I could by observing him, but I struggled to keep pace.

The BBC Westminster unit was certainly the place to get streetwise. I was there from 1993 to 1997, a beneficiary of John Major's unintended job creation initiative for political correspondents. The team of 'pol-corrs', as we were termed across the Beeb, contained not just Sergeant and Oakley but Huw Edwards, Nick Robinson, Jon Sopel, Carolyn Quinn, John Pienaar, Ric Bailey, Steve Richards, Lance Price, Carole Walker, Nick Jones and Mark Mardell. If pressed we would probably admit we thought we were red hot. But the unit was a stew of Machiavellian intrigue, more so than any of the political parties we were supposed to be reporting on.

The second most dangerous incident of my time at Westminster came when a Fiat Panda cruised through a zebra crossing, running over the tip of my shoe and coming within an inch of the rest of me. The most dangerous incident by far was when a long and flattering piece in *The Times* suggested that either I or Jon Sopel would be the next BBC political editor. It ran alongside two large and rather stately photos of us and took up a whole page of the newspaper. I remember doing a little jig of joy when I saw it, not realizing what the consequences would be.

Unfortunately both Sopel and I had the day off, which meant that by the time we resurfaced in the office we had been comprehensively filleted by colleagues anxious to ensure the article had no credibility. The *Times* piece had given positive mention to Sargie, but did not even contain the name of the talented and self-assured Edwards.

I learnt later that Huw had held an impromptu briefing for my colleagues where he announced: 'I now know for a fact that this article has been very damaging to *all* concerned.' Sopel and I were suspected of planting it. 'The organization does not like this kind of vulgarity,' Huw concluded, with total conviction.

Following him at a suitable distance, Sargie struck a woeful tone, quietly telling everyone who would listen: 'The person I feel most sorry for is Huw. Not even mentioned.'

To avoid the impression that this book is a biography of John Sergeant, I shall move on, save to underline the key point about my former boss: he understood completely that since journalists do not know humility, they benefit from regular humiliation. Nothing is so likely to destroy a broadcaster as the recognition of his or her abilities, so in a way he was helping us survive.

If you aspire to be a famous person on the air, a broadcaster or presenter or newscaster or reporter or whatever, do not expect to become important. Fame just gives angry people a licence to speak to you. Glamour never existed anyway. Embrace humiliation: it is good for the soul. Your parade needs regular rain. It is in your interests to be constantly reminded that you are less important than the story, and the moment will never come when you have truly made it. If you are dizzy enough to decide on a Monday that you have done, the following Thursday you will just begin to worry about losing everything: I guarantee that.

All careers have two phases – the *get* phase and the *keep* phase. Half your career you spend accruing whatever it is you set your heart on. The second half, if you have got what you wanted, you spend all your time worrying about losing it. That is a Rule, too, for the mindset displays itself again and again when I read interviews with distinguished people you would think have nothing left to prove and nothing left to worry about. Nicky Campbell, announcing he was moving to Manchester with Radio 5 live, told a newspaper: 'It is about security of tenure. We are all "here today, gone tomorrow" presenters.' He had previously reflected candidly on the sacking of Jimmy Young. 'The BBC is like that. I'll be the one who is shat on in five years' time. We're under no illusion here. It is a wonderful organization, but a ruthless one.' He was only wrong about the timing – he was 'shat on' one day later for giving the interview.

Even the totally sussed Fiona Bruce, one of my favourite people in the entire organization, airs self-doubt when the chance arises. 'I know there's going to come a point in the not-too-distant future when I will be quietly dropped from something,' she told the *Daily Mail* in 2008. 'There's going to come a time when my face won't fit any more, for whatever reason. When I got the job of presenter on the *Six*, other people were being fired. I got taken in one door and I was hired. Other presenters were going out the other door. I just thought, "That's how it will be for me one day. I will be the last person to find out about it, and, when it does happen, don't get bitter and twisted about it."'

Best of all, in a marvellous aside to top any from a senior figure in the Beeb, the hugely respected world affairs editor John Simpson told an audience at the Cheltenham Literary Festival that the BBC was in its 'last stages' and he hated his bosses. All careers ended with a loathing of management. 'That's what you do,' he explained. 'I shall no doubt be sacked in horrible circumstances.'

I once saw Sir David Frost in the horseshoe car park at Television Centre. Since he was born in 1939, he was close to seventy, and certainly a multi-millionaire. But he was rushing to a meeting about his Sunday programme. 'David,' I said, 'do you never stop?'

'You've got to make hay while the sun shines,' was his urgent reply.

Well, confession time. I am the same. Since I absolutely love doing the lunchtime show on Radio 2, I absolutely worry about it being taken off me. With every day my admiration grows for my predecessor, Sir Jimmy Young, who was forty-four years older than me and fought off all attempts to dislodge him until, with a record twenty-nine years in the chair, he hit the age of eighty-one and his line managers attempted a frontal assault on the studio (we will return to this later). Combining an analysis of everything I know about the current trajectory of the BBC, my own particular assessment of Radio 2's strategic direction, as well as a cold, hard look at my own ability to shield myself against a change in the weather – and passing over the very real chance of something completely unexpected dropping from a blue sky next Wednesday – I calculate that the person who is going to dislodge me from Radio 2 will be graduating from a university course somewhere in the north of England next summer.

It is like the plot from *The Terminator*. I have to find them before the BBC does.

*

And another thing. If you are a broadcaster you must get used to every mistake made at the office being magnified by transmission. In that respect it is very different from, say, librarianship. But the differences do not end there. The potential for embarrassment extends beyond the studio to any place where the broadcaster can be recognized.

Far and away the most excruciating moment of my career came not in front of a camera, but on a train. At the time I was a *Newsnight* presenter, and labouring under the realization that although I was the youngest in the programme's history (that again), I was highly unlikely to become the oldest. Broadcasting is full of cast-iron Rules that have not yet been discovered: *Never join a current affairs programme if someone else is already there with the name Jeremy* is not one anybody had previously brought to my attention. But along with *Never overtake Colin Firth in the Hall of Mirrors* (a Rule I was unaware of until my children caused a hideous breach of protocol at a funfair in Chiswick), and *Do not prod anyone's toast*, which cropped up this morning during a chaotic family breakfast, I would like to think that the Rule of the Maximum Number of Jeremys will stand the test of future generations.

So, the train.

I was heading from London to Hitchin. The occasion was the christening of my godson, James. During the journey I went to use the lavatory for what might be described as a serious purpose. And let this incident be a warning – it was the kind of loo that had button-operated doors.

The button locking system, rolled out in the nineties, joins the long list of developments which no one asked us whether we wanted or not. Had there been a referendum on this, or on the medical advances which have extended everyone's life by ten extra years which they cannot remember, I suspect there would have been massive majorities against.

As everyone now knows, in new models of train toilet the user presses a button to close the door and a button to lock it. The key word here is 'button'. It is not a latch or a bolt or a chain. The locking happens on a silicon chip somewhere; there is nothing mechanical to the process that I could see. You have to place a great deal of trust in that silicon chip.

The door slid closed very slowly. The LOCKED sign lit up.

Three minutes later, while I was in a seated position where the buttons were out of reach on the far wall, I heard the door click unlocked, and then watched as it started to slide slowly open.

Two people at a table on the other side of the carriage looked gently over and quickly back again. At full stretch I hit the button, and the door did close. But with a dismaying lack of urgency.

I wondered how I was going to get back to my seat without actually dying of shame. Could I prise the window open and bale out? It was almost worth trying, just to avoid having to face the other passengers ever again.

There was a consolation. When I finally emerged from the lavatory and walked past the woman who had seen all this, I heard her whisper to her friend, 'Wasn't that ... *Jeremy Paxman*?'

*

Soon after I joined the BBC I was stuck in a queue at reception. An angry man who might have been seventy was at the front, leaning across the desk.

'But – this is *ridiculous!*' I heard him exclaim when I moved round to hear.

The receptionist was not flustered. 'I'm sorry sir, those are the rules.'

'But it's absurd!'

A supervisor arrived to explain.

'Sir, we cannot let you into the building without a pass.'

I was not sure whether to feel sorry for the elderly gentleman, standing there in a beige raincoat and a silver-red moustache, but his next words were a life lesson for everyone who works near a microphone.

'Why won't you let me into the building? I have been broadcasting for *forty years!*'

He did not understand that broadcasting for forty years, or even four hundred, does not mean you will get into the building tomorrow. Listening to the exchange was a sobering experience for the young me. I did not recognize the irate presenter; possibly he was on the books at Radio 3. More importantly, the organization he worked for did not recognize him either, *because he did not have a pass.*

When the man continued, waving desperately at the uniformed men by the turnstile, 'The commissionaires here know me. They all remember my face – for God's sake, ask them', the supervisor responded in a steely tone: 'Sir, as I am sure you'll understand, they are not allowed to remember people's faces.'

The lesson? The receptionist outranks the broadcaster. And this principle extends throughout the Beeb, from top to bottom. There are two very different careers you can have and the firewall between them is never crossed. The BBC divides straight down the middle into the power and the glory.

The people who broadcast – who are airside, you might say – get the glory. They appear in front of microphones, speak with the organization's voice, meet real people and have all the fun. However, while they may appear to be in charge, they have no power whatsoever. They do not hire or fire. They cannot get the air conditioning turned down, and they certainly cannot enter the building without a pass.

On the other side of the dividing wall are the people who can do all of that. But those with the power – producers, editors, receptionists, the clerk in the stores who bought that faulty Radio 2 kettle – are never seen or heard on air.

Among the most powerful are the technicians, the intense and often bearded types who operate the faders, volume controls and transmitters. In radio they are known as studio managers. You must never, *ever* answer back to one of them, because by moving an index finger they can take the whole station off the air, or make you sound like the 'Mash get Smash' men.

When Anne Robinson sat in at lunchtime on Radio 2 a few years back she was, shall we say, as demanding of the staff as you would expect. She had already annoyed the studio managers by referring to one of them as 'the monkey behind the glass'. The following day her SM was Graham Bunce, among the network's most highly decorated.

Anne was wearing her headphones but, to her frustration, there was no sound coming through them.

She looked down at the headphone socket and realized they were not plugged in. Holding the headphone cable in one hand, she waved it at Bunce, asking caustically: 'And am I supposed to plug this in myself?'

He replied, 'It works better if you plug it in the desk.'

This is the beautiful paradox. In an organization of highly visible people, the ones who matter most are those you cannot see. It was never better exemplified than when the controversial John Birt was in charge. Birt was a visionary and might even have been a genius (he reminded me of Steve Jobs in some ways) but he suffered a single, crucial flaw – he was unable to communicate. It was like John the Baptist appearing in Chapter One of the gospels, but instead of making thrilling speeches he starts passing memos around. For most of his years at the helm I knew Birt only from photographs. Despite being arguably the most significant broadcaster in Europe, he barely broadcast a single word himself. He was like a silent movie queen; we did not even know what his voice sounded like.

One day John Birt appeared on the internal ringmain to make an announcement. The screen went blank at the appointed hour, and as we gathered round it in silence a disembodied voice suddenly said one word.

'Hello.'

The director-general, actually speaking! It was a rare moment.

Birt had extraordinary power. The power to shape the entire

organization. In the end producers run the show. But presenters *think* they run the show, and the audience think they are right. These intersecting lines create an atmosphere of unbearable tension.

Because broadcasters tend to get carried away with themselves, they need constant reminding that they do not really matter. Robinson relies on Bunce; the veteran presenter needs ID.

So we have landed, awkwardly, via a headphone socket and John Sergeant and a train toilet, on the first prayer of broadcasting: *Lord, where there is no humility, may you grant humiliation.*

Chapter Three

EVERYONE WANTS SEX

It always amazes me that when a broadcaster writes his or her memoirs, they begin with at least one chapter on their childhood. I always peek at those books in the shop, and think it shows how deluded those on-air types are: *they actually think their childhoods are interesting.* But now I'm writing my own book, I feel I should do at least a couple of paragraphs about where I came from and who was responsible. I will try not to tax your patience ...

In four words? My childhood was fine. To extend the four words to a paragraph, I had a loving mum and loving dad who gave me, my brother Tim and sister Sonya every chance to flourish where we lived in Cheam village, fifteen miles south of Piccadilly Circus.

Actually it was better than fine. My parents were – still are – truly wonderful. They are the least materialistic people I have ever known. To them, the most important thing is showing kindness. Their whole theory of life is that you treat everyone the same, rich or poor, northern or southern, nice or nasty, clever or not-so-clever. They would strike up conversations everywhere: they always returned from family holidays with new friends. People who came to our front door to sell double glazing, encyclopaedias or Jehovah ended up being invited in for the rest of the day. Our young lives revolved around the local church, where Mum and Dad were both so active they probably should have qualified for a Church of England pension. My father was a lecturer at the local technical college; my mum a housewife and, after we all left home, a doctor's receptionist.

I only once in my life felt naked fury – when a team of con artists told Mum and Dad that the roof of their house needed work. You know the scam. They say, 'we were just passing', they go up a ladder, rip off some of your tiles and lead flashing, then say it's worse than they thought and they will need a deposit to start work.

Of course my father believed them. Of course he was marched to a cashpoint and withdrew the £400 they demanded. Of course they drove off and never came back, and the mobile number they left put you through to an electronic howl. And he, being my dad, just thought it was the best story ever. The penalty of seeing the best in people is that you get scammed by roofers. The upside is that you are the only one who can laugh about it afterwards. When I said I would get Trading Standards onto it and write a long newspaper piece exposing the rotters, my mum said: 'Darling, I'm sure they have struggles in their lives too.'

Again and again my parents told their three young children, 'You do what you want in your lives, whatever it is, and we'll support you.' I only discovered the limits to this when, as a student, I told my mum I had seen a job advertised with the satirical magazine *Private Eye,* and might apply. It had been atrocious to a friend of hers from the church, so she told me I was not allowed to.

Fuelled by permission to do anything we wanted except work for *Private Eye,* Tim, Sonya and I plunged into the world with gusto, if not out-and-out naivety. My brother, a creature blessed with quite infuriating levels of talent, became Tim Vine The Comedian. One of the proudest sensations I ever felt was when he won the Best Joke Award at the 2010 Edinburgh Fringe, for: 'I went on a once-in-a-lifetime holiday. I tell you what, never again.' (The next day, he appeared on the *Today* programme and when the colleague interviewing him said: 'It's amusing – but really, the best joke of the Fringe?' I felt that roofer-anger for only the second time.)

My bro has written more than a thousand one-liners that I now seem to hear people retelling everywhere: 'My best friend dreamt of being run over by a steam train. When it happened, he was chuffed to bits' . . . 'Police have said the thief stealing T-shirts in order of size is still at Large' . . . but on reflection I think I'd better spare you the other 997, because when I tell Tim's jokes I seem to massacre them.

My beautiful sister is the youngest, born in 1970. She works as an actress, artist and mum. If Tim or I ever have a crisis, we always take refuge with Sonya. She is the one with her head screwed on and her heart in the right place.

People sometimes say to me, 'You're on the TV. Your sister acts. Your brother's on stage. How did that happen?' And the only possible answer I can give is that Dr Guy and Mrs Diana Vine gave their three children so much love that when we went out into the world beyond Cheam we looked to replace it with wider appreciation. Either that, or sheer coincidence.

What else?

I was beaten with a cane on my last day at school for dressing up as a pantomime cow and charging past the final assembly of term. I was the front of the cow. My friend Mark Reading was the rear. Evidently the incident inspired him to look for a career where he could be inside the back half of cows on a more regular basis, because he later became an eminent vet.

As Mark and I tried to lumber off across the playing fields the cow-head slipped, so the teacher who ran out to accost us came into view only at the outer edge of my right eye-slit. The housemaster had almost been prevented from reaching us because all the doors of the building where the assembly was taking place had been locked by a co-conspirator whose name was Tony Fernandes. He later introduced cheap air travel to Asia, bought QPR Football Club, a global hotel chain and the Lotus F1 team, but that is how Tony's career in management started, by locking those doors. Mark

Reading heroically told the teacher the caning should be applied to his bottom only and not to mine, as he had been in the rear end of the costume. The offer was turned down.

Six strokes, since you ask. And . . . yes. It did. Quite a lot actually.

Anyway, with the exception of one extraordinary incident from my teenage years – which we will come to later – there really is no need to bother you with any more scenes from my childhood. I shall sum the whole period up in one word: Cheam.

Similarly, I have tried to frontload the big stuff in this book so we get to it quickly. As a result, the most important revelation I can give you about journalism is contained in this chapter. So when you get to page 33 you can shelve the book or take it back for a refund, while still being confident that you will know all there is to know about my early years and the most significant discovery of my career.

I spent twenty-five years working this out, and it is yours in thirty-three pages.

In journalism you discover stuff all the time. That is the joy of it. The first thing I found out was that everyone wants sex.

It was 1986, halfway through Mrs Thatcher's premiership, and I had arrived in Coventry to commence training at the *Evening Telegraph.*

This was still during the golden age for newspapers. The *Coventry Evening Telegraph* took three trainees each year and incredibly they appointed me despite my having never been to the city before. I had not helped my case when a fire alarm went off during the job interview, causing an evacuation which I took as a cue to go shopping. When they finally located me and asked where on earth I had gone, I realized the trouble I was in and said I was trying to investigate the source of the fire.

The joys of working as a *Coventry Evening Telegraph* reporter in 1986 were so manifold that I feel my heart beat slightly quicker as I picture them.

We used manual typewriters, creating second and third copies by feeding triple-sheet carbon paper through the roller. Yanking the carriage return made a ratchet noise as satisfying as pulling the handle on a Las Vegas fruit machine. I remember one bright summer day when so many typewriters were being pounded and yanked so furiously by so many writers that it sounded like the office had burst into metallic song; if the newsroom had been a church the lame would have picked up their mats and started dancing.

As a trainee I was given very particular instructions. If my story ran for more than about twelve inches on the paper, I should type *mf* – more follows – then rip the page free using the serrated edge at the back of the machine and continue. When my copy was done I had to impale the bottom sheet, which was pink, on a spike beside my typewriter. Then the other two, which were green and white, I must take to the newsdesk. At this point I would be ritually humiliated by the deputy news editor Geoff Grimmer, who would complain about almost every line I had written.

During my first week I was sent to the Crown Court to cover the prosecution of a local man who had run up to a woman in the park and shouted, 'I want sex.' She pulled one of her shoes off and managed to beat him away.

Confident this was a story I could not mess up, I rushed back to the office and banged out the all-important first paragraph:

> A Coventry court heard today how
> a man ran up to a woman in a park
> and shouted: 'I want sex.'

I typed the rest of the story with enthusiasm, spiked the pink sheets and took the rest to the terrifying Grimmer.

To my surprise he read the opening sentence and put a thick red line through it.

'No, that's not a story,' he said firmly, 'because everyone wants sex.'

He told me the story was that she fought him off with a shoe. I should rewrite my account with footwear as the top line. In that brief exchange I must have been exposed to some kind of cosmic truth of journalism, for I have never forgotten it and never will: *Everyone wants sex.*

On another occasion I was sent to the train station to speak to a group of students, dressed as bears, who were raising money for the local children's ward. I asked them every single question I could think of – their names, why they were doing it, how much they were trying to raise, the hospital name and location and even the ward number – but when I returned with the story Grimmer asked me, 'Why were they dressed as bears?'

When I said I didn't know, he sent me back to the station to ask them.

He is dead now, Geoff. But if he is reading this somewhere I would like to thank him for being the greatest tutor I ever had, and apologize again for my paragraphing, syntax, grammar, lack of clarity, spelling, shorthand, clothes, background, haircut, hairstyle, hair colour, accent, as well as the copy I once submitted which broke the most basic tenets of local journalism: not only was the surname of the principal character spelt wrong, his first name mysteriously changed from Arnold to Albert halfway through. Grimmer was so overwhelmed by this error he could not speak to me for several days.

The only time I made him laugh was when he upbraided me for missing the point of yet another story and I gravely replied, 'Lessons have been learnt.' Eventually he regained his composure and said, equally seriously: 'I should hope so.' At that moment I knew he accepted me. The exchange of my copy for his advice three or four times daily brought to mind the much-quoted Bill Shankly line: it was not a matter of life and death. It was much more important than that.

Once Grimmer had his two sheets, he would spike the green, walk to the sub-editors across the office and hand over the white one. Yes, I know, the technology was pretty basic back then – he actually walked the copy across the room *using his legs*. Smoking copiously, the subs used thick pencils to cover my copy in some kind of code (I always assumed it meant, 'This one's the tosser from Cheam.') They then rolled up the annotated copy and, amazingly, inserted it into a plastic tube at the end of their desks that sucked the article up and over their heads to the other side of the building where the typesetters would go to work with tiny bits of metal. The suction tube was the closest thing we had to an innovation, and I was quite confident the newspaper industry was not going to be shaken up by it.

What else? Oh, so many things. And I list them for a simple and very important reason: they are gone now. If I close my eyes and go back to that newsroom, I can feel the room shake and sing with the very physical business of banging out news. I can recapture the smell of fresh ink and 170 armpits. I can remember learning Pitman shorthand and eventually reaching the same speed as my own hand-writing. Please forgive me if I sound nostalgic – I am, and for painful reasons. It is nearly all gone.

Whenever a fire engine raced past, the deputy news editor shouted: 'They're playing our tune.' We received majestical weekly memos from the editor, a godlike persona called Geoffrey Elliott, on points of style. One read, 'Do not use the words "incident" or "situation", for they have no meaning' (my producers were baffled when I repeated this edict at Radio 2). Elliott would definitely have corrected 'majestical', too.

On the front of the building the words COVENTRY EVENING TELEGRAPH were bolted to the wall in a Frankenstein-Gothic font which spoke of 100 years of civic history and at least 1,000 more to come. Walking out below those letters day after day to find stories, carrying the classic toolkit of reporter's pad plus chewed biro, I crossed the paths of many people whose paths I would never other-wise have crossed, people in poverty or in mourning; people who had been in accidents – never incidents – or whose lives had been suddenly changed by luck or disaster. Turning up at a council house that had been burnt down or a shop robbed, meeting someone whose entire existence had been randomly dashed against the rocks at twenty past ten on an ordinary morning, I often murmured to myself, 'Other lives.' And in essence that is journalism: discovering the other. Because a local newspaper is the only show in town, every story in it is a scoop. Which makes working there the purest and rawest and truest form of reporting.

Print journalists loathe broadcasters, because they cannot take seriously anyone who packs hairspray for an assignment. I once heard a features writer at Coventry say there should be a law preventing people with no background in newspapers from describing themselves as journalists. At the time that made perfect sense to me. Journalism was *ink*. Back then, the *Evening Telegraph* had final salary pensions, a personnel officer called Tom Duckett (he always answered the phone in throaty Brum: 'Doockett-ear'), and the budget to more than do its job, with sprawling features, sports and business desks in an editorial team of eighty-five.

It is now down to fifteen.

One day in 1987, not long before I left Coventry for the BBC, I descended the stone staircase at speed and because I was not looking where I was going I tripped over some large boxes in reception.

Looking more closely, I saw it was a delivery of computers. Computers? Well, I supposed they might be a good idea. They would allow us to type more quickly. The paper would have more stories and sell more copies. It might even publish in colour. Maybe the editor would take on five trainees a year instead of three.

More than two decades later, we know what disaster those machines spelt. It would have been fine if only the newspaper got computers, but sadly the readers did too. Their technology allowed them to look elsewhere for news, and advertisers followed. Buying freshly inked paper just off the press from a bloke with a shouty voice on a street corner suddenly seemed like one option of many, and not a very good one.

Fresh copy is no longer walked. It is forwarded.

I went back to Coventry two years ago with Roger Harrabin and David Shukman, BBC colleagues who had also worked at the paper in the eighties. The building was locked shut; gone was the day when reception was open on a Saturday. In fact we could not even see a reception. The office block sat across the road like a bedraggled giant. We were told that while the staff of the paper took up all four storeys in the eighties, they were now pushed to fill half a floor. Just to annoy Geoff Grimmer, since he is not in a position to give me any kind of dressing down for this hideous cliché, I will write here that my beloved deputy news editor is probably spinning in his grave. Sorry, Geoff.

Like me when I tripped over the computers in reception, the newspaper was not looking where it was going. The outcome is sad indeed.

*

I promised this chapter would contain the most important lesson of my career. Now is a good time to write it down because it was a lesson I think I started to learn at Coventry. I then stupidly unlearnt it in some of the jobs I did at the Beeb – *Today* programme reporter, political correspondent, Africa correspondent, *Newsnight* and *Panorama* presenter – and only grasped it finally and completely when I reached Radio 2.

The lesson is this: *The audience have better stories than we do.*

I remember at Coventry telling Geoff Grimmer that a woman had turned up at reception wanting to talk about her brother who had died suddenly. 'Go down and speak to her,' he instructed, thus coining the first commandment of journalism in six short words.

At Coventry the lives of reporters and readers were deeply intertwined. They were neighbours; friends; sometimes lovers. On one occasion a group of us had been to the pub in a black Mini driven by a colleague. On the way back we saw a fire engine and followed it to a disused office building that had been set ablaze. Firefighters were there already. We asked them what was happening and, with not much to relate, sped off into the night in our Mini. The story was followed up the next morning by a reporter in the office who had not been at the scene and got her information from the police. Her headline

MYSTERY 'BLACK MINI' IS SEEN RACING FROM BLAZE

was quickly pulled from the second edition.

The trouble starts when reporters and readers stop sleeping together. When the command 'Go down and speak to her!' is either not issued or not obeyed. This is often the case when you gather a group of brainy people in a room and call it an editorial meeting. Suddenly they think *they* decide what the news is. The smarter they are, the bigger the problem. A helpful rule of thumb is that if the people in the room are outnumbered by their university degrees, they should be separated immediately and the meeting ended. There is no problem in the world that is not made more intractable by a panel of experts.

The joy of Radio 2 is in accepting that it is highly unlikely a combination of me, three researchers, an editor, a mock leather sofa and a jug of equally mock coffee will know more than six million listeners. They are smarter. We do not know what the story is until they tell us.

When they do, either by text or email or on the phone, I often find myself quietly roaring appreciation at just how many streets ahead of us the audience always is. It is not us telling them what's going on. It is them telling us.

It is hard to select the greatest lines from all the great ones, but a compendium would have to include this classic from Trish in Redditch:

'The only way to stop these complaints over animal testing is to try out all new drugs on animal rights protesters.'

On another occasion we booked a so-called 'panel of mums' to decide sentences for serious criminals because judges so often get it wrong. They are inventive – they keep saying, when the worst scenarios come up, that serious criminals should be '*forced to wipe the bums of elderly people in retirement homes*'.

We then get a complaint from a retirement home:

'*This comment was grossly offensive to old people who do not want to come into such close contact with criminals, and who do not believe that any part of their body should be used to punish crime.*'

When Alan Johnson was health secretary he arrived to answer listener questions about a new £780m drive to curb obesity. Callers lined up with comments – you need to spend more money, less money, the policy is crazy, it's not the job of government to stop people eating chips, etc. Then we get Doris in Rotherham on the line.

'Health Secretary?' she starts.

'Yes?' Johnson leans forwards, presses the headphones to his ears to hear better.

Doris loads, aims, and fires.

'*If you give obese people seven hundred and eighty million pounds, they're just going to spend it on food.*'

That has to be in the top ten.

Another day, we reported how Manchester University students changed the signs on their toilet doors because the words 'Ladies' and 'Gents' were upsetting transgender students who felt they did not fit into either category. The signs now read: TOILETS and TOILETS WITH URINALS. An exasperated Douglas in Carlisle left this comment:

'*If these people don't even know which toilet to use, how the hell can they have been given a place at university?*'

We do an item about how people in cul-de-sacs tend to be heavier than average. Eddie from Somerset rings to say:

'*This research cannot be true. I live on a main road, and I am fat.*'

There is not enough space to properly credit the listener who emailed to say that 'Gary Glitter should be humanely destroyed', or the one who argued the best way to avoid future train crashes at level crossings would be to ensure the 'front three carriages of every train are empty, and made of rubber'. Attacking the Health and Safety

Executive, a pensioner from Swindon called them 'worse than useless' because they had 'not even been round to look at my wife's
stairlift, which is squeaking'. After a pitbull tragically mauled a young
girl in Llandudno, a listener insisted by email that 'if people want to
keep these dogs they should be forced to have all their teeth
removed.' (And the pitbull . . .?)

During a discussion on how to save money at home, a poverty-
stricken Kate rings from West Lothian:

*'I have no carpets in my house, and being on benefits I cannot afford
them. So what I do is tape two squares of carpet to my feet in the
morning. When I walk around my home it feels densely carpeted, and
it is much easier to change the colour or style of carpeting in your
house with this method.'*

I had that thought again: Other lives.

Similarly, when Monica from Liverpool rang in about Islamic
dress her comment was more poignant than it at first appeared.

*'You are discussing how Moslem women cover themselves from top-
to-toe in order to become "sexually invisible". In this country there's a
much easier way to do that – just turn forty-five.'*

When we discuss a government initiative to build a safe room
inside the homes of victims of domestic violence, so a woman whose
ex-partner suddenly turns up can retreat to a secure locked area
and call the police, Tom from North Shields objects:

'This idea is a non-starter. Two words: THE SHINING.'

It is a revelation to me. You have probably known this all along,
but suddenly I realize – the listeners have all the best lines.

One day we got a call from a man who said, 'I went to put flowers
on my grandmother's grave and found the tombstone had been
knocked over.'

He rang up the council to tell them the cemetery had been vandalized, and they replied, 'Oh no, that wasn't vandals, that was us.'
They told him they were using a machine called a Topple Tester to
check the gravestones were stable, because three children had been
killed playing in British cemeteries in the last ten years. The Topple

Tester pushes the stone and if it is not safe it falls over – the council then leave it flat and *you* have to pay to get it repaired.

Based on our caller's account, we run the story and it turns out this is happening right across the country. We are sent a photo of a graveyard in Northumberland where every stone is horizontal. Then a cemetery safety spokesman arrives who comes out with the usual line: 'Three deaths is three too many.' Now it is actually very difficult for an interviewer to come back on that, but the listeners do and they are hopping mad. Of course they have the right answer – the same phrase crops up in email after email:

'The way to stop children being killed in cemeteries is to tell them not to play there.'

And I find myself thinking, this is the way to do it. This is what news is, people telling us what's important, not the other way round.

Stories don't belong to us, but to them. The customer is king.*

---

* Not always. John Ware, my colleague on *Panorama*, made an investigative film in Northern Ireland and received a complaint which read, 'Dear Mr Ware, I would rather eat dog shit than watch another one of your programmes.' John Ware's reply was two words long: 'Bon appetit.'

Chapter Four

LUCKY TO BE ALIVE

I originally wanted to use a Woody Allen line for the title of this book and call it 'The Most Fun You Can Have Without Laughing'. Because it has often struck me that is exactly what you get when you put journalism and broadcasting together.

But the title became impossible when I looked back on all the many laugh-out-loud moments.

And also the times when there was no fun at all. In journalism you sometimes have disasters, proper life-or-death ones.

Sometimes, if you're lucky, you nearly get killed.

Straight off the news trainee course, with my Coventry experiences now yellowing cuttings in a photo album which I still have, I had some good fortune. During spare moments in the traineeship I had been pestering the *Today* programme team for work. I did the odd piece for them but made no headway.

Then one day, walking towards Broadcasting House, I noticed that a handful of shops in Carnaby Street were selling Nazi memorabilia.

Eagerly, I returned with a hefty reel-to-reel tape machine to describe the stock on display, thinking it might make a good feature.

As I stood in Carnaby Street commentating on the iron crosses, swastikas, SS badges and the like, a furious shopkeeper emerged. He attacked me with a plank of wood. From working in a timber yard in Sutton in my gap year before university, I recognized the weapon as a piece of sawn four-by-two. The man smacked me on the shoulder with it. Then he started jabbing the wood at my tape recorder. Instinctively I turned to protect the machine and got hit on the back.

I had not realized this, but being hurt while trying to defend BBC equipment is regarded as one of the most significant professional sacrifices. The people who ran *Today* were not remotely interested in the attack on me, but the fact that the man had tried to assault a BBC tape machine – known as a Uher – was regarded as uniquely despicable.

I was mentioned in dispatches for having put myself in harm's way. The package was aired with me shouting, 'Now he is banging me with the plank of wood, stop it,' and suddenly I sensed I had started to exist. Even if only infinitesimally. A BBC amoeba.

Then a reporter called Ron McCullough left *Today* for *Breakfast News*, and they asked this hyperactive trainee to fill the gap on a one-year contract. As things panned out, I look back and think the moment that shopkeeper pounced was the single luckiest break I ever had. Did he know that by hitting me he was launching my broadcasting career? If I saw him now I would give him a big hug and present him with a length of commemorative timber.

So I was now in the proper working world, a trainee no more. In at the deep end, too. No sooner had I found a spare desk on *Today* than I was sent to a war zone. They wanted me to go to Yugoslavia as it collapsed.

For me back then, that was quite a stretch. That was – *the world*. I was not sure where exactly Yugoslavia was, so in those pre-internet days I had to go via home (luckily I knew where that was) to consult an atlas. Inside my house, BBC taxi revving outside, I swiftly fetched

my passport and leafed through the bulky volume my grandmother
had given me.

The atlas was beautifully inscribed:

Dearest Jeremy, the world is your oyster.
May it be kind to you.

A tender sentiment from my father's late mother, whom we all called
Nanny. But journalists are on a mission to seek out unkindnesses. A
political earthquake had happened in Yugoslavia: the bit on the left
of the map I was hurriedly examining, Slovenia, had declared independence, effectively breaking away from Serbia, the bit on the right
where all the people in uniforms were. The Yugoslav (but really
Serb) army had immediately flown over Ljubljana, the capital of
Slovenia, and bombed it.

I arrived in Slovenia with two tape recorders and a file of cuttings
about President Tito, Croatia's support for Hitler and an obscure
fourth province called Bosnia of which I had never previously heard.
I was twenty-five, single, on the make and without a care in the
world, so I might as well have marked in my diary: *Tuesday – Get
killed*, because anyone observing this frighteningly inexperienced
war reporter would have assumed I was on a suicide mission.

This was one of my first experiences of the BBC's extraordinary
ability to pour resources into a foreign story. As I set off, my con-
temporary Justin Webb was trying to get into Serbia with a
cameraman. To my consternation, he had already broken through
into the apparently more glamorous world of television news. But
his trip suffered an early hitch. The cameraman who met him
halfway to Gatwick was one of the BBC's least competent.

Justin asked, 'Have you been to Belgrade before?' and the man's
jaw dropped in astonishment.

'*Belgrade*? I thought they said Belgrave Square.'

So I got there just ahead of Justin, which, such was the smallness
of my mind back then, mattered to me. When we laughed about it

later on a squash court, Justin gave me his version of the Gore Vidal line: 'It is not enough to succeed. Friends must fail.'

Having landed in the Slovenian capital I found that single-minded residents had repulsed the tanks of the Yugoslav army with virtually no armour on their side. So much for my war story. I thought I should at least try to see the invaders leaving, so I took a hire car directly from the airport and raced madly to the border. And there was an unforgettable moment for this young reporter – as I drove the car along an uneven ridge of road cut into hillside, I suddenly drew level with a group of three tanks on their way out. They moved parallel to my car in the baking sunshine. Trying to work my tape machine with my left hand while steering with the right, moving at speed along the edge of an overhang, I commentated hysterically. One tank swivelled a gun barrel towards my car. It seemed to nod up and down but did not fire.

I filed the piece, but I had got the BBC politics badly wrong.

Apparently when you arrive in a foreign capital you should always report in to the senior correspondent in the area. The BBC once had a South West of England correspondent, David Smeeton, who was so territorial that it was said all reporters travelling to America had to clear their assignments with him because their flights passed over Bristol.

So after I had rather proudly sent over the tanks piece on a system known as traffic – an internal ringmain to which it seemed half the news department was tuned at any one time – my boss, the *Today* editor Phil Harding, was patched through and remonstrated with me for 'not communicating with Diana Goodman and Cathy', an award-winning senior correspondent and her producer who had wedged themselves behind a desk in a press room in Ljubljana. Seeking redemption, and trying to change the subject in what was effectively a public conversation, I told him confidently, 'Well, this war seems to be over after two days.'

Oh dear. If newsrooms owned plots of land where careers were buried, they would be running out of space for all the journalists who committed the cardinal error of saying there is no story when there is. After a long time in news I did finally work out that if you say something is a story when it's not, everyone just thinks you're overenthusiastic. If you say something is *not* a story when it is, they decide you are an incompetent buffoon who should not even be trusted to fetch a half packet of digestives from the kitchen cupboard. Working on *Newsnight* on 9/11, the day had misfired from the start. We were due to lead with a routine domestic item and as the duty editor wandered into my office with the prospects (the list of stories already in the diary), he saw that the first plane had gone into the World Trade Center. 'Oh, don't worry about that,' he breezed, barely looking up. 'The sprinklers will come on in a minute.'

Well, he was wrong about the sprinklers and I was wrong about Yugoslavia. The Serbs now turned their attention, viciously, to neighbouring Croatia. Just as I was packing in Ljubljana, having met and formally apologized to Diana Goodman, violence flared between Croatian police and minority Serbs in Tenja, a suburb of Osijek 260 miles to the east of where I was. The Yugoslav soldiers had not had ethnic Serbs to 'defend' within Slovenia. But now they had a purpose. They piled in and fought the police.

Before I write any more I have to plead for your patience with me. What I am going to tell you verges on utter madness. But being twenty-five in a war zone can go one of two ways – it can either be the most exciting experience you have ever had in your life, or you can die.

*

My decision was to drive across Croatia into Serbia and back again in a day, to see what it was like to cross what was now no-man's-land.

Inside the hire car the last customer had left a tape of songs by Barry White. As I played them at full volume, driving far too fast for my own good on the road from Ljubljana, I thought I saw metal spikes protruding out of the tarmac ahead. It was an upturned road sign I was going too fast to avoid. When I slammed on the brakes the car went into a skid.

The rented vehicle shot across the road and span across the grass. It was like the famous moment of rallycross commentary by Murray Walker: 'And here he comes, you can see he's cleverly dug two big circles in his windscreen to improve visibility – *oh, and he's over the embankment!'* I saw road, embankment, then nothing but clouds. I was airborne. Did I just go off the side of a cliff?

Crash. The drop off the ledge had been a dozen feet. The impact as the car dropped like a rock into a farmer's field seemed to concertina half the discs in my spine.

Sitting there for a few seconds, I gasped for air. I was not dead; I was in the middle of a long line of Croatian potatoes. When I got out of the car in the bright sunshine I saw the impact had dislodged the front bumper, which was now attached at one end only. A back wheel was bent at an angle, and the chassis had dropped an inch or two. As I stood there, the farmer approached me, wearing dirty green trousers and a pristine white vest. He spoke no English, but I could tell he was more concerned than angry. We stood there for a moment contemplating a shared fragment of time in an infinite universe – the reporter, the farmer, the hire car flumped in his potatoes with its sagging chassis, and through the open driver's door, Barry White singing 'Can't Get Enough Of Your Love, Babe'.

The farmer saw the word PRESS spelt out on the side of the car with pieces of masking tape and, perhaps grasping the PR opportunity, was embarrassingly kind. He pulled off the pristine vest, stretched it and tied the loose end of the bumper up. Then he fetched his tractor and pulled the car out of the field.

The crash had cost me precious time, and the sun went down. I should have called off my plan to drive across the border, because that night the sun almost went down on me for good.

As I passed the last silent Croatian village in the darkness I remember thinking I was out of my depth. My heart pounded as my damaged car creaked and yowled its way down an empty road, headlights picking out trees and – nothing.

Someone would be watching. The silence was deafening. Would they fire? Of course they would. I felt real fear for the first time in my life. With the car's interior light on, I slowed to a crawl and dipped the headlights. None of this had been covered in my driving test in Wallington.

After twenty minutes I saw lights: the other side of the border. In a village called Sid, a group of Serbs stopped and roughly searched me and then, laughing at the vest on my bumper and how jumpy I was, produced guns and insisted I drive back the other way. Again my car crawled across the no-man's-land, interior light on so anyone lurking at the roadside could see there was nothing but a bewildered Englishman inside.

Years later, I met an experienced Croat journalist and told him the story – back and forth between the two countries on the outbreak of war?

'You are lucky to be alive,' he said without a smile.

But I was alive, and more so than ever. I spent the night in the first Croatian hotel I came to, where outside every door on my floor was a pair of black boots – the hard-pressed Croatian police had taken over the place – then set off for Osijek, the largest town in the east, and a pressure point.

Ten miles from Osijek I was told by a villager that there were rooftop snipers in the town up ahead. So when I got to the hotel car park, I exited the car by sliding out of it onto the tarmac.

I then crept round another parked car, trying to stay low, and finally sprinted towards reception with my body bent almost double, bursting through the open doors of the hotel. To my embarrassment, as I skidded to a halt on the polished floor of the hotel and picked myself up, a group of bored-looking journalists glanced round at me with a slightly bemused, *what-on-earth—?* expression. It turned out there were no snipers.

But, as I say, I was twenty-five. So young. These days, working on

Radio 2, I look back at that ravenous young professional and want to give him a big hug, thank him for everything he did for me and tell him to calm down and see a bit more of his mum.

On that trip to Croatia and another soon after, I was on a mission. I was alone in a war zone and I wanted at last to matter, to be spotted by the BBC and singled out for greater things.

Incidentally, I did not have a flak jacket. This was before the shooting in Bosnia of the young radio reporter John Schofield, who was the same age as me and undoubtedly destined for great things. More than any other event, John's death made the BBC look again at safety in the field.

I slept in the Hotel Osijek. To be precise, I slept in my room at the front of the hotel. Most reporters and crews were sleeping in the corridors in case the place was shelled, but I chanced my own bed. I was fortunate with that, too – three days after I left, the hotel façade was hit by Serb rockets. A piece of film was shown on the news, and watching in Cheam I saw that half my floor had been gouged out.

My plan in Croatia was to get a package for radio that conveyed the war. The tanks had been good, but the incident with Diana and Cathy had taken the shine off that slightly. So what I needed, I reasoned, was to go out with my tape recorder and find some fighting.

Later in my career I would work out the key signs of a person about to take too much risk. There is a great line from Jeff Foxworthy, the American comedian who lampoons the Deep South, which goes:

If someone in your family died after shouting, 'Hey y'all! Watch this!' – you might just be a redneck.

A South African cameraman was nearly killed with me in Lesotho after shouting 'I love action! Let's rock!' and driving straight into a lethal firefight between local soldiers and South Africans. A 25-year-old with a point to prove is probably not the safest bet.

If I had been lucky crossing the no-man's-land between Serbia and Croatia, I was now about to test my good fortune to the limit. Aware that a group of freelance photographers in the hotel were seeing fighting almost every day, and that all around my hotel were flashpoints where soldiers and locals were killing each other, I told my producers in London that I would be reporting on the risks taken by journalists to cover the conflict.

No alarm bells rang, with them or with me.

The next day I went out in my hire car with three freelance photographers. In any war zone, they are – I hope they will forgive me for saying so – the maddest. They only sell photos by getting close to the action, and even the most expensive lens in the world will not work at a safe distance. Today this group said they were going to head to Vukovar, a Croatian town under siege. There would be no way of getting there without going through the Serbian positions. How would we do that?

The answer was simple: by getting in my car and driving. The four of us set off. Two Americans and two Brits. Pete, the other Brit, had the most time for me. 'What's happened to this car? Is it going to make the trip? Why did you get a bright red one, Jeremy? If we get fired on, stop the car and get out. It's dangerous to stay in the car. The bullets go right through it.'

That was news. For some reason, possibly the diet of American cop shows consumed when I was a boy, I had thought car doors stopped bullets. The notion that we might have to abandon the car gave me that feeling in my stomach again. Fear. But also a thrill.

We were stopped on the road by burly but friendly Croats, clad in camouflage gear. 'No further,' they said. 'Too dangerous. Serbs.' They waved us back.

At this point I hoped my new friends would call the trip off, but that would have been to underestimate the incredible bravery of people who compete for publication in war zones. Worryingly, they may even have seen my presence as an incentive to press on. So instead of reversing, they rearranged the seating. One of them took over the driving and I went in the back.

'We will go via the cornfields,' said Pete.

Whatever was about to happen, I did not want to miss the chance to have it witnessed by the huge *Today* programme audience, so I switched on my Sony cassette recorder and taped everything that followed.

The car lumped off the road and, exactly as the photographers described, came to a cornfield. A path was worn down the middle. We took it. But the path gave up on itself. And now, surrounded by corn as tall as the car, shooting started.

I still have my tape of what followed.

'Out!' Pete shouts, stopping the car. 'Go on!'

The doors fly open. The shooting intensifies. 'Out!' I shout. 'Out! We're getting out the car right now! We've just been sniped at—'

The gunfire was coming through corn to our right. A Serb position had been set up to stop the field being used as a route to the town. Now we had been ambushed.

More shooting, louder.

'They've got an RPG,' says one of the photographers: rocket-propelled grenades.

'That's incoming fire,' I say on the tape. 'They're firing on our position.'

'It's coming in!' shouts Pete.

'Can we get down the road?' I squeak. 'Can we get out of this position?'

Crouching low, bullets whistling overhead, we backed through the corn and found a small dip in the ground where six inches of earth had been scooped out.

The American photographers were trying to take pictures but there was nothing to see. Bizarrely, one of them sat bolt upright adjusting his camera, asking if anyone had mosquito spray (I did say mad). The car should have been between us and the gunmen, but suddenly a volley of very precise fire came in.

'Incoming!' shouts one of the Americans on my tape. Even mosquito man flattens himself.

And then it happened. A bullet came in so close to my head that it showed up as three bars on the recording meter of my machine.

There was no bang, just a hiss like a can of soft drink opening; it cut the air so close to my face I felt the breeze. It is clearly audible on my tape.

I shout, '*WO!*'

In Cheam this means: alright, that's enough now.

But it was not the end. A van with Croatian heavies arrived and they started blasting back at the Serbs. This actually put us in more danger. A bullet smacked our hire car and blew the back window out on the far side. Then a sound I will never forget: a distant, inoffensive crump, like a sack of encyclopaedias hitting the ground.

For a second the mortar bomb would have travelled in the air towards us. Then it hit the ground just behind our position and exploded. The blast made my ears ring.

'That's incoming,' says another voice on the tape.

Pete says, 'Shall we go? Jeremy, do you want to go?'

Another mortar, another explosion, closer this time.

'Yeeeeah, yeah, yes,' I say, 'let's go, let's go,' ever more decisively.

At this point I think death was very close.

We run back to the hire car. We still have to turn the damaged, bright red vehicle around and get past the jeep the Croatians just arrived in. Pete jams the car into reverse. Dust is kicked up. He manhandles the creaking vehicle into a violent three-point turn.

Vrrrrrooom – Pete guns the accelerator and we are gone.

I say onto my tape, 'We're going, we're gone, we're going at a hundred miles an hour, well done Pete . . .'

A strange sight as we pick up the road again. A local man does a *Sieg Heil* salute at the car.

Later, I would read the Churchill quote and understand it completely: 'Nothing in life is quite so exhilarating as being shot at without result.'

When I got back to the Hotel Osijek my new friends went straight to the bar to tell the story, but I had to go and cut the package I hoped would finally get me noticed. Aware that I was lucky to have survived the day, I went to my bathroom and looked in the mirror.

A strange thing happened. As I contemplated my face, a thousand thoughts rushing through my head, two lines of blood came from my nose.

I did not know if nosebleeds could be caused by stress, or shock. Sometime I must ask a doctor friend if they can. Standing in that hotel bathroom I watched the blood make two short lines to my mouth and then pool in the crevice between my lips. Drop by drop, it fell to the white porcelain basin.

Not moving, I watched the lower part of my face cover itself in red.

I was now – I knew this – a real reporter. I had shed blood.

Chapter Five

THE GREATEST SHOW ON EARTH

When I returned from Croatia I more or less expected garlands to be thrown at me from upper floors by besotted researchers and the pavement outside Broadcasting House to be spray-painted with a long line of red emulsion, which would lead a trail all the way up the stairs to my desk on the fourth floor. My radio package in which I was nearly killed had been aired – albeit cut from eleven minutes to three – and the bullet was heard all round the country. Surely the Reporter Who Shed Blood, even if it was only through a nosebleed, would be someone special now?

Of course not. The most pressing item on the agenda, I discovered, was why the *Today* programme was being billed so much by the Slovenian branch of Hertz. And my dreams of spending the rest of my twenties showing up only on glamorous foreign assignments, possibly wearing a camel jacket, were dashed when I was told to do a piece – for the very next day – about the return of the cycling proficiency test.

But journalism is like that: a world of contrasts. Light and shade, heavy and light. The ordinary and the extraordinary. A famous headline on the front page of the *New York Daily News* screamed **KIPS BAY TENANTS SAY WE'VE GOT KILLER MOLD** – famous because the following day was 9/11; from killer mould to the end of the world, all in the same font size. Journalists benefit from having a range of fonts, from deadly serious to not-so-serious to possibly-quite-silly, but I was once advised by John Sergeant that 'the only thing They will never forgive is misplaced humour.' In twenty-five years at the BBC I never worked out who 'They' were, but some years down the line I did have a professional car crash when I forgot Sargie's vital insight. As we say on the radio, more on that later.

Sometimes the sheer range journalism gives you is giddying. I was booked to sit in for Andrew Marr on his Sunday show in 2011. In the studio would be the politicians Danny Alexander and Douglas Alexander – not much range with a double Alexander, you might say. But the producers explained there were two extra interviews to be recorded in advance, and there was a problem. One was with the deputy prime minister of Israel, a veteran of decades of wars and peace processes, Ehud Barak. The other was with the biggest movie star in the world, Johnny Depp.

'So what's the problem?' I asked. 'That sounds great.' From the Middle East peace process to Edward Scissorhands.

The issue, I was patiently informed, was that Barak was at 2.30 and Depp was at 3 p.m., the appointments were immoveable and they were in different hotels. The interview with Barak would take fifteen minutes. So it would end at 2.45, even if it started bang on time. There would be no chance of dismantling the equipment, moving hotels and setting up for Depp, whose people said he was only available for *nine* minutes as we were one of twenty-two crews he was meeting that day.

One of them was going to have to shift hotels.

But who do you ask – the film star who has earned $75m in the previous twelve months, who has shot some of the highest-grossing movies in cinema history including the *Pirates of the Caribbean* franchise . . .

Or the Israeli politician whose personal security detail must be among the world's most complex, and who – just to show this is not someone you mess with – had famously dressed as a woman in the seventies to move around Beirut and shoot members of the Palestine Liberation Organization?

It's a good question. I present a quiz show called *Eggheads* on BBC2, and I could imagine this one coming up in the traditional *Eggheads* multiple choice format. Who ended up changing hotels? Was it:

(a) Depp, (b) Barak, or (c) Vine?

You've guessed it. Because we could not get between the two men ourselves, in the end the deputy prime minister of Israel had to shift. No small thing, because the security measures taken on Barak's behalf were as comprehensive as any I've seen; there were dogs, and his protection staff had to do an extensive electronic sweep of the new room before they could declare it safe. They also needed a car revving outside.

On my way in I clocked some of the Israeli agents – the one who looked like a businessman, sitting in reception with his eyes fixed on the revolving doors. The young and earnest chap who searched my bags outside the lifts. Another just by the door. Two more big Israelis with suits inside the room. Then:

'Good afternoon, Mr Barak!'

And we were away. At two thirty I sat in the chair and we commenced.

It says something about the world, I guess. The politician makes way for the movie star. Depp, by the way, kitted out in denim, hung with motorbiker's pendants and wearing a hat, was cool and charming and curiously un-aloof. He wanted to tell me about his film, *The Rum Diary*. But also about why he keeps working when he has already made enough money to give the grandchildren of his great-grandchildren's grandchildren a life of ease: 'Oh, I like the process,' he said, eyes smiling behind blue tinted glasses. I thought I heard echoes of all the presenters I have written about: *You've got to make hay while the sun shines.*

But it turned out to be the Israeli politician who gave us the best sound bite. Here it is, with my question first.

Vine: In 1973 did you dress as a woman in Beirut to assassinate members of the PLO?

Barak: If needed, but not as a hobby.

*

So – range. Back in the eighties, light and shade were what made *Today* such a lively programme (the breakfast show on the greatest radio station in the world is always likely to be special). The most bizarre combination of stories I ever did back-to-back went from neo-Nazis in Germany to sheep racing in Dorset, via a report that Elvis had been seen in a car park in Telford.

Often reporter packages were used to lighten the load placed on the listener by a diet of heavyweight political interviews, so when I was sent out to do a piece on 'Is it really possible to learn Italian in four hours?' or 'Is Dudley the most exciting town in Britain?' I could hardly complain, even if the answer to both questions was no. One day I had to interview the Foreign Secretary at Heathrow – he was on his way to China, and none of the regular presenters could get to the airport. Was that progress? Evidently not, judging by the story I was assigned the following day: 'Why are the Bay City Rollers big in Japan?'

Sometimes the range of subjects you cover is bewildering. On *Newsnight* I once had to interview the Israeli prime minister and then rush to a hotel room in Kensington to speak to a man who had received a hand and forearm transplanted from a dead motorcyclist in pioneering surgery. The new limb had failed to make itself at home and was decomposing.

When we arrived in the half-lit hotel room the interviewee was sitting at a table with a towel covering the arm. He greeted us with, 'I will take the towel off, but I have to warn you, there will be an unpleasant smell' – a line so magnificent it just begged to be chosen as the title of this book, because in a sense it captured what journalism is all about.

Under the editorship of Phil Harding – who practised tough love, but was dedicated to his band of reporters – the *Today* programme flourished. Harding worked beneath the combative Jenny Abramsky, who gave him an inspired if slightly crackpot deputy called Rod Liddle (nicknamed 'Jenny's bit of rough'). Liddle was to the BBC what the Sex Pistols were to Jim Reeves. He loved to play the insurgent. While working on *The World This Weekend* he had got the über-serious presenter Gordon Clough to say funereally at the end of a package: 'That was Iggy Pop, with "Your Pretty Face Is Going To Hell".' Rod's arrival on *Today* was marked by Sue MacGregor having to credit Carter The Unstoppable Sex Machine at twenty to eight.

One night Liddle arrived with a new girlfriend, Rachel, and very ostentatiously snogged her in front of the reporters' desk (since none of us was of sufficient social standing to have a girlfriend, it was doubly unfortunate). He would sometimes sit on the floor of the corridor smoking to collect his thoughts, knees up to his chest and arms wrapped around them. He sent me out on what in retrospect were a series of madcap assignments: 'I want you to do a piece on why Haiti is such a horrible place,' was his instruction one morning. And another: 'Jeremy, you've got a great day's work ahead of you today. I want a six-minute feature on the New Den.' That piece, on the stadium built for Liddle's beloved Millwall Football Club, ran at full length in the prime slot allocated for elections and earthquakes.

Rod Liddle has his own place in BBC history because years later, as editor, he signed up the newspaperman Andrew Gilligan to get the *Today* programme noticed more. It certainly worked. Rod had left by the time Gilligan famously reported that Number Ten had 'sexed up' the intelligence on Iraq. The end result was a suicide, a BBC–government brawl, a public inquiry and the toppling of a director-general. Many times since, I have heard BBC types describe all this as 'Rod's mistake' – as if he could have triggered the avalanche from a remote location – but so sharp were the editorial sensibilities below that untidy mop of black hair that I actually believe the reverse is true: none of it would have happened if Liddle had still been in charge.

*

When I was on *Today*, from 1989 to 1993, Gilligan was just a twinkle in the programme's eye. Phil Harding left and was succeeded by Roger Mosey. Whereas Harding was a fretter, whose habit of anxiously rubbing his hands together during big stories was cartoonists' material, Mosey was altogether more complex and self-possessed. He missed nothing, combining John Sergeant's gift for nuance with a truly terrifying grasp of whom you had to know to get on. It was said of Peter Mandelson that the instant he walked into a newsroom he could tell you where the power was: the same was true of Mosey in the BBC, except he did not even have to walk into the room.

But I was lucky – he and Steve Mitchell, two of the Beeb's most doughty editorial leaders, as well as a rather humane executive called Richard Ayre, all seemed to decide they would help me get along. I hate to say it, but such things matter.

For me the days spent slaving away on *Today* were not just a first chance to report for a national audience; they were also an opportunity to observe the corporation from below decks. Brian Redhead, Sue MacGregor and John Humphrys stood on the prow of the programme as presenters – I watched them like a hawk, and jealously. As a large manual typewriter was heaved onto the desk every morning for the arrival of the one presenter who refused to use computers, no one could have guessed how close to the end of his life Brian Redhead was.

A listener to *Today* had a fairly clear line of sight: there were presenters, who were famous; reporters, who wanted to be famous; and producers, who were unknown. But in truth, before the efficiency drives of John Birt kicked in, the corporation did seem to have an over-elaborate superstructure.

Job titles are often a clue to what is going on inside an organization. In 1980s Romania, the wife of President Ceauşescu was known by the title 'The Best Mother Any Nation Could Want'. That alone would have been reason enough for a revolution. At Basingstoke railway station I once noticed a plaque on a door that said 'Field Manager, Zonal Performance Assistant'. Some old-style BBC nameplates could probably compete. There is a saying on the *Financial Times* that a person is not important if their job title is more than two words long, yet in those days some of the senior bods seemed to have essays for job titles.

In radio news there was a kindly gent called Roy Walters – Deputy Editor, News and Current Affairs Radio – who was known as DENCAR. Alongside him worked John Williams, the Managing Editor, known as MENCAR. They both had an office next to Jenny, who was Editor, News and Current Affairs Radio. So when I went to see Roy one day, the secretary asked, 'Are you here for ENCAR, MENCAR or DENCAR?'*

One day Princess Anne was booked to appear for a rare live interview. In the twenty-four hours before the royal arrival, there was a flurry of activity. People we had never seen before streamed in and out of the office. Then a team of men in suits entered the green room and removed the coffee-stained *Today* programme furniture,

---

* I have checked, but sadly the famous story Terry Wogan tells about the Caversham-based Europe & International Engineering Information Officer, who was known as E-I-E-I-O, does not appear to be true.

which was dark mauve with all kinds of unexplained blotches. They
slid a pristine cream-coloured leather suite into its place.

We could not believe our luck. The royal visit had triggered a
sofa-and-chairs upgrade for the staff! Princess Anne duly arrived
the following day. She spent about a minute in the room with the
cream settee, and then went through to the studio and did the
interview.

Immediately she was gone, the same suited characters bustled
into the office and removed our beautiful new suite. Back came the
coffee-stained mauve sofa and chairs, unceremoniously dropped
into place.

'I thought we were supposed to have grown up by now,' I heard
Humphrys growl.

The complexity of the place could emerge through the simplest
incidents. One night I found the top drawer of my desk jammed
shut. I rang maintenance. An hour later two workmen in blue over-
alls arrived with tools and levered the drawer open.

I thanked them, but just as they were leaving I tried to push the
drawer closed again and found it would not budge.

'Hey sorry, excuse me—' I called them back in. 'The drawer's
open, but it won't shut now.'

'Sorry mate,' they said. 'You need someone else for that.'

It was not just the drawers that needed shutting. I was doing a
piece on Muhammad Ali and wanted some original recordings of the
Rumble in the Jungle, the great fight between Ali and Foreman. So I
asked the switchboard to put me through to the boxing department.

After some clicking and ringing, a woman at the other end said:
'Hello, boxing?'

'Hi. Do you have the soundtrack for that fight between Ali and
Foreman? The one where—'

She interrupted me. 'No, sorry love, we're nothing to do with
sport. This is the department that puts things in boxes.'

*

Reporting on the *Today* programme was fun but never easy. The crew complained regularly about the hours – Phil Hay once telling Harding at a team meeting that 'our shifts are like *Night of the Living Dead*' – but I have to admit I would have done the work for free instead of the £19,600 p.a. I was getting (this included an 'unpredictability allowance' which I assumed was to offset the possibility of being shot, either abroad or in reception). My colleague Michael Crick once gave as his golden rule, 'Every piece should contain one fact and one joke', and I tried to ensure the factual content of packages was mixed in with any show-stopping material that would arrest the attention – archive material from LPs in the Beeb's vault, or better still, a recording of something actually happening; preferably happening to me.

Reporting in Russia on a dangerous free-for-all in the post-Soviet arms market, I secretly taped myself going undercover to strike a deal with a Moscow arms dealer and got Radio 4 a good price on a secondhand MIG fighter jet. 'And will the plane be very fast?', asked in a Cheam accent, seemed to cause my colleagues endless amusement.

Nothing is quite so powerful on radio as the reporter suddenly experiencing the event firsthand. In a piece about roller coasters, you simply have to ride one. Just don't volunteer for the item on tasers, waterboarding or the medicinal effect of drinking your own urine.

One of the prime exponents of the technique was Jonathan Maitland, who placed himself on the edge of frame in so many stories that he could have been the inspiration for the film *Forrest Gump*. Maitland was in Australia when Prince Charles was shot at by a man carrying a starter pistol. The show was on air when it happened. They rang Jonathan, who was at the event.

In the studio, Sue MacGregor begins to read the dramatic introduction:

'We have just heard news of an attack on Prince Charles.'

As Maitland waits to go on, the editor in London says, 'She's going to ask you about the shooting.'

Maitland replies, 'What shooting?'

The introduction is reaching its conclusion and now Roger Mosey, sensing an emergency, has reached for the talkback and is reading wire copy off a screen.

'Jonathan, listen, all you need to know is that a man ran onto the stage, he fired a gun in the air, Charles is unhurt, the man fell over, he's now been arrested.'

In the studio Sue MacGregor announces, 'We can now hear the latest from Sydney. We're joined live on the line by Jonathan Maitland.

'Jonathan, what happened?'

The voice on the other side of the world comes back as clear as a bell. 'Sue – a man has just run on the stage, he fired a gun in the air, then he fell over, he's been arrested, Prince Charles wasn't hurt.'

MacGregor asks, 'What was the reaction of the people around you?'

'Believe it or not,' Maitland replies, 'some of them weren't even aware it had happened.'

The programme seemed to be constantly on the brink of disaster. One night an extraordinary piece was filed via traffic from BBC Radio Bristol. Sitting there in the early hours of the morning, the team of night producers were baffled. Nowhere in the diary had the day team left any note that it was expected.

They listened as a local radio reporter told the story from a farm in Wiltshire: 'Five cows were taken from here to an abattoir in Salisbury. They were slaughtered in the abattoir, but then they came back to life.'

As the piece was played on the ringmain the night team drew closer to the loudspeaker, looking at each other in astonishment. The reporter was now interviewing a scientist who explained the cows had been grazing in fields where victims of the Black Death had been buried. 'It appears the heavy residue of nitrates in the field gave their nervous systems a back-up.'

The reporter signed off without hanging around to talk on traffic. The producers got the tape ready for broadcast by labelling it, cutting the ends with a razor and sticking a length of yellow leader at the start of the reel and red-and-white at the end.

At 5 a.m. John Humphrys appeared to be briefed on the programme's contents, and when the abattoir story was mentioned his eyes lit up.

'Wait, that's a bloody big story. We should lead on it.'

Congratulations to Humphrys, because in that instant the hoaxer was undone. When the producers tried to contact the reporter they could find no record of him. The scientist did not exist, and the farm was fictional. The tape was pulled.

An inquiry was launched and the culprit was discovered to be Chris Morris, who had worked at Radio Bristol and was making a spoof show on Radio 4 called *On The Hour* (he would go on to give the world *The Day Today* and *Brass Eye*). Let's just pause for a second and think about how mad that is – a silly part of the BBC trying to hoax a serious part, with catastrophic consequences for *Today*'s credibility had the silly part succeeded.

Morris did have greater success that same month with a different target. A piece filed through GNS, the central hub for BBC local radio, went out on nearly all stations – the 'reporter' describing how a boy in north London had been suspended from school because he was an Arsenal fan and had moulded his head into the shape of a cannon.

*

For me the best part of working on *Today* was the obvious one – just reporting. The cumbersome reel-to-reel machine gave way to the more compact Sony Walkman. Although the contents of the cassette would still have to be dubbed across to quarter-inch tape for editing, at least the Sony did not cause permanent musculoskeletal disruption (known as 'Uher shoulders'). Pulling out a blank cassette and heading away from the building with my recorder, I constantly recalled Geoff Grimmer's injunction: 'Go down and speak to her.'

Veteran field reporters like Malcolm Brabant, Joe Paley and Tim Maby would allow me occasionally to look over their shoulder. Martin Bell, the vanilla-suited, super-stylish war reporter – probably the greatest ever maker of television news packages – once said 'hello' to me in a lift. Why was Bell the best? His staccato script lines are still quoted verbatim in newsrooms:

'Their wake-up call came from the barrel of a gun.'

'They said this was the last ditch, but the last ditch – just keeps on moving.'

Or, returning to Belfast and narrating over what should have been rather boring pictures of new office blocks: *'Thirty years on, the conversations on these street corners have not changed. All that has changed – are the street corners.'*

There were many other artisans. On the floor below our office a radio genius called Hugh Sykes worked on *PM*, which was like having Michelangelo paint your kitchen. Alongside me on *Today*, Sue Pennington, Mark Coles and Dominic Arkwright were fascinating to observe, whether for journalistic acumen or the craftsmanship with which they assembled lush radio soundscapes. Long into the night they would be making marks on quarter-inch reel-to-reel with an oily yellow pencil called a chinagraph, cutting the tape with a razor blade and reattaching the loose ends with sticky white tape. And at the desk right beside me sat Allan Little, without question the finest writer of my generation, and with a sense of humour to match.

After we had both left the programme I paid Allan a long-deferred compliment, telling him: 'You are one of the five greatest radio reporters of all time.'

He looked at me a little too perceptively, then asked: 'Who are the other three?'

The *Today* programme took me all over the Middle East, the former Soviet Union and Europe. Most assignments were not dangerous – they were just fun, although you couldn't ever laugh. On the trip to Russia, I saw firsthand how the so-called 'shock therapy' advocated by brainbox western economists had caused rampant inflation, a mafia takeover and the collapse in the rouble. It led me to a deep-seated mistrust of anyone who describes themselves as an expert – on which subject, as I might have typed at the bottom of my page in Coventry, *mf.* In Moscow, taxi drivers had a sign on their dashboards saying 'The fare displayed on the meter will be multiplied by forty.' By the end of my visit the 'forty' had been replaced by 'sixty'.

The local correspondent, Kevin Connolly, told me how he had been having his hair cut. At the moment when the barber had cut one half of his hair but not the other half, the clippers were mysteriously switched off behind Connolly's head, leaving him looking like a crew member from Star Trek. When he asked what the matter was, the barber came out with the most popular phrase in the country: 'The price changed.'

It wasn't just the barbers. Our own Moscow driver had initially bagged our business by producing a sheet of A4 with very competitive prices on it, all under the heading

OUR PRICES ARE DEFINITELY THE LOWEST IN THE WORLD

Four days in, a huge row blew up between the translator and the driver and I asked what was wrong.

'This,' said the translator.

He handed me a new sheet of paper with revised prices that were at least triple the original quote. The new slogan at the top of the page was:

OUR PRICES ARE QUITE LOW

*

One Sunday night in 1994 I was watching the television news at home when the presenter said something I was not expecting. Up popped a photo of Brian Redhead on the set behind him as Chris Lowe, the newsreader, read the item announcing that Brian had died.

I never had that much to do with Brian personally. The relationship was as between the emperor and the shoeshine boy. I knew producers were often hurt by his infuriating self-confidence; once, when I watched his attention drawn to a briefing on his desk that someone had spent half the night working on, Brian dismissed it with a chuckle and told the producer: 'I've never read one of those.' But the news was unexpected and, to my surprise, I cried.

My wife Janelle saw me. 'Are you okay?'

'Yeah,' I told her. 'They just said Brian Redhead died.' To my surprise I could barely get the words out. This was not me mourning a friend, because I could not claim Brian had been that. He had been friendly to me, and once or twice gave me good advice ('I know you're keen, but don't shout into the microphone'), but that was it. No, my emotion was more the shock of losing that intimate beaming voice, full of life, with which I had woken up on so many mornings.

I realized I was grieving Brian as a listener, and in that moment understood just how powerful the connection between presenter and audience can be.

Chapter Six

TAILGATING
THE GREATS

At university, I remember most clearly a single sentence from one tutor.

Studying the ancient and difficult *Beowulf*, we veered briefly into a discussion of who was on the throne in England when the poem was written. Then she broke off abruptly.

'In the end, kings and queens don't matter,' she said. 'Only poets do.'

As they say in darts: *One-hundred-and-eighty*. My tutor was bang on target. And it is true for the Beeb as well. The kings and queens – the people who run the place – are highly inspired and committed individuals who, with few exceptions, are quickly forgotten. The poets are the ones who live on: whether or not you liked his poetry, Redhead was one.

In saying this I am not even tangentially attacking the beleaguered managers of the Beeb, who seem to be up there with investment bankers and estate agents as everyone's favourite distressed asset class. Quite the opposite. With the rise of media as a career in the nineties – and, in parallel, an unfortunate collapse in the reputation of politics – a wave of super-bright people washed up in broadcasting. The producers around me were always high calibre, usually higher than the politicians I met. And as for the broadcasting executives at the very top, although the organizational machinery they worked with makes the DeLorean look roadworthy, they are mostly more impressive than the Cabinet.

But that is not the point. If we look solely within broadcasting, you find that presenters work in the certain knowledge that they, not the backstage crew, are the gifted ones. Producers, directors, editors, even the most powerful executives have all suffered a terrible twist of fate which must never be mentioned. At some stage they took a wrong turn, and the excitement of being at the microphone was snatched away forever. The deal is this: they pretend to be happy, and we pretend it doesn't matter.

Occasionally someone blows the gaffe on it. Nick Robinson was an upwardly mobile deputy editor of *Panorama* when he suddenly showed up in Westminster and demanded to appear on the air. It was not a breakdown, it was a career move. He joined the team of pol-corrs I was in and his brave manoeuvre – the equivalent of trying to flip a Scalextric car from one track to another, virtually impossible – paid off handsomely. He could have run the place, but running the place is no fun.

At certain junctures I became more and more convinced of the tragedy of all off-screen careers. My close friend James Stephenson, a first-rate deputy editor of *Newsnight* who in 2003 launched the *Politics Show* with me on BBC1, always seemed like the exception to my rule: he, it appeared, had chosen production and production had chosen him. Affable, intelligent and with an editor's gift for seeing trouble before it careened into you, surely he was the born producer? He assured me he had no desire whatsoever to be heard or seen on the air, and I reluctantly accepted his reassurances, thinking he had destroyed my theory.

One day he told me he was switching from Westminster to the

Middle East. He had been appointed bureau chief in Jerusalem. This was an off-air role, so there was nothing in the move to prove me wrong – until I rang his office to see if we could hook up for a drink before his departure.

'He is not around today,' said his feisty office manager, Sue Brewer, 'because *he has gone on a course to learn how to broadcast*.'

The cat was out of the bag! As Michael Buerk had said during a hilarious and very off-message address to my fellow trainees (in which he dismissed the entire generation of old-school announcer/news-readers as 'effeminate guardsmen'), why would you join the BBC and not broadcast? Buerk told us passionately: 'You might as well have gone into the Post Office.' He played us a tape of his greatest hits and our jaws dropped.

Once you are airside in the organization – which may be as little as ten per cent of the workforce – things look different. The presenters above you come into focus, and you have the chance to learn from the finest of them all. If you want to be one yourself, prepare to start tailgating the greats.

＊

I was once rushing to a story at Westminster. It was a dark winter evening. I came out of the double doors at full tilt, skidded on a heel and made off down the fog on Great Peter Street. But something in the bearing of the man standing on the pavement ahead slowed me up. When I passed him at jogging speed, he smiled at me through his glasses.

'I admire everything you have done,' I said.

'And I admire everything *you* do,' replied Sir Robin Day. 'But I don't know who you are.'

The greats are the ones who say something and make you realize they just saved you twenty years discovering it for yourself. I was speaking to Anna Ford and said, 'It's fun this, isn't it? Presenting shows? Interviewing? I feel we're lucky doing it.'

'Lucky?' she repeated incredulously. '*Lucky*? We are the luckiest people in the history of the world.'

Another time I was interviewing Anna on Radio 2 for Children in Need. 'Do the female newsreaders sometimes get together in a small room,' I asked her during a record, 'to explore their most intimate concerns, to open up about how things are going, and just give vent to their frustrations and their feelings?'

Her severe reply – 'Jeremy, don't let your fantasies run away with you' – certainly put me in my place.

Working on *Today*, I watched as Brian Redhead broke into a smile every time the red light told him his microphone was on: you could hear the smile in his voice. John Humphrys remains the towering figure – observing the way he prepped for the programme, I saw that he would dispatch a dozen items at speed to ensure he could focus all of his attention on just one interview, and sometimes one question, knowing it would be the one that counted. I never learnt from that; the morning I had to sit in on the show I was still preparing the 06.40 interview when the time hit seven o'clock.

The presenters on *Today* would sit across from each other, bantering irreverently about the management. 'Who is this Chamois Leather guy?' Redhead once said, referring to the executive Samir Shah. 'Is he working with Peter Bollocks?' Which could have been a reference to Peter Bell, or Horrocks, or both.

Watching the presenters who could cut it and the ones who could not, I want to say the secret was hard labour: undoubtedly nobody in the BBC has toiled harder than Humphrys and you cannot get there without it. But was that all you needed? Was it enough?

Last time there was a tube strike, I ran into work. Across Hyde Park from Hammersmith, seven miles.

Knackered, I arrived at our little Radio 2 office block and shambled through reception in my shorts, breathing heavily.

When I get to the lift and look to my left, there is someone else standing there – Sir Terry Wogan, at the time presenter of the breakfast show, in his perfectly pressed casual suit. Quite a contrast.

We get into the cramped lift. We say hello to each other. I am drenched in sweat, he is as cool as a cucumber carrying his briefcase. He is going to the sixth, where the studio is, and I am about to press for the second floor when I look at my watch.

'Terry,' I say, 'it's 7.28. You're on the air in ninety seconds.'

He replies, 'Yes, I'm early this morning.'

I say, 'Well let's get you to your studio before I go anywhere.' He gets out at the sixth, I go back down to my office, turn on the radio. Immediately the Radio 2 jingle plays and next, *that* voice. 'Good morning! This is Terry Wogan.'

He then says: 'One of the great things about a tube strike is that you get to meet your colleagues in the strangest places. So in the lift this morning, there was Jeremy Vine. Just finished a seven-mile run from Hammersmith. And believe me,' – an intake of breath, as if reminding himself of the bouquet – 'in a lift that size, you could tell.'

I reflected, that's the genius. He had not even thought about his show until I happened to give him the opening line.

The incident sums up the effortlessness of Sir Terry's art (and it is an art). When the Queen visited Broadcasting House in 2008, she said to him, 'How long have you worked here?' 'Oh, nobody works here,' was his reply, and if you are doing what you love then it does sometimes feel like that. I once proudly told some schoolchildren that life at the BBC was so exciting, 'I have never once looked at the clock since 1987. In fact I don't know what the clocks in the BBC look like.'

One pupil knocked me dead with the question: 'If you don't look at the clocks, how do you know when to stop speaking?'

When my wife and I went to see Peter Kay at the O2, I said the same to her about him as I say about Wogan to everyone: 'He just makes it look so easy!' Kay had entertained 15,000 people for nearly two hours with only a couple of fireworks for company. Terry entertained eight million for thirty years with no explosive materials at all, unless we count Sarah Kennedy. If not workrate, then what is their secret?

The answer most people come to straightaway is natural talent.

The Americans actually use the word 'talent' to refer to presenters – as in 'Do you want to see if the talent wants a Danish pastry?' – and producers think presenters have not noticed the word (and probably the pastry) is laced with sarcasm. It would be good to know which fragment of genetic code David Attenborough or Lenny Henry or Brian Cox or Mary Nightingale or Miranda Hart or John Peel all acquired that is somehow extra, bolted onto the other regular bits. Where is Ken Bruce's fragment? Did Fiona inherit hers from Ken?

The idea that broadcasting greatness is biological, that there is a small socket of DNA that fits all the microphones, gained traction in my own mind when my Radio 2 show adopted an 'official' allotmenteer – Terry Walton in the Rhondda Valley. It was all a bit experimental. But Terry's first broadcast was perfect; hilarious, actually. At sixty, he had never been on radio or television before and yet his rustling, bustling audio-tour of the vegetable patch could not have been bettered by a professional. In fact – and I am hoping he will not take this the wrong way – it was the sheer lack of professionalism that made Terry so real. When he got stung on the nose by a bee, or dropped his phone in a water butt, you really did believe what you were hearing. Eight years on, like the excellent Martin Lewis, Cristina Odone, David Wilson, Barbara Want, Philip Stott or Dr Sarah Jarvis, Terry is still a regular and has an army of fans. People who listen to my show mention him continually – *What's that guy on the allotment like? Have you met him? Where does he get all that energy from?* and so on. It is not only his parsnips that are completely natural.

*

I was talking to a manager about a DJ on another station who had recently found himself dumped. 'I thought he was really good,' I said, though probably without conviction. 'I mean technically, voicing over the records and all that – flawless – you know, and quick-witted.'

The manager's reply was one devastating word:

'Vanilla.'

What does vanilla mean? It means not standing out. Having a certain soullessness. Technically adept, sure. Professional (that word again). Smooth and inoffensive. Likeable – and forgettable. The biggest mistake of them all is to be flawless.

At this point we should call as evidence Russell Brand, whose magic was composed of all the opposite qualities.

Brand had to spend more time on his own allotment after getting my controller, and himself, the sack. Although he was at the wheel for one of the biggest disasters in radio history, he was a fascinating figure at Radio 2. Whatever the X factor is for radio presenters, he had it – and Y, and Z, and Q and W and every other factor too. Okay, I admit I watched him closely, seeing him as potentially one of the all-time most exciting radio voices (not necessarily incompatible with making the all-time most exciting mistake). He had been brought initially to 6 Music by Lesley Douglas, the zeitgeisty Radio 2 controller who would ultimately pay with her job.

When he was on 6, he would broadcast material that made everyone on my show recite it back to each other in amazement the following day. 'If you had a piece of fruit, where would you insert it into the Queen?' was one of his questions to the audience. 'Have you ever needed tin foil to smoke heroin in a hotel, and you go down to reception and say you need foil to reflect the lights better? Just to change the atmosphere of the room a bit . . .' all in that fluting nasal voice so reminiscent of Kenneth Williams. With the last example, realizing he was on dangerous ground, Brand then shouted: 'ALL DRUGS ARE WRONG!'

I know I should have resisted the charm, because in the end his seeming inability to do anything but filth would bring the entire station to its knees, but in the early stages there was something gloriously mental about Russell Brand. The station buzzed with rumours of his latest exploit, on or off the air – the time he had sex in the disabled toilets with a fan who came to watch the show, or the day he told his team to urgently courier a vegetarian curry from Knightsbridge.

Soon after Brand arrived on Radio 2 he asked me to be one of the guests on his Saturday evening show. Like a besotted fan, I still have the tape. I rang in from my kitchen and, just as I was about to be introduced, shouted up to my wife Rachel to tune in. This is what she heard:

Brand: Why don't you watch me on the telly?

Sidekick: I didn't know it was on. I don't tune in to Paul O'Grady every day.

Brand: (shouting) WHY? It's good. At the end of it he says (does impression) 'Go on, 'ave yer tea.' I like that.

Sidekick: Go on, 'ave your tea, luv.

Brand: I like that. He knows his audience are gonna have their tea. What are our audience doing afterwards? Go on, you poor sick pigs, go and have it off in a gutter. Go and slither around like vibrant eels you saucy bunch! I tell you who does listen to this show – Jeremy Vine.

Sidekick: Oh.

Brand: Jeremy Vine and his missus. (Starts singing) Jeremy Vine, and his wife, laying in bed, stiff and erect and all over each other. Slithering around in a sexual—

Sidekick: Play a song.

Brand: Alright, we're gonna play a song called 'Safety Dance', Men Without Hats, which I dedicate to Jeremy Vine who I believe is having unprotected sex with his wife right now. Jeremy Vine, Men Without Hats, we are playing this for the two of you … (Music starts).

Upstairs, my wife shouted, 'What the hell was that?'

For some reason I replied, 'Sorry.'

The next day I went to the press officer and was grimacing over the incident as well as a series of others for which Brand could easily have been crucified.

'How come the papers don't take him apart?' I asked.

'Oh, they love him,' was the fatal reply. We would find out just how little they loved him later.

Yet if you put aside all the offensive stuff – not easy – Russell Brand seemed to have been created purely for the purpose of broadcasting. His vocabulary and intellect were formidable. Lesley asked me to interview him for a big internal staff session and he launched into a diatribe about Wittgenstein and Dostoyevsky. Looking up at the 250-strong audience, I saw a broad grin on every single face – the first time that has ever happened at a BBC staff meeting. When I questioned him another time for the Radio Festival in 2008, this time in front of industry executives, I thought I should at least put him on his mettle. Onstage I read to him a criticism by Libby Purves of Radio 4, who had written in *The Times* that the pursuit of star presenters and the move into digital would result in a bewildering proliferation of platforms packed with what she called 'preening ninnies'.

Since that seemed aimed at Russell, I asked, what did he have to say to Libby?

'What that woman needs is a massive orgasm,' he replied.

Brand would stand outside our building smoking in a beanie hat that made him anonymous, and I would hover there and speak to him and felt just like I did when I tried to get in with the older and cooler boys at school. 'I love kids,' he said. 'Do you have kids?' I said I had two. I would have said seventy if I had thought that was the answer he wanted. Would he like to come round and see them? We fixed a date for him to meet Martha and Anna. The Ross–Brand debacle exploded at that very moment in the diary, not only blowing away our date but taking out of commission a radio voice I believe, with a little of the restraint that was sadly lacking on my radio station, could have become one of the very greatest.

How did we do that just then – move from Brian Redhead to Terry Walton to Russell Brand? That is what broadcasting does; puts a roof over all their heads. The very greatest either have the workrate or they are naturals or probably both. But that still does not quite tell the story. There are lots of hard-working and talented buskers. What is it that suddenly scoops one of them out of the railway station and into Wembley Stadium?

In the end I think the answer is that you have be an original. Original is the opposite of vanilla.

*

The greats get there by standing out. They create contrast.

Here is an example. A few months back we asked Tony Benn to speak to us about Iraq. He may be out of the Commons but he remains highly involved with politics and as sharp as a tack. On his own, he is remarkable enough.

By coincidence, Benn's arrival at Radio 2 coincided with an interview Steve Wright was doing with the glamour model Jordan. Before being taken to separate studios they met in the green room with one of our researchers listening in.

Tony Benn says courteously: 'Hello, who are you?'

'I'm Jordan.'

'What are you here to speak about?' He is like a child, wide-eyed.

'I'm publicizing my autobiography.'

Benn: 'Autobiography! But you're too young to have written an autobiography.'

'It's my second.'

The conversation ends and Benn arrives in my studio. He says, 'Jeremy, I've just met the most extraordinary woman. She was very young, and she's written *two* autobiographies.'

'What was her name?' I ask.

He says, 'I think it was Morgan.'

Somehow the act of meeting Jordan brought out the total Benn-ness of Benn; and meeting him made Jordan even more, er, Jordanian. Just as the colour-saturated Boris Johnson stood out in a grey House of Commons, or Susan Boyle set *Britain's Got Talent* alight, or Sargie brought the house down on *Strictly Come Dancing*; just as (to go highbrow for a moment) Picasso overturned the art world or Copernicus the universe; they all benefited from the contrast they created with what was around them – *they looked as if they should not be there.* That is how trailblazers always look. If you watch Sir Robin Day interviewing for ITN in the early days – when, for example, bow tie on, he dismantles an astonished Japanese foreign minister called Fujiyama in 1959 over ballbearing patents, with the poor man's translator objecting to 'this treachery' because he expected an easy ride – you see why Robin stood out. Flawed he may have been; he was not vanilla.

We should mention luck again. Every day you walk into a media employer and your staff fob works the turnstile, you are lucky. I was lucky in Carnaby Street. And very, very lucky with that bullet in Croatia. Years later I would be lucky again, moving from *Newsnight* to Radio 2 – saved from my dangerous tailgating of one presenter by a different kind of bullet that did for another.

Once you start asking what makes the greats – from JP to JY, and what a stretch that is – you find all kinds of answers come up. At a lunch in the nineties with Richard Sambrook, the boss of BBC News who would later be hurt in the Hutton crisis but survive and reach even greater heights, he asked me what made for success in

TV journalism. Quoting Brian Hanrahan's 'I counted them all out, and I counted them all back in', I told him my theory that broadcasters were usually made or broken by one defining moment.

The Moment could be good or bad, I went on. I always felt sorry for James Cox, who toiled away for a hundred years as a political broadcaster and then, because of one spicily worded question in one interview, retired to the headline:

JOURNALIST WHO SAID 'CRAP' ON THE BBC RETIRES

Richard did not go with my Theory of Moments. His reply was almost the opposite, and only a word long – 'Stamina.' That, he said, was the key component of greatness. Fortunately for him, he turned out to have it.

One mega-famous newsreader gave me good advice when I was thirty, but it was not what I expected. He leant over during dinner after a by-election and told me: 'I think you should get your teeth straightened.' I did, and wore a brace at night for two years, but it did not result in any more exclusives.

Presenters also need RAM. Computers have two types of memory. Read-only memory, ROM, is the total storage space on the hard drive – imagine a cupboard that can hold a thousand tennis balls. But there is a huge difference between having a large cupboard and being able to juggle. RAM is the active memory that allows multiple tasking. Some presenters have a vast ROM (it's all in there) but zero RAM (they can't recall it quickly). David Dimbleby has colossal RAM – like the Andrews Neil and Marr, Huw Edwards, Nick Ferrari, Paul Merton or Graham Norton. But if you remember back to *Question Time* before David, it was a different story. Peter Sissons moved to the show from traditional newsreading, which requires neither ROM nor RAM. The new job was unkind to him. He had a large cupboard, for sure, but looked out of practice with his juggling. Low RAM is dangerous in a live environment – your presenter can crash.

Yet as I write this chapter about tailgating the greats, the clearer the menu of qualities becomes, the more mistrustful of it we should feel. In the end, by definition, the shared assets of this peculiar, non-unionized bunch of slightly disturbed individuals – harder to herd than cats – are necessarily hard to pin down and probably impossible to copy. The key is to be real. And whatever cynics may say, the real you cannot be faked.

*

In 2007, for the *Radio Times*, I had to interview Sir Bruce Forsyth. It was his eightieth birthday, so I googled the biography – learnt to tap-dance on the tin roof of family home at ten; first show in 1942 aged fourteen, stage name Bruce the Mighty Atom; *Generation Game* starts when I'm aged six; hosting *Strictly* puts him past fifty years in TV.

As Elton John once said of Bill Clinton, 'When people are that famous, you just stare.'

We meet at the Palladium. He says, 'I've been on your radio show!' and I hesitate because I can't quite place the occasion, so he says to the assembled company: 'Oh great! I remember him, he doesn't remember me! Who's interviewing who here?'

Everyone around us laughs. Brucie has what he needs: an audience.

We talk for about an hour and he is charming. Every time I ask a question I notice he takes a small plastic dish out of his pocket, unscrews it and licks all round it. Inside appears to be a black blob. The spectacle starts to make me feel a little queasy.

Finally I say, 'Bruce, I've got to ask you – what is in that plastic holder?'

He says, 'Lozenge.' Apparently he licks it during my questions and then puts it away when he answers. 'I can't put these directly in my mouth, because you must never have too much menthol.' He adds, 'I did it backstage in the Palladium in 1970 and I do it now.'

In front of me he drinks a jar of Complan, the vitamin drink made from mixing water and a thick white powder. 'You must never have too much to eat in the evenings,' he muses.

I think, I am getting fifty years of wisdom here. The interview is fascinating. Sir Bruce has outlived almost everyone and he has nothing left to prove. But the performance is continuous nevertheless.

Hoping we've got on well, I ask him at the end, 'Do you have email?'

Evidently we haven't got on quite that well. 'No. Er, yeah. Well – Jeremy, feed me that line again.'

Again? Okay. 'Bruce, do you have email?'

'No, I'm far too famous!'

And once again the assembled company roar with laughter. The quip may not even be funny. It doesn't matter. It brought us joy.

Kevin Bakhurst, controller of the BBC News Channel, once gave me great advice almost by accident. I was having to make a choice between two jobs. Taking one would have meant cutting back on Radio 2. He disapproved. 'Jeremy, just think about where you give pleasure,' he told me.

Giving pleasure. It is such a simple thought. It is what Sir Bruce Forsyth has done for half a century. However much cynics dismiss him as hackneyed, they could never compete on the same turf.

When the Burmese opposition leader Aung San Suu Kyi emerged from house arrest after fifteen years she said that, despite the anxieties caused by her confinement, her life 'had been made much more complete' by a World Service music request show fronted by Dave Lee Travis. Wait – the *Hairy Cornflake*? Everyone laughed as if she must have got the wrong name. But no. He gave her pleasure.

Working in South Africa, I was poleaxed by a photoshoot at which Nelson Mandela met the Spice Girls. It should have been routine. As we watched them drape themselves over him amid peals of laughter, someone next to me asked President Mandela, 'Sir, is this a good day?'

He replied, with total seriousness, 'This ... is ... the greatest day of my life.'

But we should not be cynical. They gave pleasure. Giving pleasure is a gift in itself.

In Chapter Three I said my childhood had been fine apart from one remarkable incident. I feel this chapter is in need of a dramatic crescendo. So now is the time – in the words of Erin Callan, chief financial officer of Lehman Bank just before it went under – 'to open the kimono'.

In 1978, a tender thirteen with a choirboy's unbroken voice, I wrote a postcard to a presenter called Maggie Norden at Capital Radio, suggesting myself for a ten-minute slot she featured every Sunday called 'Teenage Disc Jockey'. To my delight, she invited me up to the station to record the segment. I came on the train with my mum. I played 'Good Luck Charm' by Elvis and a version of 'Annie's Song' by James Galway, an early error of judgement. But there were two positives. The slot was introduced by Kenny Everett with a song:

> *Don't be nervous, don't be rocky*
> *You're our teenage ... disco jockey*

meaning I can claim a fleeting association with one of the greatest of them all. Plus, it gave me first sight of a radio studio.

The effect was electrifying. Was that really *Roger Scott* in the glass cubicle in the opposite corner? I left Capital that afternoon with my mind made up – I was going to play records for a living. So I got cracking straightaway, writing a letter to every local radio station in the country asking for a job. My parents found fifty stamps and envelopes missing. They remained supportive, even while I was typing each letter one-fingered on their manual typewriter. The sound was like a dripping tap in a metal basin for days. Each letter was personal, each had a reference to the area. I was deeply interested in Northampton, in Leicester, in Suffolk, Glasgow and even more so in Derry. I was hugely committed to Newcastle and to Cardiff. I was equally fascinated by Norwich.

The station managers must have sniffed out the con, or possibly recognized the uneven typing of a thirteen-year-old. Over the weeks that followed the replies dribbled back. Every single one negative. Some not even very friendly.

But I never forgot my brief brush with Kenny Everett, surely the greatest DJ in the history of British radio. As a teenager I would go to the spare room in the family home to hear Kenny's Saturday show – sitting on the floor, radio on the bedside table next to me, loving all those doolally sound effects and sackable offences.

I feel very sad when I think that Everett – just like his friend Freddie Mercury – was taken from us by Aids only a matter of months before scientists found the drug combination to fight the virus which causes it. If Kenny Everett were alive today he would be on Radio 2, no question. I would see him in the lift (just as I see Tony Blackburn, Bob Harris and Johnnie Walker) and I would tell him that I am only standing in the lift on my way to do today's show because, when I was a teenager, he inspired me.

Maybe it all comes down to that. You tailgate the greats and try to work out what the secret is, and in the end it is no secret at all. It is the most obvious thing in the world. They give pleasure.

Chapter Seven

TO WESTMINSTER
BY U-BOAT

On 5 May 1945, as the Second World War ended, a small group of Nazi sailors committed one last, foolhardy act – they got me my first break in television.

For reasons unknown at the time, the crew of a German submarine carrying a new design of acoustic torpedo ignored the order of Admiral Doenitz to turn back from patrol duties and surrender. Instead their vessel, U-boat 534, set course for Norway. British Liberator aircraft chased it and dropped depth charges. The submarine crew managed to shoot down one bomber but they were hit by a depth charge. The U-boat took in water and sank to the seabed. Some of the crew escaped through the torpedo tubes.

Five decades later in a sun-drenched office in London, the bombed submarine was giving the editor of *Breakfast News* a headache. Bob Wheaton – who was also the boyfriend of Jill Dando – had seen that the sub was due to be pulled from the sea but had no one to cover the story. He summoned me to his office and paid me some brisk compliments for my work on *Today*. I noticed immediately that he was better dressed than any of the editors in radio.

'What do you want out of your career, Jeremy?'

'To be a presenter,' I said without hesitation.

He peered at me. 'Do you have a decent jacket?'

I said I did.

'Where is it?'

'I've got it on.'

Television, Wheaton gently reminded me, involved appearance. There is no getting away from it: the person actually has to appear. He said my double-breasted blazer with shiny gold buttons was 'fine for radio', and began to tell me about how a German submarine would be pulled from the depths of the Kattegat Sea by a team of Danish winchers, and he had no staff.

Only one U-boat had been recovered since the end of the Second World War.

'Could be good. It'll get you off radio. They start the lift on Tuesday.' It was Friday. 'You should get going tomorrow. Go downstairs to the newsroom where the crew will meet you.'

It was hard enough to find the foreign desk in the sprawling TV newsroom. The foreign editor was Vin Ray. He called over a sound man, Duncan Stone, and cameraman Brian Hulls. I was apologizing to all three for my inexperience, but they already had a map stretched across two desks. We would stay in Anholt, in Denmark, and charter a plane every day to fly us to the island nearest the recovery site. They pointed everything out. Film crews are like the military when it comes to logistics.

'Anyone know anything about Anholt?' one shouted across the newsroom. 'Yeah, it's all right,' somebody called back.

By the time our small boat bobbed close to the scene of the lift, I was marvelling at the tortuousness of the trip. We had flown from Gatwick to Denmark, chartered a plane to the island, landed after two abortive swoops on a runway that seemed too short, shot a so-called 'piece-to-camera' where I explained that we were about to hire a tug to take us out to sea, then hired a tug that took us out to sea and shot another PTC saying we had hired a tug and been taken out to sea.

But there was, as yet, no U-boat. Seasick because of the motion of the tug, I had thrown up over the side a dozen times and was suspicious that Brian might have filmed me for his Christmas tape. All we had to shoot now were some rusty barges and cranes bobbing unhappily in the water. The Danish newspaper financing the lift, *Den Blå Avis*, explained to us by phone that the lifting tackle had only just taken hold of the stern of the submarine on the seabed.

'This might take several days.'

'Right,' I said queasily, aware of the motion of the tug.

'There is, of course,' the spokesman went on, 'much speculation about what is inside.'

Speculation? I did not clock, as I should have, that the newspaper must be responsible for the speculation. Instead I asked what exactly the speculation was.

'Well, this U-boat, number 534, was part of a convoy racing away from Germany as the Third Reich fell. We do not know why they disobeyed the order to surrender. The suspicion is that there may be the bodies of senior Nazis on board—'

This was getting so bloody exciting now. I was writing in my notepad, *the bodies of senior Nazis.*

'—and they may have been trying to get away with precious works of art, Old Masters and the like, which we may find in the sub.'

Oil paintings and dead Nazis! This was shaping into something. Heart racing, still green with nausea, I addressed the camera dramatically.

'And there is now speculation that this operation going on behind me may yield a spectacular haul, because . . .'

Regurgitating the phone call, as well as the rest of my breakfast. But the story was alive. The cut piece appeared on the news the next morning. Grainy black-and-white archive of German submarines racing through the sea brought home the drama of U-boat 534's last journey. My PTC was reinforced by an interview with a recovery worker who could barely contain his excitement, and then with me rounding off:

'...so more than forty years on, the U-boat should break the surface of the Kattegat Sea by the end of the week and reveal its secrets at last. Jeremy Vine, *Breakfast News*, Anholt.'

This being the summer there wasn't much news, so the story of U-boat 534 started to excite interest. It seemed to have everything – war, Nazis, art, secret torpedoes, the open sea and plenty of suspense: the Alfred Hitchcock sort and the industrial winching sort.

A cynic would say there was just a waterlogged submarine and a cubic mile of speculation. In fact there was not even a submarine yet. But it is remarkable how uncynical journalists become when there is space on the front page to play for. The main news bulletins now wanted a slice of the story. *Breakfast News* had been shoved out of the way in the rush to commandeer me.

'What can you offer us today?' a more senior editor growled from London. It turned out to be the voice of Mike Blakey, a keystone of the BBC newsroom (years later I heard him yell across to a programme editor: 'CANCEL THE LATE BELSEN!'). I told him the winching had started.

'It's coming closer to the surface.'

'Brilliant,' he said in his gravelly voice. 'What can you send us?'

'We're going to film the recovery operation from the air.' The plane would circle over it.

'Great. And any more news on what's inside?'

'The latest is Nazi gold, but it's just speculation.'

'Gold?'

We ran on the evening news. Large pieces of Nazi gold, huge gleaming hunks too heavy for a single man to lift, had bought me my debut as a primetime television reporter. My mum saw the piece and when I rang her she complained about my 'strange constipated expression'. But the package was dazzling – aerial shots with me in the back of the plane pointing down at the sea, talk of treasure, more archive footage, drums groaning with the stress of steel cables.

'Just thirty feet to go before we finally discover what's inside the submarine. It is getting more and more exciting to be here,' I signed off.

Back home, friends and family were thrilled. I had suddenly emerged from whatever laundry basket the Beeb had been hiding me in. The newsdesk kept wanting updates. Twenty feet to the surface, then fifteen. Gold, Nazi commanders, maybe secret Third Reich documents; the speculation mounted gloriously.

With ten feet to go, Duncan had a stroke of genius – hire an underwater film crew to get pictures of the U-boat for the first time. It was expensive, and the footage came back as a luminous green wash punctuated by the occasional mysterious rivet. But as the submarine rose, so did the story, lifting itself another couple of inches on the running order.

Not for a second was I expecting it, but the moment the U-boat was pulled clear of the sea, the story died.

For me it was the start of the real news. At last we could explain what was actually inside. For the newsdesk, it was time to move on. The bulletins ran first pictures of the submarine and then I got a call from the man at the Danish newspaper.

'I'm sorry, there seems to be nothing on board. We have been through the hatch.'

'Nothing?'

'A man went inside. Condoms and some empty bottles of wine, that's all we found,' he explained.

Disconcerted, I rang London. 'We're going to file on what they've found.'

'Which is—?'

'Er, nothing.'

'Nothing?'

'Condoms and some empty wine bottles.'

'Okay, never mind. It's pretty busy today. Just come back. Nice work, Jeremy.'

I was glowing at the compliment and his use of my name, but not entirely willing to give up. Shouldn't I at least do a piece saying there was nothing in the sub? He could not see why. It was not a story. There was other news.

The camera crew showed no surprise. 'The speculation has now dismounted,' said Brian Hulls sagely, as if he had seen the same phenomenon many times before.

Back in Britain, I unlocked the front door of my flat just as my neighbour Don was coming out (he worked for Barings Bank; two years later a rogue trader would sink it faster than the submarine).

'What was in that thing after all? I missed the grand finale.'

'Just condoms,' I said.

'Bit of a wasted trip?'

'And wine bottles.'

Over the next few weeks a dozen people started the same conversation as my neighbour. 'Hey, what was in your sub?' And I would explain: nothing. Nothing was in that bloody sub. And nothing was on the news. Nothing cannot be news, so nothing had been reported. The best line in the movie *Jaws* is when Brody says: 'You're gonna need a bigger boat.' We had the right size of boat. We just needed a bigger story.

But if events in Anholt taught me a sharp lesson, they also did me a big favour. I was not to know, but at Westminster they were scouting for a temporary political correspondent to fill a gap. Luckily for me, someone had seen this rangy, constipated nerd pop up in Denmark barking about Nazi gold. Patrick Gregory, news editor at the political unit, suggested I should come and do some reporting at Parliament 'to see if it floats your boat'.

Okay, thanks, enough submarine references now. I thought that was probably the last I would endure.

But my visit to the recovery site in the Kattegat Sea would turn out to be the perfect preparation for Westminster.

*

I got ready for the BBC political unit at Millbank by buying a Wheaton-compliant jacket. Single-breasted, dark plastic buttons. My friends had only slightly rained on the parade. 'Politics is so dull,' they said. 'At least with *Today* you were jetting all over the world.'

To Dudley, I might have thrown in. But I didn't even agree with the first half of their statement. Politics is not dull. As John Cole, the man who broke the mould as political editor said, 'Politics is one man wanting another man's job.' And that was just the BBC office.

Politics is human drama. If a politician announces new bedsheets for the health service, the health correspondent will tell us the size and colour of the sheets. The political correspondent then weighs in to inform us that the knives are out for the minister because this is her third gaffe in a month and the bedsheet policy is being seen as a coded attack on the Chancellor. Allies of the health secretary claim the whispers emanate from sources close to the defence secretary who is accused of launching a plot to destabilize the prime minister, there is talk of a

SPLIT

and pretty soon everyone resigns and there is a general election – all of which generates more jobs for political correspondents who tell us that every sneeze at Westminster is a story. It is fairly difficult not to enjoy all of that, even if it does sometimes trouble the conscience.

On my first shift at Westminster I have a vivid memory of half a dozen of the pol-corrs sitting at their desks chatting. 'Why are you here?' one asked me quietly. 'Labour can't ever win again.' On paper he looked to be bang on – the Conservatives had dumped Mrs T in 1990, then fought and won the '92 election in the teeth of a terrible recession. Soon afterwards there had even been stories that the re-elected John Major was 'finding the job too easy'. Meanwhile Labour had switched Neil Kinnock with John Smith, who were like apples and apples, and the seemingly unanswerable argument being made by some of my new colleagues ran like this: if Labour can't win power when the Conservatives have driven the economy against the rocks, how will they ever win?

In other words – where's the story?

Very quickly we would see the answer unfold before our eyes, and, to quote Freddie Mercury, there was a kind of magic in the drama. The pound fell out of the ERM and John Major fell out with his Chancellor. Conservative Eurosceptics started misbehaving 'like teenagers who have just discovered sex', to steal Robin Oakley's best line. Then one morning I arrived early in the House of Commons office to be told, 'You might as well go down to Labour HQ on Walworth Road. There's nothing else happening and apparently John Smith has been taken ill.'

By the time I arrived at party headquarters, word was surfacing that the leader of the opposition was dead. His first heart attack had been six years previously; that morning Smith had suffered a second in his flat, then another in the ambulance taking him to a hospital whose A&E department he had last visited during a campaign against its closure.

A newsflash broke into the morning schedule on BBC1. Standing in the reception of Labour headquarters, clutching a payphone connected to the television studio, I heard the editor Cathy Hunt shout in the gallery: 'This is a CATEGORY ONE death', a bit of editorial jargon that nevertheless captured the seismic scale. Being cut up live on BBC1 in the days before rolling news channels was a truly rare experience. After describing the tearful scenes around me, I was asked who would lead Labour now. Broadcasting can do that: with a slip of the rota and a twist of fate, suddenly it is the new boy who is asked to pass judgement on a generation. A red-eyed Smith aide, Tracey Woolas, distracted me by appearing uneasily on the stairs. 'I think you will see the name of Tony Blair come through very strongly,' I replied, quietly hoping I had made up for my misreading of the war in Yugoslavia.

The birth of New Labour and the parallel collapse of the Conservative party were fascinating to me. I have to admit I worked my socks off (they too were replaced with a more televisual pair). With the *Six O'Clock News* showing three, maybe four pieces each day from Westminster, the ambitious team of junior pol-corrs below Robin Oakley had every chance to put ourselves about on the pitch. You considered you had 'scored' if your report ran on a television bulletin, and the goal was especially valuable if you had got the story yourself. The junior players – Edwards, Robinson, Mardell, Sopel, Bailey, Quinn, Vine, etc. – saw ourselves as midfielders, with Oakley and Sergeant playing upfront in a striking role. In football manager parlance, John Sergeant was supposed to work 'in the hole' behind Oakley as the political editor's deputy. The idea was that the midfield would get the ball off the opposition with some fairly violent tackling, then gracefully slot it through to Sargie, who would lay the ball off to Robin, who would score.

But the political editor sometimes found himself in front of an open goal, only for Sargie to slide brilliantly through him and put the ball in the net. Since Robin was one of the sweetest and most honest workers ever employed by the Beeb, this was genuinely painful to watch.

Not only that, the midfield were obsessed with getting on the scoresheet ourselves. That would mean not only taking the play through the opposition's defence – which wasn't easy, since Michael Brunson at ITN and Sky's Adam Boulton were world class players – but also to get in front of goal without passing the story to Oakley or Sargie.

One technique which worked was the Forrest Gump Method, whereby you came back from an assignment with a pile of rushes and apologized for the fact that you had stupidly strayed into every shot, and despite very clear instructions the cameraman had filmed the interview with both you and the politician in frame throughout, which had made you jolly cross, and you had exchanged some pretty firm words with him, but of course it did mean the only person who could now cut the package for the network news was you. This was effective, but dangerous if repeated too often: we were a team, after all.

That team ate, drank, slept, lived and breathed politics. Because Millbank was now churning out so much material, superstar general reporters would occasionally join us with a fanfare and, almost without exception, strike the wrong note. One destroyed her reputation in a trice by asking the person sitting next to her, 'When Margaret Thatcher became Conservative leader, were they in power or in opposition?' It might be an obscure historical fact, but to us it was like asking what that red stuff in the middle of a doughnut was. (Years later, on Radio 2, a researcher asked, 'Does Blair have an 'e' in it?' and I reflected again on how swiftly a person can dismantle themselves.)

Of the big cheese general reporters, Huw Edwards confided to me: 'I love it when these people march in here thinking they're God, then when the red light comes on it's obvious they haven't got a bloody clue about the story.' Politics is all about fine detail, but a lot of the incomers seemed to work with a supersized paintbrush and only carried tins of black and white. What they thought was monochrome was actually kaleidoscopic. Here I must quote Sergeant again. After I unwisely suggested to him that reporters could get by with 'ninety seconds of information' on any given topic, since that was the length of most television pieces, he drew himself up to his full height and protested that he was only able to condense stories to ninety seconds 'because I have spent a lifetime studying the issues'.

The pol-corr unit must have looked like a tight ship. But things troubled me. Looking back, I do think *being troubled* is a vital quality in a journalist. Let me give an example of what caused me unease and see what you think.

When I arrived at the first New Labour party conference in 1994, Tony Blair had just become leader and was about to drop a bombshell. He rose to make his debut speech in the packed auditorium, and promised 'a clear set of values on one piece of paper'.

Right next to me, but already streets ahead, Patrick Wintour of the *Guardian* turned and raised his eyebrows. 'That's Clause Four he's talking about.'

'Yeah, exactly,' I agreed – a key rule of journalism is *Try never to look surprised when you hear something you didn't know.* I watched the activists applaud. The television news machine swung into action. Abolishing the only part of Labour's constitution anyone had heard of was big stuff – Clintonization, the pundits were calling it. We started rounding up interviewees. Bulletins were going crazy for the story. Was anyone angry about the speech?

'Only the usual suspects,' the correspondents were telling them.

'Shadow Cabinet?'

'Nothing on the record, not a chance.'

'Off the record?'

'Not really.'

Discipline was tight. Late at night I ended up on the balcony at the conference centre, waiting for John Prescott with a camera. Blair's deputy had agreed to do a sound bite for the morning news. Despite his Old Labour credentials, we had no hope of anything even slightly disloyal. Prescott was no fool. He had to back the speech.

To my surprise, when he got to the top of the stairs he was accompanied by Alastair Campbell, Blair's head of communications. Campbell hovered as we made small talk.

'Is my hair straight?' Prescott asked.

'Yes, fine,' I said. 'I'll just be asking you about the speech, if that's okay.'

'Okay, hang on.' Prescott was stooping to see his reflection in the lens of the camera, running his hand across his fringe. 'Actually, I got Tony to sign my copy of it.'

'Really?' I asked.

Prescott was staring at himself in the lens, straightening his tie now. 'Yes. So I had a record of the moment he gave my party a stuffing.'

Campbell took a step forward. 'That's not for you.'

Prescott straightened up. 'Ready to start?'

I paused. Glanced at the cameraman. 'Sure.' Prescott settled himself, smiled at me. I asked him about the speech. He praised it for a full five minutes. 'Traditional values in a modern setting', and so on. No sign even of the merest reservation, certainly no sign of a deputy unhappy with his leader.

'Cheers, guys,' said Campbell as they walked off.

And then the cameraman tapped me on the shoulder.

'Hey, listen Jeremy, I got that,' he said. 'The bit where he was straightening his tie. My tape was rolling.'

I raced back to the edit suite and shoved the tape in the machine. Sure enough, there it was. Prescott's face mooning into view as he sought his reflection. Hair, tie, and:

I got Tony to sign my copy of his speech. So I had a record of the moment he gave my party a stuffing.

Now I had the mother of all moral dilemmas. Could you broadcast something that was effectively a surreptitious recording? Or was that tantamount to bugging Prescott's hotel room? Could we dump the real interview, and put out the much more real non-interview?

It would have rocked New Labour, then in its infancy. **TONY BLAIR PLUNGED INTO FIRST BIG CRISIS** ... PARTY SPLIT OVER CLAUSE FOUR ... **PRESCOTT HAS HIS LEADER FOR LUNCH** ... it was not difficult to imagine the headlines.

I thought and thought and thought. I wanted to, but I just could not bring myself to do it. Late at night I brought in a senior producer who looked at the tape in a mixture of wonder and alarm, and agreed. How could we? The next best thing was to speak to a colleague, so I quietly relayed the incident to Nick Jones, a political correspondent who never went out without a full set of spanners to insert into the spokes of any party press operation.

His eyes boggled. 'Gave my party a stuffing!' he noted Prescott's phrase. 'Thanks Jeremy. Hmm . . .'

I did not know that Nick Jones had a piece of corroborating intelligence. Prescott, he had been told, was not informed about Blair's speech until the weekend before. Jones now appeared on the BBC *Conference Live* programme and set the Catherine wheel spinning:

'At least one Shadow Cabinet member has described Mr Blair as "stuffing the party" with this speech – and it's also emerging that the deputy leader John Prescott was not even told about the plan until a couple of days ago.'

Retribution was swift. Campbell bulldozed into the press room and gave Nick Jones a high-octane public carpeting. It was the talk of the newsrooms within half an hour. With dozens of journalists looking on, the communications chief berated my colleague, veins jumping in his temple, calling his story 'bollocks' and 'a load of fucking crap' and asking him how he dared report it when he had no way of knowing it was true.

'But this is terrible,' I told the producer running the coverage that day. 'Prescott himself said that thing about stuffing the party and we even got it on tape. I'll go and get it and show you.'

My colleagues waited. I found the edit suite exactly as it had been left the night before. But where the tape had sat on a top shelf, my hand now probed a gap. It had disappeared.

I searched high and low for that Prescott interview. It was nowhere to be found. To this day I have no idea what became of the tape. Not being able to find it not only spiked the story – it also left my colleague unprotected in the onslaught from Campbell and his friends.

The next morning Donald Macintyre, political editor of the *Independent*, wrote:

Alastair Campbell, Tony Blair's incoming press secretary, could be seen in the cramped press room at Blackpool's Winter Gardens yesterday giving a loud and public dressing-down to a BBC reporter who had dared suggest that John Prescott had been told only a few days before the party conference, as a fait accompli, that Mr Blair would be seeking the replacement of Clause Four.

We all make mistakes, and the row is a sign of the highly proactive briefing style of the new Blair office. But it also illustrates an understandable desire on the part of the leadership to make clear what is true, that Mr Prescott was involved in intimate discussion with Mr Blair on the bombshell in his speech, from several weeks ago.

Excuse me: WE ALL MAKE MISTAKES??!!?! THE HIGHLY PROACTIVE BRIEFI— !!??%@!?!! The phrases made my head swim with expletives. And yes, I was more than troubled that day, I was distraught. Eventually I came to the view that I should have packaged up Prescott's comments and run them regardless of the blowback. In a competitive field, that was definitely the worst day's work I have done for the BBC. It was one thing to leave the real comments unbroadcast; it was quite another to put the unreal comments out. The news we broadcast – that Prescott backed the speech completely – made us joint operators of the smoke machine. It was a disservice to the viewer and probably not a great service to John Prescott either (he is, after all, among the bluntest of politicians). Nick Jones had made a brave attempt to correct the situation and been sandbagged. I was the coward.

But then, over the years that followed, I thought about it some more. Can you really run a tape which has been recorded without a person's knowledge? Sure, that's what happened with Mr Brown and Mrs Duffy. But it is also what happened with those people who were a bit too clever with telephones on the *News of the World*, and look where they ended up.

*

The Prescott Tape had given me the utterly fundamental lesson on politics. There are two worlds at Westminster – the sunlit world and the unlit world. And this is where our submarine lurches back into the story. Arriving at Parliament via U-boat turned out to be perfect, because in politics there is the world above water and the world below. The politicians only want you to see the world above. The reporters have to bring the rest to the surface.

Politicians divide their time between the false world of breezy waves and press releases, and the real world where all the serious business gets done: they move between Westminster, and Westminster-under-the-Sea. One Tory MP who told me unattributably, 'John Major is an utter disgrace, he must go tomorrow' drew a deep breath when my microphone was turned on and then announced: 'I back the Prime Minister and I wish my colleagues would stop this pathetic sniping from the shadows.'

Television has a serious problem because we find it so difficult to film in the shadows. No one has yet zoomed in on a policy being hatched or a minister being lined up for the sack. One of the most famous Sunday interview programmes was called *On the Record* – the title inadvertently advertised all its shortcomings, since a lot of what is said on the record is either not interesting or not true.

None of this was a problem for a political correspondent: quite the opposite. It made life joyous for us. Every day was an eye-opener, because listeners and viewers relied on us to describe what was going on below the surface. Cabinets and shadow cabinets are built like cardboard guttering, and we happily collected every leak. If we had collectively put out a programme it would have been called *Off the Record*. We became fixtures outside Number Ten, on balconies overlooking Parliament, in front of this or that party HQ and anywhere else that moved (or, more likely, didn't). Oakley once told me: 'You are the first correspondent to do a piece to camera while running down a fire escape.' I cannot remember the significance of the fire escape, or even the story, but I was probably outside yet another building our cameras had not been allowed into. Suddenly I, as a callow twenty-something, was being asked not just to relay the content of speeches by people thirty years older, but to *judge them*: this, when you think about it, is extraordinary. Effectively our job was to say, 'It may look one way, but the reality is different as I shall now explain.' Which was fine when we got it right.

After Blair became Labour leader, John Major's poll ratings collapsed. Conservatives accused Blair of stealing their clothes, but that only sounded like an endorsement. I was in the press gallery of the House of Commons when the Tory MP Tim Rathbone asked the Prime Minister a marvellous question that seemed to sum up all his party's frustrations:

> *Rathbone:* During the course of today, when the Prime Minister looks back to his trip to the Far East, did he remember seeing there a beautiful and very rare flower called the *Rafflesia arnoldii*, which is parasitic in nature, is without a stem or roots and which, with its vines, embraces any handy, strong tree? If he did, did he draw any conclusions from seeing it?

> *Major:* I saw no such flowers on that occasion.

John Major looked witheringly at Blair as he uttered the words 'on that occasion'. The Conservatives were rapidly being embroiled in scandals and disasters. An Italian journalist once wrote, 'Governments are like nappies. They must be changed regularly, and for the same reason.' Major was finding the argument hard to resist. While on the surface he made out everything was set fair, events in Westminster-under-the-Sea moved at stomach-churning speed.

In 1995 John Major told a private meeting of his backbenchers: 'When your back's against the wall, it's time to turn around and start fighting.' (One of the MPs in the room came out and told me, 'We wondered what the wall had done wrong.')

Major then called a press conference in the Downing Street Rose Garden. No one knew why.

Now, as a political correspondent, I like to think we were a fairly clued-up bunch. By which I mean, if the PM calls a news conference in a garden the media are hardly ever allowed into, you would think we would be able to ping our contacts in the hours leading up to it and find out exactly what the purpose was. But somehow the entire Westminster operation – by which I mean all the news organizations put together – failed to predict that Major would sensationally resign the Conservative leadership.

Not only that. When he did resign, we predicted he would not be challenged by anyone in his own Cabinet.

Then, when he was, we said if he failed to secure the votes of more than a hundred of his own backbenchers he would be finished.

Then, when he did, he wasn't.

As we discussed this litany of misses – all of which had been mitigated, of course, with phrases like 'time will tell' and 'too early to be certain of this, but' – I would like to say we were embarrassed, but we were too busy to be.

The leadership challenger was John Redwood. Never before have I seen BBC staff so electrified as the pol-corrs were when the story broke. They were like dogs on heat, prowling for a backside to sniff. I was learning fast. Probably too fast – my next mistake was going to teach me just how much power had been vested in these young hands.

A Conservative MP approached me in the lobby of the House of Commons and told me 'a minister may resign' to come out in support of Redwood.

Sensing an opportunity to shine, I went live on the *One O'Clock News*. I couched my intelligence carefully. 'Just a rumour,' I said, but I had been 'given information' that we could see a 'ministerial resignation this afternoon' by someone who will be 'publicly supporting Redwood.' I did not name my source or the minister; come to think of it, the source never named the minister either.

Unfortunately, someone at Reuters was watching this broadcast and flashed a very slightly exaggerated one-line message up on their city wire service:

'CABINET MINISTER TO RESIGN TO BACK REDWOOD.'

The pound started to fall.

The obvious suspect was Michael Portillo, at the time a so-called 'bastard' right-winger, who happened to be having lunch with Mark Mardell, one of my colleagues. Later Mardell told me Portillo was paged by Central Office during the dessert. Their urgent message read: 'Rumours you are resigning – please deny.'

Another right-wing minister, the late Eric Forth, was chased down the street by camera crews and a sound man who shouted: 'When are you going to say what you know about John Redwood?' a question it was almost impossible to answer. Because he had a sense of humour, Forth could not stop laughing, which only made him look more suspicious. By the end of the day the sequence of events that started with my remark on the lunchtime news had caused a collapse in sterling not seen since the so-called 'Valentine's Day massacre' of the pound the previous February.

After I got home, jangling with battlefield nerves, my darling mum rang. 'So, Jeremy,' she said, 'what did you get up to today?'

I replied, 'I drove the pound down.'

I was twenty-nine. A bit young to be doing that, really.

It is not surprising that politicians get flummoxed and more than a little annoyed. They see unelected reporters tell people what their speech was *really* about, when all they want to do is lash themselves to the camera tripod and deliver it direct.

Infuriatingly for them, reporters are also responsible for building narratives. These can be incredibly powerful. The columnist Peter Oborne once wrote about joining the *Evening Standard*'s parliamentary team at the same time I joined the BBC's, and said he expected to be sacked because initially he found he had no idea how to recognize a political story: 'I acquired a haunted look, and lost more than a stone in weight.'

Then someone explained the secret to him. An event was not newsworthy unless it was levered into a running narrative. So a story that inflation had risen by 0.2% would struggle to make page sixteen. But writing that a rise in inflation had 'plunged the government into fresh turmoil' could easily splash on the front. Once he understood this, wrote Oborne, 'my fortunes started to improve.'

The politicians regularly confronted me (and I suspect all the other reporters at Westminster) about this state of affairs. The classic question would be phrased like this: 'Why did you spend thirty seconds showing my speech and then five minutes analysing it?'

The cocky journalist could reply airily, 'If you told us the truth (in Andrew Marr's phrase, "spoke fluent human"), then you could be on programmes the whole time.' Had I been especially brave, I might even have shared my submarine story with them and told them to slide out through the torpedo hatch and ... no, you're right, they would have done the thousand-yard stare on me.

But the fact is that the media do not exactly make it easy for the politicians to come up for air.

Once, when I was presenting *Newsnight*, the luminously bright editor George Entwistle had the idea of bringing in the Labour chairman Charles Clarke to discuss why politicians hide all the interesting stuff and avoid all the key questions. 'Let's tell Clarke, "You be frank, and we won't punish you for it." Let's see what happens!'

Great idea. Next to me and Clarke in the studio were Andrew Marr and the Conservative Michael Gove. And very civilized our discussion was too. Clarke frankly brought up the difficulty of having open debate when every candid moment is described as a split or a gaffe. 'If I'm honest,' he said, 'you've got fifteen or twenty people round the Cabinet table, and on most days, on any particular issue, you've got fifteen or twenty different opinions.'

Marvellous. We sat in the green room afterwards, clinked plastic cups and ate *Newsnight* Hula Hoops to celebrate the new dawn. Wow, I thought, maybe we changed something in British politics tonight. A politician actually came to the studio and answered every single question and we didn't jump down his throat and call it all a gaffe or a split.

The next morning the *Daily Mirror* ran a story under the headline **MINISTERS IN CLARKE BLAST**, which said:

Labour chairman Charles Clarke was last night blamed for stoking a Government crisis by revealing splits in the Cabinet.

Ministers slammed his disclosure on TV's Newsnight that he 'could name 15 issues on which there is a wide range of opinions across the Cabinet table.'

An insider said: 'What's the point of a chairman incapable of sticking to any Government line and who tells the world the Cabinet is at each other's throats?'

It was, as Andrew Marr said to me afterwards, 'laugh or cry territory, really.'

*

Watching this situation crush the Conservatives – reporters only just out of short trousers constructing narratives, analysing speeches, running a commentary on all the exciting complexities of Westminster-under-the-Sea when the politicians just want us to focus our gaze on the sunlit world above it – the New Labour crew under Tony Blair took careful note. They decided to do something never before attempted: they would fight with unmitigated ferocity for control of every single paragraph, printed and spoken, hand-to-hand, tooth-and-nail. The world called it spin. But New Labour thought of it as getting even, and they were very good at it.

Chapter Eight

THE DROWNING MAN: HOW SPIN WORKS

This is how spin works. It is the best example I ever personally experienced.

Tony Blair came to visit South Africa. I was in the team of reporters travelling with him. As I listened to them talking, it was obvious they had no interest in any African angle whatsoever. The one story they were keen on was paparazzi beach photos a magazine had printed two days before. They showed Cherie Blair in a swimsuit with quite a lot of tummy and thigh, and they were not flattering.

The print journalists want to know 'how upset' Cherie is. She is on the trip too. If they find out how upset, that's a new line, so they can run the photos again.

It is the very last story Alastair Campbell wants to see published. Cherie is quite upset already. He doesn't want her further upset by stories about how upset she is, because then there might be another round of stories saying she is even more upset than she was when she was quite upset. He wants the reporters to cover

African issues. Failing that, he does not want a single column inch on cellulite.

In that breach between what the press want to say and what the politicians want them to say, the spin doctor is born.

The next day we are all aboard a plane going back to Johannesburg. Sitting next to Huw Edwards, I watch carefully what happens. Campbell threads his way down the aisle to standard class, and starts asking: 'So what are you working on, guys?'

Some of the tabloids say, 'Bit of Cherie? We gather she's upset about the—?'

Now, Campbell could appeal to them as gentlemen (they are all men), but he is too smart to bother wasting his time hoping they might find a shred of kindness. Nothing is more heartless than journalists travelling in a pack. In fact Campbell never even refers to the beach photos. Instead he takes a reporter off to one side. As if in confidence, he tells him: 'Tony saved someone's life on holiday.'

The word spreads round our section of the plane. Pretty soon reporters are out of their seats, squeezing round the food trolley, trying to get the details. And 'reluctantly' Campbell, standing in the aisle, tells us the story.

The Prime Minister saved a man from drowning in the Seychelles while conducting a Cabinet reshuffle on his mobile phone.

That is the story.

When we land, the agency and tabloid writers are off the plane like a shot to file. The TV people, myself and Huw among them, are slightly reluctant to fall for it – but we are then rung by our London desks who have seen the reports flash up on the wires and tell us: 'We need Blair on the drowning man.'

A pooled interview is fixed with the Prime Minister. Huw Edwards does it. After four questions on Africa, Huw says to Blair: 'Right. I do need to ask you about the Danish businessman you saved from drowning.'

Blair requests a pause. He turns to Campbell and says, grimly: 'Is this down to you?'

The camera is turned back on and Blair gives a clip where he says, 'Ah, anyone would have done the same, it was nothing.'

The ruse works brilliantly. The Cherie beach photos are never heard of again. All the papers run the drowning man the following day. The *Daily Mirror* had the headline **I WAS SAVED BY A BLAIR SEA RESCUE**. The article gives you the flavour:

Tony Blair was hailed a hero last night after saving a swimmer from drowning in a vicious sea current.

Danish businessman Jorge Joergensen was close to collapse when Mr Blair spotted him about half a mile from the shore.

Mr Blair, who was in a dinghy with his bodyguard and a yacht skipper, helped pull Mr Joergensen to safety.

But amazingly the Dane never recognised his rescuer.

The drama took place while the Premier was holidaying in the Seychelles with his family.

Skipper Gerard Mussard, 29, said: 'The man was very relieved. I know these waters. If we hadn't been there he could have died in 30 minutes.'

Mr Blair, who is due back in London today after his visit to South Africa, tried to play down the incident last night.

He said: 'I don't think I can make any claims for myself at all. There was a guy in difficulty and we helped him. It was as simple as that. It would be egging it very considerably to describe it as anything other than a bit of luck for him.'

That is spin. You notice there is nothing on the record confirming the story, which may be lucky for the perpetrators, because a tiny postscript appeared the following weekend.

By that stage everyone has forgotten the 'rescue' – it has served its purpose. But the Danish citizen has not forgotten, because he has been trying to understand how his name suddenly cropped up as part of a story he barely recognizes. And funnily enough I have not forgotten, because, in a slightly high-minded and otherworldly way, I have been feeling a little aggrieved that the sea rescue story stopped any coverage of African issues.

So I kept the following cutting, because it gives us a clue to what Mr Joergensen made of his one and only encounter with the Downing Street press operation.

THE SUNDAY TIMES

SWIMMER DENIES HE WAS SAVED BY PM

By Jack Grimston

THE Danish holidaymaker 'rescued' by Tony Blair in the Seychelles has denied he was in any trouble when he clambered aboard the prime minister's boat and claims he was just asking for a lift.

Hans Joergensen described claims that Blair had saved him from drowning as 'absurd and ridiculous'.

That is spin. And maybe it is funny, and maybe it doesn't matter – or maybe it matters quite a lot.

Chapter Nine

CAN I BE FRIENDS WITH PETER MANDELSON?

Perhaps your jaw dropped when you saw the sentence at the top of this page. Yet it was a genuine question in my mind back then. For the politicians to fight with the reporters for control of every paragraph of the news, they had to get up close and personal with us. Given that we were the wildlife photographers and they were the lions, why not allow them to wander right into our tent and give them a big friendly stroke?

Yes, good point. There is that.

It didn't occur to me that I might be savaged as I crept around the corridors of Parliament, barely thirty, obsessed with politics and finding that my job was to trade gossip with these gloriously psychopathic characters – none so captivating as the moustachioed Mandelson. Politics, according to Gore Vidal, is 'showbusiness for ugly people', but at least one of them definitely knew how to put on a show.

I first came across Peter during what he uncomfortably admitted was political downtime. John Smith was Labour leader and had been known to describe the former communications chief as 'so devious he will one day disappear up his own arse'. As a result the MP for

Hartlepool had been exiled with no official role. He seemed to like me. I took him for lunch one day and he sat there in a sleeveless blue pullover exchanging waspish gossip about ... fellow MPs? No, the other BBC correspondents. Afterwards we ran into a newspaper writer and I blushed as Peter told him he had never had a lunch quite so entertaining and enjoyable as the one he had just had with me. I believed him.

There was an early sign of his destructive talent. One day Mandelson asked me what I thought of the Conservative government's plan to lay on street parties to mark the fiftieth anniversary of D-Day.

I said I didn't have much of a clue. It all seemed pretty dull: there were to be some fun events – like 'spam fritter frying contests' – and fireworks in Hyde Park. But Mandelson said that Smith had allowed him to at least 'see if we can do something' on the issue.

Do something? Nope, I still didn't get it. What was there to do, Peter?

'Aha,' he said enigmatically, and, in the bright sunlight of a spring day, walked off down the street with his buddy, the pollster Philip Gould.

Over the next few days the government's planning was torn to shreds. From the outside no one could see fingerprints on the story, but suddenly the Conservatives were being lacerated for 'trivializing' the Normandy landings. Veterans' organizations raged at the plan for street parties and fireworks; even the wartime megastar Dame Vera Lynn waded in to urge a boycott. The issue may have been trivial, but it fitted perfectly with the narrative Mandelson would later help Blair to build – that, nearing twenty years in power, the Conservatives had lost touch with the public and John Major in particular had 'the non-Midas touch'.* Soon everyone was asking:

---

* A memorable phrase from Smith's best day in the House of Commons. Referring to a series of recent mishaps (none of which were anything to do with the government), he said John Major was prime minister 'in a country where the Grand National doesn't start, and the hotels fall into the sea.' Labour seemed to perfect this technique under Mandelson, realizing it was doubly effective to blame the Conservatives for things they were not responsible for, because they could do nothing about them.

how can a government be so cack-handed as to think a silly game with spam is the right way to mark D-Day?

I watched every step of the story, agog at the way the different ingredients were shaken into the brew. It did not matter that the spam contest was the idea of the Scottish Tourist Board and nothing whatsoever to do with John Major – the next report said he was in a 'crisis meeting' over the planning, and the Culture Secretary Peter Brooke was facing the sack. The fire spread with questions in the Commons. The *Independent* then added petrol by reporting a poll showing the public did not appreciate the way the government was disrespecting the war dead. I dug the article out for this chapter, and marvelled again at how a few fritters of spam had been flambéed into a crisis in the hands of a master chef:

Our NOP poll shows 65% of electors agree with criticisms that such events would 'trivialise' the 50th anniversary next month, suggesting John Major's government has seriously misjudged the public mood . . .

The Prime Minister's office said planning for Hyde Park was going ahead. Ministers are keen to salvage the event in the face of calls by veterans for it to be cancelled and a boycott threat by Vera Lynn . . .

Peter Brooke, but more especially Iain Sproat, the Minister of State for National Heritage, were being blamed last night for the debacle . . . [Also involved was] Sir Tim Bell, whose public relations company was hired by the Government for £62,000 to help promote D-Day. Labour MPs yesterday called for Sir Tim's dismissal . . .

Peter Mandelson, Labour MP for Hartlepool and a prominent critic of the Government's plans, said: 'I am glad that the veterans' organisations are now back in control.' There could now be a programme 'the country can unite behind.'

The date: 22 April 1994. This young reporter was being wowed by the master. It was impressive stuff – no, it was actually hilarious. How had Peter caused a multiple vehicle pile-up without ever being seen on the carriageway?

My admiration increased. And there was that question again, ticking away – can I actually be *friends* with this guy? I am a correspondent, he is a politician. But my job is to report on the most interesting things on Planet Westminster and this particular alien is the most interesting of them all. Could it hurt? To be mates? Really? Peter encouraged my enthusiasm. He had oodles of time to talk. The MP who described him as 'pathologically addicted to briefing journalists' got it spot on. He would range far and wide in his planting and harvesting of information, as interested in my colleagues as I was in his, all charm and secrets.

Once he asked me, 'I need a tip from you as a natural. When I appear on television, how do I stop frown lines appearing on my forehead?' Next he stopped me in the lobby to make the comment which needed no reply. 'You are the only person in Britain who wants to be on television more than I do.'

I was wondering if the spam incident would lead Smith to bring Mandelson out of the cold, when suddenly the Labour leader died. As Tony Blair was crowned, I immediately saw the utter folly of my idea that Peter Mandelson and I could be, or had ever been anything like, friends. The charm was still there. But it was simply the scabbard on the rapier. If you helped him, he would pump you up. If you crossed him, he would run you through. Blair's arrival was the culmination of all of Mandelson's political dreams and the stakes were raised stratospherically. He became the Third Man; the rest is history. And by the way, if you think history has done him a disservice with its dark and menacing caricature, I would agree. He was far more dark and menacing than that.

One day Harriet Harman, a colleague Peter was close to, ran into trouble with her choice of a selective school for her child. Selection was against Labour policy, and Blair's team were trying to damp down flashpoints with the old guard (who had answered the birth of New Labour by restyling themselves 'Classic Labour'). Walking down one of the dim, wooden-panelled House of Commons corridors, I saw the unmistakeable figure leaning against the woodwork in the gloom ahead of me.

I smiled a greeting. Set like death, Mandelson's face loomed out of the shadows.

He said, very threateningly, 'I know what you want, and you're not getting it.'

'Peter, what do you think I want?'

'You want Harriet to resign – and she's not going to.'

'Actually,' I said, 'the BBC doesn't have a view on Harriet Harman's future.'

Eyes drilling into my sockets, he said, very softly, 'I don't mean the BBC, Jeremy. I mean *you*.'

For good measure, he added: 'We have read all your scripts.'

You always felt like you were in a bad TV mini-drama with him. At Blair's first party conference as leader, Mandelson was everywhere. A dangerous story was running that Labour's links with the unions meant policy was effectively being written by the barons of the GMB and their brothers. Still not quite used to the idea that the two of us were Not Friends Any More, I approached Peter in the crowded reception of a conference hotel. 'Are you busy spinning?' I teased. 'It must be exhausting, pulling all those strings.'

He glared back at me, unsmiling, lip trembling.

'Let me make it clear to you, Jeremy. I do not spin. I do not operate "puppet strings"' – he was rising to his theme – 'I am not a dark lord of manipulation, or whatever it is you people are saying this week. I am not working behind the scenes, I am not Machiavellian, I am not plotting or planning and I am definitely NOT SPINNING.'

His speech was interrupted by his mobile phone. 'Excuse me.' He turned away from me to answer it, listened for a moment and then hissed violently: 'This. Must. Be. Defused.'*

At any point, Peter would be involved in about twenty highly personal run-ins with political journalists, so I never felt left out.

---

* I told my colleague Stuart Maconie this story while appearing with him on a Radio 5 live programme called *The Treatment* in 1995. He grasped the hilarity of it much quicker than I did, and has repeated it on various shows as if he was there and the incident happened to him. One day I resolved to complain to him about this. But as I began my snotty email I realized nothing, but nothing, could be more humiliating than having an ownership dispute over a Mandelson story.

The BBC's Nick Jones pointed out the way Campbell and Mandelson worked as a pair – the baseball bat and the stiletto. 'If they don't like your story, Campbell screams down the phone at you while Mandelson quietly goes to the Director-General,' he said.

With me, Peter seemed to use a more direct approach (see how even now I fall into the trap of thinking I was special?) When he saw me talking to an MP he did not approve of – Diane Abbott or Clare Short were good examples – Mandelson would walk deliberately close to us and make a loud hooting noise, a sort of derisive whoop, throwing his head back and then looking over his shoulder with his eyes popping in mock amazement. He also made great play of 'punishing' me for reports he did not like. I walked up to him in Parliament while he and Jon Sopel were in conversation. Without looking over at me, Mandelson told Sopel: 'Would you please tell the person standing to my left that I am not speaking to him.' Another time he beckoned me with a melodramatically outstretched finger that kept beckoning until I was but twelve inches from his face. 'I am In . . . can . . . descent with you,' he hissed. About what? Some package that had run on The World Tonight.

Matters came to a head when I tried to use my influence on Peter (which was zero, although I had not yet understood that) to get Blair to do his first interview about his faith. Campbell had famously said, 'We don't do God', but I reckoned there was a chance. Over several weeks I carefully laid the ground. Then the mortar bomb hit me.

Mandelson walked up to me in the Millbank office. 'Tony has asked me to tell you he will not be giving you an interview about God. I drew to his attention the item you ran on the radio this morning,' – which had suggested, quite correctly, that the more torrential the Labour attack on the Conservatives became, the fewer policy differences anyone could find between them – 'and he agrees with me that you would not be the right person to do this interview.

'I am so sorry,' he added, with pure pleasure.

I fulminated over the injustice for days. How could he? After sulking, I got angry. Late one night, still furious, I bumped into Peter outside Parliament. He wore a dark overcoat so long it looked like a cape. I gave him both barrels.

'You are so totally out of order with that religion interview, Peter. I am really, really upset about it. Really upset with you.' For the first time in my career, I was trembling with anger.

He peered at me with – was it? – the faintest smile. 'I bet you think I'm a right bastard.'

*

With relations cool, we were about to be thrown into the same bed, or at least the same hotel. New Labour put Mandelson in charge of an electrifying campaign at the Littleborough and Saddleworth by-election, caused by the death in 1995 of the sitting Tory MP Geoffrey Dickens. Simultaneously the BBC sent me to the area alone to cover the entire four-week run-up. As I drove into Littleborough for the first time, my car must have registered on the Mandelson radar – my bleeper went off.

The message said 'RING PETER', and gave a local number. I did so. He picked up. 'I have a very large by-election in my hands here, Jeremy. I am going to need you to *ride close*.'

I responded non-committally. As the days went on the campaign became a festival. The Lib Dem candidate, Chris Davies, a somewhat nerdy fell runner, was rocked by a Labour leaflet accusing him of being 'soft on drugs', which must have baffled most of the locals as well as him. The Tory, John Hudson, turned out to be a high-spir-ited, end-of-the-pier character it was impossible not to warm to (on the doorstep with him, I heard him tell residents in one street: 'What a lovely view you've got of the gasworks.'). Labour's candidate was Phil Woolas who, many years down the line, would get his ears boxed by Joanna Lumley over the Gurkhas and then lose a court case that saw him banned from Parliament.

Gradually national attention turned to Little and Sad, as it became known. The poll would be a perfect way of finding out if real people were taken with Blair's technically perfect relaunch, but it was Mandelson's moment to shine, too – the chance to prove that his genius and chicanery could be put to the service of his party without the normal attendant destruction. Could he lift Labour from third place in the seat to second or even first?

During a hectic last weekend of campaigning, I was following Jeffrey Archer around the constituency. The novelist had not yet been convicted and jailed, so he was one of the Tory big guns sent for the final push.

While I was with him I got a strange call from one of the local Labour officials. 'This is a bit embarrassing,' he began, 'but we have lost one of our open-top buses, have you seen it?' I said no, I hadn't; what was the problem exactly? But he would not elaborate.

Labour had two double-decker open-top buses, painted red and yellow and emblazoned with pictures of Tony Blair and the slogan 'New Labour, New Britain'. And it turned out that on this particular day, they had put all their big names – including Donald Dewar, Mo Mowlam and the local mayor – into bus number one.

But the other bus, which they had initially forgotten about, had been boarded by local yobs and was now being driven at speed around the constituency. This had the potential to wreck Mandelson's weeks of fastidious preparation.

Ten minutes after this mysterious call, sure enough, Lord Archer is turning off the high street with us to be filmed walking along the canal. Over the brow of the hill comes the second Labour bus.

We can hear the shouting on the top deck. There is swearing and jeering. Our cameraman, Chris Marlow, is onto it straightaway. He swings his camera round and gets a peach of a shot – in the open top of the bus, above the words TRADITIONAL VALUES IN A MODERN SETTING, are a bunch of yobs who have now spotted Archer. They are making V-signs at him from the top deck and yelling abuse. The words 'Dickhead' and 'Tory tosser' were the politest they shouted.

Then comes a brilliant camera move of the kind reporters dream about. With the camera on his shoulder, Marlow pans from the louts jeering at the top of the bus to Lord Archer. As he pulls focus we see Archer glaring at the yobs, stony-faced. The bus disappears off down the high street, and Archer turns dramatically to the camera lens.

'If that is what New Labour has in store for this country,' he says, 'then heaven help us all.'

The devastating sound bite could not have been crafted better by Mandelson himself. We put the piece out on the BBC1 Saturday evening news, reaching the biggest audience of the entire by-election. In the edit suite the louts-to-Archer camera pan works even better than I dared to hope. It is magnificent.

Within three seconds of the piece ending, my bleeper goes off: 'RING PETER.'

I dial the number. The phone picks up immediately at the other end. All I hear is Mandelson's voice, a slow whisper.

'Well, well, well.'

As if it was a personal betrayal.

*

The Lib Dems ended up taking the seat. Labour votes did not pile up in quite enough numbers to give Mandelson the stunning victory he coveted. But his campaign took Labour from third to second place and increased his party's support by fifteen per cent. The Conservative vote plunged by a fifth. In its own way, the result was a predictor of the coming Labour landslide.

*

The first rule of the spin doctor is: know your enemy. The second, less well-known rule, is to make the enemy think you are their friend. Peter Mandelson and I did not become friends, because we could not, not only since that would have been calamitous on so many fronts; I doubt friendship was being offered, anyway. We did remain friendly, though. In 2001 *Newsnight* sent me across the country in a 1976 Volkswagen camper van, painted in the programme's shirt colours and with *NEWSNIGHT* on both sides. The editorial team of Sian Kevill, George Entwistle and James Stephenson had sat in a small room for an hour and emerged with what initially seemed like a completely hare brained scheme.

But the *Newsnight* Van turned a dull general election – where hardly any seats changed hands – into an enlivening journey on both sides of the camera, and achieved cult status as well as a place in BBC News folklore. I was instructed to drive from the Sutherland lighthouse, just north of John O'Groats, to Land's End in Cornwall. Along the way I would run into politicians, visit key seats and try out what Hunter S. Thompson called Gonzo journalism: where the reporter tries to put himself at the centre of the story.

Among many surreal incidents was an encounter with the Conservative frontbencher Oliver Letwin in Somerset. Letwin had gone missing after an election gaffe on public spending cuts, but that day he was due to take part in a novelty hustings in his constituency, where the theme was ancient Rome. No reporters would be present, or so he thought. So he was dressed in a Roman toga when he saw the *Newsnight* Volkswagen – in the same shade of mauve – lumber over the brow of the nearest hill and lurch to a halt, camera pointing out of the window.

At that moment, from another direction, the indie rocker and political activist Billy Bragg arrived to spring his own surprise. Bragg – who lived nearby – was dressed from top to toe as a Roman centurion, with elaborate feathered headgear and a spear. He appeared shouting, 'My name is Tacticus. I say to you, Senator Letwinius, surrender unto Thatcher that which is Thatcher's.'

Oliver Letwin just said, 'No, no, no. No. No, no, no, no, no. No. No—' and, in front of his bemused constituents, removed the toga to reveal a tie and a neatly pressed shirt underneath. He then conducted a serious *Newsnight* interview with me while being heckled by a Roman centurion, as if nothing out of the ordinary was happening at all. Hunter S. Thompson had been kicked around the park by a man who smoked a pipe at university.

What exactly was Gonzo journalism, as defined by the *Newsnight* Van? Our vehicle had to be inserted into as many stories as possible, and not just the ones we were doing. When it was seen doing a laborious three-point-turn in the background of an ITN interview, we had hit the jackpot.

The trip inspired an army of imitations at the following election in 2005 – Michael Crick had a helicopter, *BBC London News* had a boat, the *Today* programme had a battlebus (yawn), the *Politics Show* had a barge, and *Channel Four News* went campaigning in a pristine Winnebago. After that, the question 'Why don't we do the election as a journey?' went drastically out of fashion.

However, in 2001 I spent five hilarious weeks in that van, along with cameraman Frank Considine, picture editor Herbie Graham and producer Isobel Eaton. It collided with a lamppost in Bristol, disrupting a press call across the street with the Lib Dem leader Charles Kennedy (the shout went up: 'He's crashed the *Newsnight* Van!' as Kennedy was explaining education policy). It also blew a gasket in Hull.

But Hartlepool was the place where we had the most fun.

As we drove towards Peter Mandelson's constituency, smoke started pouring from the dashboard. One of the problems of driving a 1976 VW is that it tends to break down a lot. No one in London had thought of that. White smoke floating upwards we could handle, but when it turned black and drifted downwards we pulled in on the hard shoulder.

The AA patched up the engine eventually, and escorted us into Hartlepool. Frank Considine took his camera to find Mandelson on foot. Peter had agreed to see us, but he wasn't expecting what limped round the corner – a battered camper van with an AA escort, and me leaning out of the window, waving.

Newsnight being *Newsnight*, we had thought long and hard what to ask Peter. He had been having a rough time at Westminster – his first resignation from Cabinet had been on 23 December 1998, and now he was giving everyone the implausible line that he was happy to represent the people of Hartlepool and leave it at that. Obviously there would be some mileage there. But *Newsnight* delights in finding the one unanswerable and *unforeseen* question, and a researcher in London faxed us an article Mandelson had written in a newspaper which gave the slyest hint that he disapproved of Labour's election strategy. The strategist was a minister called Gordon Brown.

Writing this makes me remember so many wonderful *Newsnight* production meetings at which we slaved over the one, unanswerable question. What was it for Peter?

Finally, Isobel and I thought we had cracked it.

Is Gordon Brown having a perfect election campaign?

This, we reckoned, simply could not be answered.

The appointed hour arrived. Mandelson came with us as the van kangarooed its way to the interview location. The interior still smelt of smoke from the breakdown, so he asked if he could wind the window down. 'Sure,' I said, 'just pull the handle on the door there.'

As he pulled the handle it came off in his hand.

'I *hate* Newsnight,' he said, wearily.

When we had parked up, he and I climbed into the back of the van. It was a squeeze – Frank had to mount his camera behind me and operate it from the driver's seat. I asked Peter various questions about Labour policy, and then whether he was truly happy just being the honourable member for Hartlepool? He said, 'Yes, yes, I am actually,' not entirely convincingly. And then the following:

Vine: How often do you speak to the Prime Minister on the phone?

Mandelson: I don't, er, speak to the Prime Minister. He's a bit busy, he's got an election on you know.

Vine: Is he taking your advice?

Mandelson: Ha. No. He doesn't need to take my advice.

Vine: Do you think Gordon Brown has run a perfect election campaign so far?

On the tape his jaw juts out, he tuts and looks out of the window.

Mandelson: Right. Now. Let's stop this. Because I'm not going to do this interview.

The item ran on *Newsnight* (the same day as the Prescott punch and the confrontation between Blair and an angry voter called Sharon Storer, so the menu at the top of the show, with Jeremy Paxman asking 'Plus – what made Mandelson storm out of our van?' was one of the liveliest ever) and then, with doubtless a push and a shove from a BBC press officer, the newspapers were full of it the following day.

I felt bad for Peter. *Newsnight* had plotted our journey through his constituency, which he would have enjoyed, but the actual encounter would have left him feeling he had played along and been suckered. Not only that, but there was no way of furiously exiting a 1976 Volkswagen camper without losing your dignity, and pictures were spread across the papers too.

The following day my phone went. Isobel was driving and I took the call in the passenger seat. 'Hello, Jeremy,' said the familiar voice. 'I just want you to know I don't mind what happened.'

'Thank you, Peter,' I said.

'But I've seen the papers.'

'Ah.'

'And what I hate, about all of you, *is the way you spin.*'

Said without even a hint of irony, it was probably the highest compliment he had ever paid.

Chapter Ten

A Disruption
of the Norm

Let us, as they say, back up a bit.

What exactly is news, anyway?

Once you get into a ruck with a character like Mandelson – who wants to send you into a spin, tries to convince you he knows what the news should be and you do not – you do start to wonder.

What is news and what is news not?

'News,' it was said, 'is what someone else doesn't want you to know. All the rest is advertising.'

Beautiful. And quite wrong. I used to have neighbours who argued all the time. They didn't want me to know that. It doesn't mean them arguing is news.

In fact, once you try to find a definition, you discover exasperating contradictions almost immediately.

For starters: news is *not* what is new. The fact that the sun has just risen in the east and Burger King have served their 18,679,552nd Whopper may be new, but it is not news.

My shoes are new. They are not news.

And news can be old. If Malcolm walks into the pub on Friday night and says, 'I got thrown out of university for having an affair with the Dean's wife,' his mates at the bar will all crowd round to hear the story and hush at the other drinkers to shut up. The fact that it was seventy years ago, Malcolm is nearly ninety and the poor Dean and his missus are both dead does not matter – it is a story about the living and it is news. It is news because his mates did not know about it before.

So news is *what is new to me*. One person's news is another's old hat, because very few events are new to everyone. Editors make decisions on what to tell their readers based on what they think those readers do not yet know. If they assume nobody knows anything, then everything is news.

Crucially, if an editor judges that an earlier piece of news might have slipped the audience's mind, they are free to repeat it.

I have seen that last point cause massive confusion among people who feature in the news. For example, I did an interview for *Newsnight* about a scandal over the Elgin Marbles. A newspaper reported that the Marbles had been cleaned with wire brushes, a very stupid act that caused them serious damage. The revelation whipped up a storm. Greece renewed its demand for the return of the Marbles.

The British Museum protested. The wire brush fiasco, they insisted, happened *nearly seventy years ago*. The 'revelation' was nothing of the sort, since all the facts emerged in the sixties. There had been questions in Parliament when Alec Douglas-Home was prime minister.

So the British Museum rang to demand we explain why this was a story now.

'Because the Greeks are cross *today*,' they were told (never mind that the Greeks are always cross about the Marbles).

Despite his fury, the man in charge of the museum came into the *Newsnight* studio.

'How do you defend using Brillo Pads?' I asked him.

'This story was revealed in the sixties,' Robert Anderson replied.

'You are, if I may say so, evading the question.'

'It wasn't Brillo Pads, it was wire brushes,' he tried.

Occasionally I jump awake as a dream replays that memory. Every programme and every newspaper covered the wire brushes, because they were news. *They were news because people had forgotten them.*

So news can be old.

Which is why the revelation that Elvis had a distant relative called Andrew Presley, who worked as a blacksmith in Aberdeenshire, arrived on our television screens 250 years after the poor man died. Is two-and-a-half centuries pushing it? Not at all – in October 2003 the bulletins carried news that the universe 'may have begun with a whistle rather than a Big Bang' after a physicist recreated the sound by analysing radiation left over from fourteen billion years ago.

'The noise is rather like a large jet plane flying 100 feet above your house in the middle of the night,' said Dr John Cramer of the University of Washington in Seattle, unwittingly setting a record for bringing us the oldest piece of news ever broadcast. Slippage by a day or two hardly matters when Dr Cramer managed to get a story past the newsdesks that was 14,000,000,000 years old.

*

A complaint landed on my desk at Radio 2 once. It turned out to be the best example of news being all the stuff we forgot we already knew.

The complaint was not primarily directed at me. The writers – let's call them Ted and Phyllis Stangate – actually wanted my help. The Stangates were upset about a story in *The Times* reporting how their neighbour had died and had bequeathed her house to her cat.

After *The Times* published the story on 6 May 2003, every other newspaper and broadcaster followed up. To give you a flavour, this was the take in the *Western Mail* the next day:

A wealthy widow has bequeathed her cat his own £350,000 detached house and a £100,000 trust fund to pay his expenses.

Black cat Tinker (pictured) is a former stray who befriended Margaret Layne, 89, according to the Times. Like many who come into money he has acquired hangers-on – two other cats have moved into the three-bedroom house in Suffolk Road, Harrow, north west London, since Mrs Layne's death.

The *Times* story had described the living arrangements in some detail:

The sliding door to the summer house – where Tinker likes to go 'for a bit of a lie down' – is left open to save the indignity of him squeezing through a cat flap. And just in case Tinker or his friends tire of the sedentary life, there is also a bird bath in the back garden, providing a never-ending parade of potential fast food.

Nothing wrong with any of that, you might think. So did I. Until I read the Stangates' letter. Not only did they enclose the *Times* piece, they also enclosed one from the *Daily Mail* from *eight months earlier*. Plus a copy of the complaint they had just sent the managing editor of *The Times*:

Dear Mr Brock,

I would like to ask how it has come about that your paper has resurrected the story of 'Tinker' when it had already been published in the *Daily Mail* [eight months ago] on Saturday 14th September. Your story is not news, but history.

Your valuation of the property is well wide of the mark . . . as for 'Tinker's' wealth, much was invested in the stock market and as a result there is a very substantial shortfall.

Thanks to the press, we have had telephone calls threatening my wife, threatening to kidnap 'Tinker' and a large number of silent ones.

Other comments I would make are:

1. The will was made public long ago.
2. To date no work has been carried out on the house.
3. The sliding roof is to the greenhouse not the summer house.
4. It is Lucy who likes to laze in the summer house, not 'Tinker', who much prefers the greenhouse.
5. Your statement about the birdbath is in very poor taste and nothing short of an insult to animal and bird lovers.

Mr Stangate also pointed out that when the *Mail* ran the first story with a large picture headed **TINKER THE MOGGIE** stretched across the whole page, the photo was not of Tinker.

Now he was asking me for help.

Dear Jeremy,
Having recently been contacted by Dutch television and the *Evening Standard* on the subject of 'Tinker', we are beginning to wonder as to when this matter is likely to end. With the story already published in 2002 and 2003 – see enclosures – are we in for further publication in 2004?

I did not need to give the Stangates my answer, because they already had it. By the time they had posted their letter, sadly my own pro-gramme had also covered the story, because we did not know it was coming round a second time. It could well run a third, and a fourth – maybe a tenth, who knows? – with the Stangates trapped in a news nightmare. There is even the possibility that the very same TV crews and reporters could be camped outside their home on suc-cessive occasions. Tinker could alternate with the British Museum's Brillo Pads and we could all happily continue the cycle forever.

*

Staying in a hotel, the phone jolted me from sleep at five-thirty. Rang like it was trying to jump off the bedside table. I was trying to remember where I was: which country, which continent?

Okay, I had it. In the middle of South Africa, where we had been filming. Kimberley – that was the place. Shooting for the hundredth anniversary of the Boer War. Dawn was starting to warm the hotel curtains.

But the phone call from London was not about a forgotten war. They were waking me about a helicopter crash in Cape Town.

'You and Milton are going to have to get down there,' the assignments editor at the other end was saying. 'It crashed yesterday and killed both people on board.'

'Right,' I said, bleary-eyed and more than a little confused. 'Fell into a street, did it? Killed pedestrians as well?' I was wondering why I had heard nothing of it.

'No, just killed the two men on board. It happened on the roof of a tall building. They were taking off and the chopper clipped a hoarding. Went out of control. Boom.'

Boom. But I really was mystified. London were calling because of a helicopter crash thousands of miles away from them, scrambling us to file a report on an incident in which, frankly, only two people had died? And died yesterday?

It sounded like the famous *Financial Times* headline: **SMALL EARTHQUAKE IN CHILE, NOT MANY DEAD**. I was sitting on the edge of the bed now. 'I don't quite understand – why do you want a piece on this? Were they well-known sportsmen or something?'

'No, we think they were maintenance men.'

'So why do you want a piece on—'

'*Because someone filmed it.*'

That was all I needed to know.

'And,' the editor went on, 'I'm being told the pictures are great.'

I rang my colleagues in other rooms and dressed quickly. We left as fast as we could, speeding south to file the story. Why was it a story? It was a story because someone filmed it. A guest in a Cape

Town hotel on the other side of the street had been experimenting with his video camera, taking pictures of the helicopter. The maintenance men were repairing a unit on the roof. The hotel guest had seen them land and filmed the attempt to take off. He kept rolling as the rear propeller clipped a billboard and the chopper went into a rocking spin, dawdled in the air, and finally fell back onto the roof and exploded in a shower of burning petrol.

The two dead had been maintenance men working on air-conditioning. A tragedy for them and their families. They were not diplomats, sports stars or international bankers. But they were a story because they died on camera.

We raced there, hoovered up all the footage we could, and filed. Back in Britain the evening news ran the dramatic piece, which included three viewings of the explosion, one in slow motion and another very slow. In airing the report the programme made an important point as we search for a working definition of what news is.

News is what you can see.

One day, I was leafing through the local paper in Johannesburg when I saw a dramatic photograph. It showed a saloon car with two huge balls of fire spurting from both sides. The accompanying piece explained that this was 'The Blaster', a defensive accessory for cars invented by a South African entrepreneur called Charles Fourie. A gas canister in the boot of your car connects to a pedal in the footwell. When the pedal is pressed down, a pilot light ignites flumes of gas which are propelled from nozzles fitted below the two front doors. Any person trying to hijack the car gets burnt to a crisp.

'Hey, we should do this,' I told a producer. We duly filmed the Blaster and interviewed the inventor, who said drivers should put their hands up when carjacked and then step on the pedal: 'It is a choice. Either you get shot, your wife is raped, your child is murdered – against him getting burnt.'

The report also featured a burns specialist who confirmed that, yes, fire is both frightening and dangerous. Finally a police officer stressed the risk of violent hijack in Johannesburg and concluded, 'Not only is this device quite legal, two of my colleagues have already purchased one.'

We filed the piece. It caused one of those flurries at the Beeb where every single programme wants a version. It then, amazingly, ran on outlets all over the world. It was pictured in *Time* magazine and televised in Japan. I lost count of the calls we had to the bureau from foreign news programmes – Indian, Mexican, Chinese – wanting contact details for Mr Fourie. I had never before filmed a story which got picked up so universally and so effortlessly. But this was the same simple principle we saw in action with the exploding helicopter: there were pictures, and they were dramatic. News has to be seen.

Or rather, *it really helps if you can see it.*

While home on holiday from Johannesburg, I had a meeting with Tony Hall, then chief executive of BBC News. Some days later it emerged that he was about to leave to run the Royal Opera House, and I wondered afterwards if that might explain why I seemed to catch him in a deeply reflective mood in his suite of offices by Shepherds Bush.

'How many stories do you think we're missing in Africa?' he asked.

I had what could be described as an A. J. Ayer moment. The late philosopher, who wrote the brilliant *Language, Truth and Logic,* was famous for long silences and thoughtful replies in which each word was carefully weighed. His watershed book had explained a new way of dealing with the problems of philosophy: essentially, he believed we should redefine the meaning of all words. When asked at a press conference how many of the issues philosophers had struggled with through the centuries were solved by his new theories, he paused for a very long time, and then said:

'All of them.'

So when Hall asked me how many stories we were missing in Africa, I was tempted to run the Ayer Reply just to see his reaction. But during my pause it struck me that this was the kamikaze option, since I was the correspondent responsible for the coverage. So all I managed was the long silence.

'The Congo,' I finally blurted.

In 1998 the Democratic Republic of Congo, formerly Zaire, had fallen into a calamitous war which had dragged in its neighbours and cost the lives of more than a million people. Despite the vast swathe of African life bound into the disaster, the country had hardly rated a mention on any television bulletin.

'Why do you think this is?' Tony Hall asked.

'Because the conflict is too difficult to film,' I said, warming to the theme. It was true – reporters were not allowed up-country. The collapse of the Mobutu regime in Zaire two years before had attracted correspondents from all over the world, as rebel soldiers fought their way to the capital. But this new war was impossible to find.

Hall confessed this troubled him. I confessed it troubled me too. He and I talked about how we could get pictures so the story could finally be told. I rashly promised to write up a proposal for filming the war in Congo. After the meeting, sensing the impossibility of it, I sat down by a bank of televisions in a BBC reception area known as Stage Door.

And then I was goggling at one of the screens.

'Injured – the woman whose husband tried to catapult her across a field,' the newsreader intoned.

A few minutes later, the story ran. The woman, dressed eccentrically, had been placed in a large catapult somewhere in rural England and then flung forty yards. She shot through the air and missed a safety net, breaking her collarbone. People rushed to help.

The story cannot possibly have been the fourth most important event in the world that day, but it was running because – here we go again – someone grabbed a camera when the catapult was released.

At that moment, it seemed to me the flying wife had landed directly on that piece of news space reserved for the war in Congo, and I bristled with anger. But the plain fact is that television struggles to broadcast news without pictures.

We are dealing with the tree falling in the forest here. Unless a camera is present, it makes no sound at all.

*

A professor in Florida made a splash in 2007, announcing that 'household cleaning equipment such as dishcloths and sponges' could be most effectively decontaminated by being zapped in a microwave.

Gabriel Bitton explained that although *bacillus cereus* spores – bacteria in fruit and veg – are resistant to radiation, heat and chemicals, they are completely eradicated after four minutes in the microwave.

Professor Bitton said this effect was caused by the way microwaves 'excited water molecules'.

When I heard the item I remember wondering if it was news. But the findings were covered across all the papers and channels and I now reprint, word for word, the lengthy announcement they subsequently had to make on the BBC News Channel.

Newsreader Louise Minchin said the following, in full:

'We recently transmitted information about a report by Professor Gabriel Bitton, a expert in environmental engineering at the University of Florida. The professor claimed that 99 per cent of germs contained in a kitchen sponge or dishcloth would be killed if the item was placed in a microwave oven on full power for four minutes.

'Shropshire Fire and Rescue service have today, at 13.08 hours, attended a fire in the Telford area which involved a dishcloth in a microwave oven. The occupier was attempting to sterilize the dishcloth in the manner described by Professor Bitton. Fortunately the fire was contained within the microwave oven.

'Attempting to sterilize a dishcloth in this way is extremely dangerous. There are too many variable factors. Shropshire Fire and Rescue service strongly advise the public not to attempt to sterilize sponges or dishcloths in this way. Attempting to do so may result in your home being destroyed.'

This incident raises all kind of problems, not least for the person who nearly burnt down their own house. The story here was initially that you could clean dishcloths in the microwave. This then paled into insignificance compared to the report that someone had actually believed the original story and almost destroyed their home. If news is what you get when people set their houses on fire because they have heard a story that probably isn't true, then we are in a very strange world indeed.

But strange it is – I sat next to the editor of a national newspaper at a concert in 2011 and we bonded, discovering we had both trained in that pernickety world of regional newspapers.

He told me how he had recently had lunch with the agent of a very well-known model, whose name I shall not give but feel free to have a guess. The Tiger Woods sex scandal had just broken, and the model's agent quietly told the editor: 'My client is prepared to be one of the lovers.'

What he meant was that the paper could run a headline along the lines of: **EXCLUSIVE: I WAS TIGER'S NUMBER TEN** with a big picture of the famous woman (photographed as if embarrassed, sunglasses on, rushing between buildings) and she would not complain or deny it, even though she had never even met Tiger Woods. This would serve all of their purposes. Tiger's reputation was so damaged he could never object. Who would lose?

The editor, a charming guy, told me: 'I actually sat discussing the possibilities of this with him for a full ten minutes – thinking about how I'd put 50,000 on our circulation with that headline – and then I remembered my local paper, where you'd get sacked just for spelling someone's name wrong, and I wondered what the hell I was doing.'

He changed the subject and we never did hear about Tiger's Number Ten.

So news is inconsistent. Sometimes full of meaning and value but sometimes, in the wrong hands, vacuous.

At Coventry one sub-editor had a sign above his desk which read, TRUTH IS OFTEN ECLIPSED BUT NEVER EXTINGUISHED. There goes an optimist. The contrary view is that news is a shortened version of the truth; compression and reduction always distort; and that which is distorted is not true.

Sometimes the distortion is wilful. There is no journalism without impact, because with no impact there is no audience. But exaggeration is used too often to enhance stories. After news broke of Wayne Rooney's gambling problem, an editorial in the Nigerian *Daily Sun* said:

> Rooney's gambling debts are an indelible stigma that the entire waters of the Atlantic cannot wash away

and I remember thinking it was the perfect example of the exaggeration habit. Succumb, and pretty soon you are writing stories from another planet.

The dishcloth incident? It was news eating itself. One of the first laws of quantum mechanics is Heisenberg's Uncertainty Principle. Expressed simply, it states that scientists change things simply by observing them. Journalists can do the same. When I travelled to Northern Ireland to report on clashes between Catholics and Protestants over a marching route, I found the Orangemen hoisting a banner at the end of a Catholic street in Drumcree which read: 'KATE ADIE'S HERE SO IT MUST BE WAR'.

News is rapacious and devours its own. Graham Riddick was a popular Tory backbencher until he was flattened by the cash-for-questions scandal. I bumped into him in a lift inside Parliament, looking hunted. The lift was tiny and there was no way of avoiding each other's gazes. 'You lot,' he shook his head. 'You're like a gigantic herd of wildebeest, and we all look at you from a distance and we laugh at how slow and how stupid you are. But when you charge, it's over.'

So the news world is unpredictable and self-cannibalizing, and a long spoon can be necessary. When James Hewitt boasted he had been the lover of Princess Diana in the nineties, the *Sun* found a man who had built a hangman's scaffold in his back garden on which he said he would gladly execute Hewitt. Under the headline **HAVE I GOT NOOSE FOR YOU** the paper carried an interview with him.

The following day I happened to see the *Sun* and roared with laughter when I noticed a large photo of an angry woman below the words:

SCAFFOLD MAN IS LOVE RAT SAYS EX

The more we explore the news, the more we find that trying to define it is a bit like walking into that house of mirrors in *The Man with the Golden Gun*. You can end up with everything the wrong way round and mortal injuries. Even so, let us keep going, for at least a couple more pages, before we surrender to Scaramanga.

*

I want to say that news is the unexpected. That proposition seems pretty simple and surely it must be true, so let's give it a paragraph of its own and a fancy font:

News is all the stuff you don't expec

t

Whoops. But even as I write that, I remember watching the most recent Royal Wedding. That was expected. But it was news, surely. It was scheduled, yes, but it was still news. The satellite channels called the vows 'BREAKING NEWS' in bold captions even though, with that many royals and dignitaries and politicians packed into an abbey at the appointed hour, it was fairly likely that the chap in the uniform and the woman in the white dress would say something important to each other when they met at the end of the aisle.

Worse still, from the point of view of my starting proposition, the Royal Wedding was one of the most organized events of the year. The balcony wave, we were told, would happen at 1.24 p.m. But it was also one of the biggest news stories.

This raises the frightening possibility that the biggest news stories are not the most unexpected, but the most expected.

Sure, if Kate had called it off at the last moment (the unexpected), then it would have been a bigger story. Or would it? You would not have had the flypast. Anyway, thankfully she did not call it off, and it was big.

When I was at Westminster, *Newsnight* sent me to follow a group of Conservative Eurosceptics around Brussels. They were there to protest at a meeting of Euro-Commissioners.

It was the kind of trip where you despair at the lack of pictures. But as we were driving behind their car, we saw it collide with a delivery van. Nothing serious. In fact, in television terms, just a little bit wonderful – the Eurosceptics cannot even set foot in Belgium without crashing into someone! The wheels have come off! I was already drafting the script in my head as the hapless MPs piled out of their car, inspecting their creased bonnet and the buckled bumper of the van. The other driver was shouting and pointing and they were trying to reason with him. Beautiful little sequence for our feature.

It was over in a couple of minutes and I was looking for the cameraman.

'Great pictures for our piece,' I laughed. 'How much of it did you get?'

'None of it,' he said.

'None of it?' My heart sank. My dream of a film from Brussels that was not dominated by footage of large wet buildings evaporated. 'Why not?'

'Well, it wasn't planned, was it?' the cameraman replied.

Given that every newsroom has a very strange object called a 'news diary', a book of upcoming events to prevent us being surprised by anything, we should at least contemplate the frightening possibility that the cameraman is right – news is not unexpected at all. It is all the stuff we can see coming.

Three days after Kate and Wills blew us all away, American special forces gave Osama Bin Laden the same sensation. I happened to be in the ITN newsroom, because the BBC hired one of their studios for the local election graphics extravaganza which I do, and there I ran into one of the great newsreaders, Alastair Stewart. With the words 'BIN LADEN KILLED' flashing on the screens, we put this proposition to each other: the special forces shot him three days earlier. The news emerges the morning of Kate and William's wedding. What then?

We were unsure. One event has had all the planning, all the cameras, that balcony kiss, all of that organized joy. The other is unscheduled, kiss-free, bloody, unfilmed but world-shaking.

I won't say we came to an answer. Alastair said ITN might stick with the Royal Wedding, for all the obvious reasons. I said I thought you had to lead with Osama, because in a dead heat between two massive stories, you ask this tiebreaker question:

Which story is the most surprising?

And there is a precedent. Every newsroom in the world did brilliantly in 1994, successfully setting up scores of camera positions and hundreds of satellite feeds in South Africa to bring us the scheduled inauguration of Nelson Mandela as president of South Africa after twenty-seven years in jail. It was a massive event, superbly covered.

The coverage was so well-organized that the newsrooms missed the biggest story in the world. A hop by plane from Johannesburg, in a tiny country called Rwanda, 800,000 people were hacked to death in three months. Where were the cameras to show us these victims of an unscheduled genocide? Where were the reporters? Almost all of them were in Pretoria. I even know of a correspondent who refused to redeploy from South Africa because, as he protested to his editor, 'The inauguration is a story I have waited all my life for.'

Well, precisely. The story you have waited all your life for is not the one you should be covering, my friend. We have barely a single frame of the most horrendous butchery since the Second World War, because something else was in the diary.

*

The World at One presenter Nick Clarke, a model of shrewdness and impartiality who was taken from us prematurely by an aggressive cancer, took me on one side at a Labour party conference while I was a pol-corr. Grimly he said, 'This lot just don't get it. They think we have to report what they tell us. But journalists are built differently. News is a disruption of the norm. They won't accept it.'

News is a disruption of the norm – Nick's very phrase.

Does that define it?

We may be getting warmer; it certainly sounds right. Not long ago I went to a big railway awards ceremony full of station managers, senior timetablers and zonal performance managers. They sat in a sprawling dining room as I handed out awards for stations, timetables and zonal performance.

Looking out at all these fine people, working in an industry with a certain gritty honesty – it is not exactly a dotcom – I felt a pang of conscience. Why does every news item on the railways tell us our trains are late, crowded, dirty or dangerous?

No sooner had I had the thought than it was coming out of the mouths around me.

'You work for *Newsnight*, do you?'

'I did till recently. Then I moved to—'

'Because they did an absolutely disgraceful piece on rail safety the other day. They actually claimed that . . .'

'Mr Vine,' said another, 'why does the news only report the five per cent of trains that run late? Why does the news only report the cancelled trains?'

'Listen, journalists destroy British Rail and then, when the system changes, you actually manage to hypnotize people into believing it's worse. I mean, on maintenance for example, Jeremy . . .'

And then the killer question, from a woman in a tight business suit who did the accounting for one of the big track operators:

'Why don't you report the trains that run on time?'

Well?

The answer is vitally important, and simple. Punctual trains are not news.

Working hospitals and good schools and free-flowing roads and holidaymakers not being delayed and lift doors opening on the right floor and everyone getting out safely, and nobody having their leg trapped or being stabbed, and dogs biting men, and moderate weather or moderate anything – nope, not news either. Normal life is not news. Trouble is. The extraordinary is. News is a disruption of the norm.

Yes, it is news when an underground train runs on time in Houston. But that is because Houston does not have an underground system.

If the answer seems simple (my thanks to Nick Clarke), it still did not seem to get me out of that hole with the train people. They were concerned that ninety-eight per cent of news describes two per cent of trains, which gave the viewer a topsy-turvy picture of the world. I could have asked them, 'You want a news flash every time someone serves the right temperature bacon roll at Darlington?' but I did not, because it seemed unfair. Maybe the news is unfair.

I caught a black cab home that night. 'Where you been, Jeremy?' the driver asked.

'A railway awards ceremony,' I told him.

'Can't have lasted long!' he roared.

Yes, the news is definitely unfair.

No sooner had I put the train experience behind me than I was attending a Society of Editors conference as a guest. There I heard a speech by Mr Justice Judge, the deputy Lord Chief Justice of England and Wales (superb name – he was born Igor Judge).

He stood up and made exactly the same point to a gathering of editors, just switching the word 'judges' with 'trains'. Why were the reliable judges not praised? Why did journalists not say 'well done' when a judge handed down the right sentence? Why were they only ever castigated?

We come back to the Nick Clarke answer again. News is a disruption of the norm. That covers the Royal Wedding, Bin Laden and Rwanda. And the chump who put a dishcloth in his microwave.

*

It also covers the Flared Generation. Probably the most quease-inducing episode of my youth, but a lesson worth noting.

Like most sixteen-year-old lads, I was in a band. I could play drums a bit, and sing not at all, so I thought I was Phil Collins. Everyone in Cheam, Sutton, Rosehill, Morden, Carshalton, Wallington and all the surrounding areas was in a group of some kind. A missile strike on that unfashionable blob of south London in the early eighties would have taken out at least six hundred wannabe Paul Wellers.

To ensure I fulfilled my musical commitments, I spent my first years as a driver ferrying drums around at high speed in a small car. There is no sight less cool than a lad of seventeen tearing up the street in a Mini Clubman with his view obscured by a bass drum. If there had ever been a crash I would have needed intestinal surgery to remove a hi-hat.

But the bands I joined were impressively serious. By which I mean the ambition was there. We were not mucking about. I was the drummer with the Sharp Suits, which had John Hillman doing a

superb Elvis Costello on guitar and Pete Firmo on bass. My brother
Tim was on keyboards. And there was Wait & See, me drumming
again, this time with Simon Williams on guitar and Tim Thompsett
on bass. We would practise every Friday at Simon's house – he had
very patient parents – then be collected by local schoolgirls to go to
the pub at the end of the road, the Drill. Our best song, written by
Simon, was called 'One Good Thing'. Our aim was nothing less than
world domination and we worked on the principle that the more
bands we formed, the more likely that domination was. My brother
and I set up several other groups with a variety of line-ups: we were
The Last Wave, Killer Sons, and Two Can Talk. The last was just me
and Tim, a Paleolithic synthesizer and a 1983 TASCAM Portastudio,
for which I saved up with my job at the timber yard.

Totting them up, I reckon at one point I was in five bands simultaneously. They were all focused, dedicated, mean, and completely
useless. We modelled ourselves on the Clash, the Fall, Joy Division,
Theatre of Hate, the Undertones, the Jam, anyone else with a snarl
and an amplifier – but nothing we played went anywhere. We could
not even get booked in local pubs. We had no talent, no fans, no gigs,
no future, no past and no hope.

Faced with the imminent death of all our dreams, my brother and
I sat down with Simon Williams to discuss matters.

The key, we decided, was to spring some kind of surprise: to
be different. Every band we knew of was a wannabe Sex Pistols or
Stranglers or Clash. So as long as we pursued that route we would
never be heard outside Simon's bedroom. We had to swallow our
pride and reverse what everyone else was doing.

So we formed the Flared Generation.

The idea was simple. Cheam had finally produced a punk band,
but the town was so unfashionable the band had missed the point of
punk completely. I became Kevin Evans, with a pair of jeans whose
flares had been dramatically extended by thirty inches. My brother
was Justin Beams. Simon became 'Wilma' Cooper.

Dressed in kipper ties, hideous shirts with wing collars, wigs, horn-rimmed spectacles, university sweatshirts and enormous flares, we announced our intention to make a music video for a song entitled 'Sensible Shoes' on a local roundabout in Sutton.

The effect was remarkable. Suddenly the local newspapers wanted photographs of us and interviews.

Being seventeen and having reporters turn up at your parents' home to ask you questions is quite exciting. We stayed in character throughout, at one point telling the *Croydon Advertiser* that we were 'already bigger than the Beatles, in Cheam certainly.' We spoke in a way that made us sound utterly square – Cooper assuring the baffled reporter this was a 'glad day indeed' and telling him the point of the music was 'to celebrate university'. The fact that we had no real songs did not seem to matter. When I wrote a letter to the Mayor of Sutton demanding a new law to make the wearing of flared trousers compulsory, his refusal was a news story. When we announced that the release of our first single, Flared Revolution, had been delayed because the first 500 copies had come out oval (we fleetingly had a manager who actually told us this), again it was news. Suddenly The Most Unfashionable Punk Band In The Country were in teenage magazines, *Smash Hits*, then even the *Sun* newspaper. To cap it all, television cameras came down to Cheam. Danny Baker reported on us for ITV's *Six O'Clock Show*. Even Radio 1 wanted us on and we came up to Broadcasting House sporting ludicrous side partings to be interviewed. In those analogue days, this was close to celebrity.

The mistake came when we actually thought we were a band. My brother wrote a selection of songs and we booked ourselves as the headline act at the local Secombe Centre.

We knew how the concert should begin. Tim and I would lay down a rhythm on guitar and drums, then Simon would appear dramatically onstage, dressed in outlandish flares, wearing large women's sunglasses, riding on a skateboard with bangers taped to it. As the bangers exploded, he would jump off the skateboard and start singing. But after Tim and I had been playing for what seemed like at least five minutes, catastrophe struck. Simon shot onto the stage on his skateboard then off the other side. A crash and a series of loud bangs offstage followed. When Simon reappeared, looking shaken, one of the lenses of his sunglasses had been blown out.

The *Sutton Guardian* described the concert as 'memorable – but for all the wrong reasons', and the Flared Generation quickly bit the dust.

However, the experience was formative. All those attempts to be mean and serious, which fitted so well with the time, had failed utterly.

But when we presented a completely ludicrous proposition, we effortlessly spread ourselves all over the papers, radio and television. Accidentally I had stumbled on Nick Clarke's Rule that 'news is a disruption of the norm' and brought it down to four short words:

In punk, wear flares.

Chapter Eleven

QUESTIONS TO THE PRIME MINISTER

So you catch up with me back at Westminster, feeling my years at thirty-one, and gearing up for the huge election of 1997, at which Blair would win his landslide and the Conservatives would tumble from power after eighteen years.

And I am about to sit down for breakfast with Alastair Campbell. I notice nearly all the food that comes to the table has been ordered by me, although, as Labour's director of communications, Campbell has a lot more on his plate.

Before I explain the breakfast with him, I should say that there are two great jobs in broadcast news to do before you start presenting.

One is to be a political correspondent. The other is to be a foreign correspondent. For me, the foreign posting – a gem – would come later.

When I was at Westminster, I reported on power. When I was in Africa, I reported on weakness. Both are vital for an understanding of the world beyond the studio. Once a presenter is locked in a studio, they bank their real world experiences. The account may attract interest, but nothing more is deposited. So there needs to be as much in the bank as possible.

Moving to the studio too early can be catastrophic. I don't think Peter Snow, my hero, even contemplated the studio until he was in his forties. When he finally folded his hand and arrived in the *Newsnight* office as a presenter you could see the desert dust on his shoes. By that stage he was an absolute titan in the field. It is better to be a titan than a twit.

Reporting allows you to present with conviction. You did not stumble over the name of that foreign city on the autocue because you had never heard of it, you stumbled because you were remembering the first time you dived for cover there.

Let's go a step further, and see how this sounds. No one should be allowed to present a news programme until they can supply a battered passport and documentary evidence showing they have been to Jerusalem, Belfast, Washington, Moscow and Tokyo. Actually, strike out Tokyo: I haven't been there myself. Oh, and add Westminster. And surely you've got to have an African city in there ...

Yeah, I agree. That is getting a little complex to enforce. Maybe it can't be a Rule.

But we can sum the whole thing up like this:

There are terrible presenters who have been great reporters, but there are no great presenters who have been terrible reporters.

Reporting on power is crucial because journalists will regularly meet the people who wield it and have to understand who they are, how they use power and why they seek it. The who is easy. The how is tricky. The why is usually completely and utterly impenetrable.

There is really only one thing to remember when you interview a prime minister: try not to be scared. To misquote Robert Duvall in *Apocalypse Now*, politicians love the smell of a sweaty palm in the morning.

Take Tony Blair. I knew him a bit from before he became Labour leader, just to chat to; I could not claim to have seen into his soul. He

always appeared clever, polite and serious. He would stop for a conversation in the House of Commons lobby while he was Labour's
home affairs spokesman ('Tough on crime, tough on the causes of
crime'), but would lean back very slightly from the waist while he
was talking to me, as if I was emitting an unpleasant smell. He was
always a little brisk – that could have been the aroma, or maybe he
knew, even then, where he was headed and how quickly.

I put him down as a nice bloke overall, who was nevertheless The
Complete Politician. If he cut his nails or licked a postage stamp, I
imagined he would do it in a political way. He could probably ski or
iron a shirt politically. For that reason I studied him closely at every
opportunity, and with fascination.

Once, when he was prime minister, he came to my Radio 2 studio.
It was soon after a bout of heart trouble and I was not sure what
state I would find him in.

As a record played, I tried to put him at his ease.

'If you like I can play some music, Tony, after we've spoken on the
air. Just suggest an artist.'

In that instant I recalled him giving a lifetime achievement award
to David Bowie at a huge, televised awards bash. Blair had praised
his hero lavishly, saying something like, 'He is not just one of the
greatest musicians of my life, he is one of the greatest artists of all of
our lives.'

And so I said to him as I sat opposite him in the studio, 'What
about some Bowie? Because I know you love your Bowie.'

We were not on the air at this point; a song by Beverley Knight
was playing. But at that instant, as I watched Blair, I saw the question
had dropped into the wrong side of his brain. It was not Tony Blair
Nice Bloke who had heard it, it was Tony Blair The Complete
Politician. And as I watch him he seizes up and starts stalling for
time.

'Sure ... errrr ... Bowie. Yeah, I mean, who doesn't? Absolutely.'

Sensing I am not going to get anywhere, I try prompting him.

'Look, Prime Minister, it's just so we can pull out a song you like – I saw you give him a big lifetime achievement award so I thought—'

He is still stalling. 'Bowie. Great artist. Well . . . Bowie.'

'Can't you just name one of his tracks you like?'

That seems to snap him out of it.

'Oh, sure. "China Girl"?'

And then I remembered: it was not the only time it had happened. During that momentous election campaign of 1997, when his concentration on the politics was total, I was on the Blair battle-bus as it went round the country. (There were actually three of them, each painted with a huge word – when they travelled in the right order, it read 'BRITAIN DESERVES CHANGE'. Blair repeatedly told the story of how a supermarket lorry nipped between the back two on the M40, and the slogan briefly became 'BRITAIN DESERVES WALL'S CLASSIC PORK SAUSAGES'. If it happened, I didn't see it.)

The press pack travelled everywhere on those buses, only realizing later that it was a way of keeping us in lockdown: a Labour insider was quoted after the election saying, 'The whole bus thing worked brilliantly. The reporters on it didn't have a clue what was going on.' I decided I should do everything I could to secure an interview with Blair's wife, Cherie, whom I saw a lot of on the bus.

At one point I said to her, 'If you gave me an interview it would clear the air.'

She was tremendously flirtatious. 'I don't think there's any air that needs clearing, Jeremy.'

'But,' I pressed, 'if you gave me an interview it would cause a sensation.'

Cherie replied: 'I can cause you a sensation anytime, Jeremy, but only in private.'

We watched Blair speak an awful lot. The reporters used to joke with him that we knew which phrases would come in the speech, and we would bet against each other on the order. He took all of our nonsense in his stride. One day he travelled to Southampton to talk at the university. Since the journalists had heard the speech a dozen times, we ducked out and sat in the student canteen. I was eating a large piece of chocolate gateau.

Suddenly, Alastair Campbell emerged from the hall, walked past my table, picked up my fork, took a chunk out of my cake, put it in his mouth and walked off almost without breaking his stride.

We all laughed a bit and carried on talking. Then there was some applause and we realized Blair had finished the speech. Seconds later he came out, walked right past us, saw us and said: 'Hey guys. Glad you all made it, hope everything's all right.'

And I replied, 'Not really, because your press secretary just ate half my gateau.'

Which is when it happened.

This remarkable man, who had been fielding questions on the Euro, Northern Ireland, the minimum wage, the health service – *he could not process the gateau comment at all.* Blair looked startled. His eyes darted as if he was calculating the electoral impact of the scandal.

He finally said, 'We're making progress.' And walked off.

*

Leadership is language. Prime ministers come in all shapes and sizes, but they must all pick from the same set of words and we can get closer to understanding them by listening carefully. In some countries leaders govern through the barrel of a gun; here they do it through the barrel of a microphone. Thus, to be the one entrusted with holding the weapon on the public's behalf is a rare honour.

But the job of the media is not just to wire up the willing. For better or worse, we are there to choose what gets heard and what gets left on the cutting room floor. Interviewing is just live editing; that's why it is hard.

Blair's 'We're making progress' must, I reflected, be the answer you get when all systems fail. Ronald Reagan, American president in the eighties, used a very similar phrase – supplied, audibly, by his wife Nancy when he was stumped by a question thrown from left field.

'We're doing everything we can,' she hissed.

'We're doing everything we can,' he said.

Reagan was lampooned for his apparent airheadedness (unfortunate, since he may have been in the first stages of dementia while president), but his gift for the telling phrase, perfectly delivered, was unequalled. I was in my teens when he arrived at the White House, but I remember being fascinated by this snappily dressed ex-actor's ability to weave a spell with words. His head would nod hypnotically as he spoke.

When the space shuttle Challenger exploded in 1986, killing all on board, Reagan went on national television. His remarkable words about the astronauts paraphrased a sonnet written by John Gillespie Magee, a young American airman killed in the Second World War.

'We will never forget them,' said Reagan, 'nor the last time we saw them this morning as they prepared for their journey and waved goodbye, and' – here comes the unforgettable line – 'they slipped the surly bonds of earth to touch the face of God.'

There was a similar moment when George W. Bush was president, in 2003, when the space shuttle Columbia exploded, again killing all on board.

Mr Bush went on national television and said, 'We should never underestimate the dangers of travel by rocket.'

That is not to denigrate Bush Junior's use of words, a practice which became so boringly fashionable during his time in office that he even attacked himself at one point. True, he promised American troops would go into Liberia to 'restore chaos', and, signing a $400bn defence spending bill on 5 August 2003, said: 'Our enemies are innovative and resourceful, and so are we. They never stop thinking about new ways to harm our country and our people, and neither do we.'

But outsiders failed to understand that the magnetism of this unusual president stemmed in part from his use of language.

His appearance with talk show host David Letterman during his first election campaign to announce 'the top ten changes I will make in the White House' was a case in point. He joked that he would 'make sure the White House library has lots of books with big print and pictures.' And then, in a reference to Bill Clinton's affair with an intern:

'I will give the Oval Office one heck of a scrubbing.'

When we previewed Bush's second election campaign for my *Politics Show* on BBC1, I was sent to the heart of the oil-rich Permian Basin in Midland, Texas. My assignment, in the neighbourhood where he was brought up, was: 'See if you can work out what makes George Bush tick.' So I went round his childhood home. To try to get into Mr Bush's mind, the team had me buy a cowboy outfit from a local outfitters and I was filmed walking down Main Street in Midland in it: Stetson, leather leggings, boots and all. I remember thinking it was a funny way to earn a living.

Strangely though, the best insight into President Bush came when I returned to my hotel room one evening.

I turned on the cable TV and there he was, speaking live outside the White House about the progress of the War on Terror.

Bush was running through the names of captured Al Qaeda leaders. Standing at a lectern he said, 'Thanks to coalition activities we've caught Khalid Sheikh Mohammed, Abu Zubaydah, Ram-bay al—'

He could not get the name out. 'Ray-bay bin Mel—'

'Raya El Binban—'

'Raybin—'

And then, leaning into the microphone, in a Texan drawl:

'I'm sorry, Ray, I got yer name wrong.'

Words are a window into a leader's soul. Even the most gifted can stumble on the basics and give themselves away. Reagan made a series of gaffes (example: 'Mr President, what do you know about rumours that the other candidate, Michael Dukakis, suffers from depression?' Reagan: 'Look, I'm not going to pick on an invalid.' And later, his apology: 'I was trying to make a joke and it didn't work.') He also came adrift badly in the Iran–Contra scandal, giving the following statement in March 1987 where the key sentence is the last one.

'A few months ago, I told the American people I did not trade arms for hostages. My heart and my best intentions tell me that's true. But the facts and the evidence say it's not.'

Above all, the greatest leaders wield power through language. The cleverest are fiendishly hard to interview because of their powers of evasion. The more leeway they give themselves, the more power they have. Every precisely answered question is a loss of power.

The best evasion I ever had to a question was from Bill Clinton himself. The lobby pack had travelled to Washington with Blair while he was opposition leader and Clinton was president. We ended up in that White House sitting room with the yellow sofa, and I thought if I could get Clinton to say something even mildly endorsing Blair it would make all the news back home. I spent ages working on what question to ask.

Finally they got to the junior reporters. Choosing every word with care, and trying very hard not to look scared, I said, 'Mr President, do you feel you're sitting beside an ideological soulmate?'

Sitting deep inside the armchair, Clinton just half-turned, half-looked at me, and said, 'Well. I'll leave that to you.' It was the most masterful, effortless evasion of a direct enquiry I had ever heard.

*

If leaders reveal themselves through what they say, reporters can sometimes expose themselves through what they ask.

I have questioned every prime minister since James Callaghan (admittedly with Callaghan, it was short. I approached him at a dinner and asked, 'Could I interview you about the Budget?' He stared at his seafood starter and replied: 'No.' It was the first time I have been outranked by a group of king prawns.). I only interviewed Mrs Thatcher once, sadly, and that was in order for her to pay tribute to Sir Keith Joseph, so it would not have been appropriate to say, 'Clearly you are not prepared to answer that question, so I'll try another.' John Major once called me a 'very impatient boy' when I shouted a question at him while he was visiting a factory in Basildon (I was actually a very impatient thirty-two). But with Blair, Brown and Cameron there have been numerous occasions.

Westminster was superb training for this. Our news editor for much of the nineties was Joy Johnson, a short and overheated character with inspirational and sometimes confusing flashes of temper. She did not walk into rooms, she burst into them. One day she saw six of the pol-corrs at our desks. A quarter per cent rise in interest rates had just been announced and Joy pounced on us with the immortal rocketing: 'WHAT THE HELL ARE YOU SITTING AROUND FOR?? THE ECONOMY'S OVERHEATING!!!'

Johnson was interesting, because she was being groomed for greatness after making her mark as the BBC's Chief Shouter. The unofficial role became almost a part of the constitution during the Major and Blair years. The Chief Shouter had to stand across the street from the door of Number Ten and yell at ministers on their way in. The two most common questions were: 'When are you going to resign?' and, during a reshuffle, 'Are you about to be sacked?' John Major reportedly asked a Downing Street aide, 'Who is that woman who makes me feel like a criminal every time I walk in here?' It was Joy. When the remark leaked, she was marked out for greater things.

What she did was an art. Getting the timing of the Shout just right, and making sure the question was succinct enough to allow space for an answer, is not easy.

I discovered the difficulties for myself the day I was sent urgently to 10 Downing Street to do the Shout for Robert Mugabe.

At the office, Patrick Gregory had explained the purpose: the bulletins had been on the blower; no one saw this coming; they needed a question linking the Bruce Grobbelaar scandal to his national football team. But crucially, it needed to be safe from any danger of defamation as nothing had been proven against Grobbelaar.

Breathless from running all the way, I took my place at the barrier next to only two others, both extremely courteous journalists from Zimbabwe.

Mugabe drew up in a limousine. I cleared my throat like an opera singer as John Major opened the front door of Number Ten to greet him.

'PRESIDENT MUGABE,' I yelled from across the street, conscious that my two Zimbabwean colleagues were shrinking back in alarm, 'DO THE SUSPICIONS THAT BRUCE GROBBELAAR DELIBERATELY LET GOALS IN FOR LIVERPOOL, AS ALLEGED IN AN ONGOING LIBEL CASE, BUT THEY ARE JUST ALLEGATIONS, MEAN THERE ARE DOUBTS ABOUT HIS PLACE IN GOAL FOR ZIMBABWE WHEN YOUR SQUAD BEGINS THE QUALIFYING ROUNDS FOR THE NEXT WORLD CUP?'

It must surely have been the longest Shout in British political history. By the time the question was finished, Mugabe and Major had shaken hands and disappeared inside Number Ten. The door had closed on them before I even got to my first mention of Zimbabwe. The two African reporters looked dumbfounded. When the stills photographers came out, one asked me: 'What the hell did you shout out here? The two of them were laughing so hard we almost couldn't do the photo.'

Sometimes the question works best when it is unexpected. I was standing in Downing Street the day Ian Paisley and his hardline colleagues from the Democratic Unionist Party emerged furious after seeing a first draft of the Downing Street Declaration.

They were in uproar about everything – the Declaration was a sell-out to the IRA, they had not been consulted, and (it was claimed later) they had been told there were too many of them to use the Downing Street lavatories. The DUP leader was enraged. His colleagues looked fit to burst. They rushed towards our microphones, coats flapping. Paisley's normal speaking voice is volume eleven, but this was loud even for him.

'IF THIS DOCUMENT EVER SEES THE LIGHT OF DAY, THE

Christmas 1970, with my brother and sister. I was looking into Camera One; Tim was already favouring the live audience. Sonya effortlessly upstages us both.

Preparing for a fancy dress party in suburban Cheam. The extension behind me was built by my grandfather. I just threw that in to distract you from my outfit.

TV break for local group

Flares gospel widens appeal

THAT tantalising step from local stardom to national recognition was taken by The Flared Generation last week.

By courtesy of London Weekend Television's Six O'Clock Show, the three young men, who have left an indelible mark on local fashions in the last year, will be preaching the flared gospel to millions of hitherto unconverted viewers this Friday.

A camera crew from the popular Friday evening show spent two hours last week filming the group in what has become the local Flare hunter's paradise, the Help The Aged shop in Grove Road.

"Danny Baker (one of the show's presenters) seemed like a rather flared sort of person to me," said Kevin Evans, the group's lead singer and lyricist. "He showed a lot of potential by wearing a pair of pink suede shoes and by the end of filming he was impressed enough to invest in a pair of his own.

"We were keen to provide our beloved home town, Cheam, with plenty of publicity" added guitarist and fellow songwriter Justin Beams. "Fortunately, on the day of filming Cheam seemed to be full of young people wearing flares and fortunately they were all spotted by the camera crew and interviewed."

Drummer and dark horse of the band, Wilma Cooper, was more interested in the effect the publicity would have on the nation's sartorial habits. "If it means that, as a result of this, more people than ever will wear wide ties and massively flared trousers then we'll be happy," he said.

■Six O'Clock Show presenter Danny Baker examines the Flared Generation.

The Flared Generation: undoubtedly Cheam's biggest band in 1981. Having tried and failed to form a successful punk group, Tim, Simon Williams and I created the Most Unfashionable Band in the Country. It worked: Danny Baker put us on TV.

And JEREMY VINE reports on how some people just can't leave him alone

Someone has taken my car again — for second time

No car: Jeremy Vine holds the keys to his car — which was stolen

I AM the latest victim of Coventry's rocketing crime figures. For the second time in a month my car was stolen from the city centre.

This time the police found it ploughed into a wall in Coundon. The time before it had finished up against a wall in Bedworth with only superficial damages.

Now it's a mangled heap that can't be driven.

The latest theft is the fourth time city yobs have broken into my Ford Escort in just two months.

in Upper Well Street. It was broken into and the stereo cassette player I'd installed only the week before was torn out.

The lightning theft left the indicators damaged and wiring hanging down to the floor of the car.

Estimates

So I bought a portable radio to listen to in the car and hid it under the seat.

But it was stolen along with the car and speakers worth £100 when thieves again successfully

industrial estate in Bedworth and crashed. Police who arrived at the scene arrested a youth making off with a can of petrol which I locked into the boot. He tore out the back seat to get to it.

My insurance company was trying to assess the damage done to the car — at least £500 worth — when the fourth theft left the Escort an outright right-off.

It was stolen from St Columba's Close, off the Radford Road, two minutes' walk out of the city centre.

Now my insurance company is

A steering lock didn't save the car. Nor did the absence of any valuables on display inside it.

I suggested to a police officer who found the car that more bobbies on the beat might cut down the city's spiralling crime figures: 95 crimes a day.

Laughed

There is a crime every 16 minutes in Coventry and in January 27 cars broken into or stolen every day.

But the officer laughed and

Reporting for the *Coventry Evening Telegraph*, 1986. This was one of my regular investigations into the theft of my own car.

Scary. The young reporter, with the jacket purchased for *Breakfast News*, just back from hunting U-boats.

Foreign correspondent in Lesotho, 1998. The mountainous kingdom kicked off in the most terrifying way, only 200 miles from the bureau in Joburg. Cameraman Alistair Lyne almost died the day after this picture was taken. On the left is producer Tony Wende.

One of the last BBC interviews with President Robert Mugabe. I asked him why, since he was messianic about family values, he had taken a mistress while his wife lay gravely ill. The atmosphere soured after that.

My mum and dad in Cheam, with Rachel (back row) and Paulina next to me. Some of her BBC friends flew Paulina over to London and we all took turns to show her round.

The Rule of the Maximum Number of Jeremys: the *Newsnight* presenting team in 2000. If you look carefully you can see that the dot has fallen off the 'i' in the programme's name behind us. I stayed in position a little longer.

The *Newsnight* Van was a killer idea and gave us improbable amounts of fun during the 2001 election. Billy Bragg had just confronted Oliver Letwin dressed as a centurion. Producer Isobel Eaton is studying the shot.

2 | Media

The Guardian Monday June 3 2002

So Newsnight's Joy Division-loving presenter Jeremy Vine is to replace housewives' choice Jimmy Young on Radio 2. **Maggie Brown** on why it will be like taking over from the Queen Mother

Jeremy, the new Jimmy

The contract is issued. It's all over, bar minor haggling. The Jimmy Young show becomes the Jeremy Vine show from Monday, January 6, 2003. A veteran is being replaced by a dashing presenter of 37, who is expected to quietly stir "interactivity" and youthful "dexterity" into Radio 2's daily two-hour current affairs and music slot.

A formal announcement is being delayed, however, because – after last year's unseemly brouhaha when Nicky Campbell claimed he'd been sounded out for the job – everybody involved at the BBC wants to treat octogenarian Sir Jimmy Young with the dignity 50 years of professionalism at the microphone deserves.

So first Young must go to Buckingham Palace on June 27 to be invested with his knighthood – another means of soothing displeasure – and then he will be awarded the consolation prize of a new one-hour current affairs programme, at tea-time on Sundays. Until then, the BBC is sticking to the technical figleaf of saying "no contract has been signed".

Vine's agent, Alex Armitage of Noel Gay, nevertheless confirms the deal is done: "It is a fantastic journalistic job. Jeremy will become the senior journalist of Radio 2, at the middle of the day – the nation's village pump, where people get together".

Armitage rang up Vine when he was the BBC's correspondent in South Africa after catching him on screen and deciding he was "something special" then and there: "He was full of beans and just very good. I have been doing this job a long time and knew he had this undeniable quality."

The job is a passport to making a tidy fortune. Vine will leave the BBC staff and more than treble his pay. The rate for the five-days-a-week show is likely to be north of £150,000–£200,000 a year, and juicy TV presenting opportunities are mooted, such as fronting The State We're In, a satire show recently piloted on BBC Choice.

But many Newsnight viewers, watching Vine handle Stephen Byers's resignation and the cabinet reshuffle with aplomb last week, might justifiably wonder: what's in it for him? Why would a TV anchor on the BBC's most high-profile current affairs programme elect to go to chat and spin discs on Radio 2 at lunchtime?

Easy. Audiences for the Radio 2 slot are five times that of Newsnight. And for Vine, it's a chance to escape from the long shadow of the other Jeremy and to star in his own show. Jeremy Paxman, 52, with the impetus of the interviews with Tony Blair behind him, seems set to rule the programme for the next 10 years. Kirsty Wark is second in the Newsnight pecking order. Some think Vine has tried too hard to emulate Paxman's minister-kebabing style, although he actually possesses something different but equally valuable – an accessible, friendly, engaging side – as his election coverage last year from a battered purple camper van proved.

The Jimmy Young Show's production team praise Vine's "emollient voice" and "sense of fun", with one observing: "Each time he's stood in for Jimmy he got better." He also endeared himself by bringing his own stack of CDs into the studio, and Armitage stresses Vine's deep love of music – although his enthusiasm for performers such as Elvis Costello, Joy Division and the Fall

On the same wavelength . . . Vine's accessible, friendly and engaging manner won him the job

Thunder Road here we come. The 'secret' got out when the editor of *Newsnight* held a team meeting to say I was leaving.

Jimmy Young, who started as a pop star, was derailed by Elvis. Yet he was still broadcasting a live daily show fifty years later. This was his final programme.

One of the most brilliant quiz show formats ever devised. As I throw questions at them, I often think that if we could harness the combined brainpower of Chris, Daphne, CJ, Kevin and Judith – the Eggheads – there would be enough energy to drive the national grid.

Can I be friends with Peter Mandelson? Here he is in my radio studio. 'I tried to put your van in my memoirs,' he told me sweetly, 'but it just wouldn't fit.'

In broadcasting most things should be tried at least once. Sadly we stumbled on one of the few that shouldn't. For the record, it was the 2008 council elections and the graphic was about the Lib Dems.

A seminal moment as Labour slumped from power. Gordon Brown listens to the 'bigotgate' tape I am playing him as, unbeknownst to either of us, a camera shows his reaction live.

The swingometer, 2010-style. The birth of the coalition government, and I can't see any of it. A computer fills in the graphics on your TV and I remember where they are using chalk marks – until they move, that is.

All in an hour's work. With the deputy prime minister of Israel, Ehud Barak, in one hotel room . . .

. . . and thirty minutes later, Johnny Depp in another. Barak had to shift hotels for Depp. The biggest film star on the planet doesn't move for a mere statesman.

The best job of the lot. With Martha and Anna, who I work for.

Milton Nkosi on a visit to London in 2002, amused to see just how much welly Greg Dyke's BBC was putting into my Radio 2 launch. This hoarding in Shepherds Bush was one of thousands.

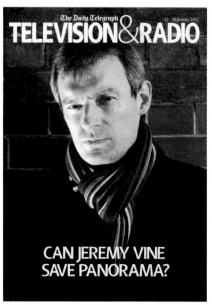

Written by someone from the Department of Silly Questions, I presume. *Panorama* never needed saving.

Chasing a paedophile for *Panorama*, 2008. The man in the red cap had been trying to fix a date with a girl he thought was 14 (he was later convicted). I seem to be running fastest, so why am I in last place?

STREETS OF ULSTER WILL RUN WITH THE BLOOD OF INNO-
CENT FAMILIES AS THE REPUBLICAN DEVIL SMITES THE
LAND—'

Or words to that effect. When the shouting stopped, a *Daily
Mirror* reporter standing next to me piped up.

'So it's a cautious welcome, then?'

But I was never very good at doorsteps. Try as I might, I just
could not get the knack of the Shout. When Tony Blair arrived at
Tate Britain to speak about the economy, I again mistimed my
question:

'Mr Blair! What is your comment on the change to the public
sector deficit forecast given the fact that you were using the previous
figures as a basis for your spending plans over the next Parliament?'

Blair sailed past, smiling at me, followed by Campbell, who
swerved into me like a rugby player and knocked me backwards.
'Oi – he's come to make a speech, not listen to one,' he said.

*

When you travel abroad, you do realize the strangeness of what we
do here. Chancellor Kohl was involved in a huge German financial
scandal in 2001 and I had to try to catch up with him in Vrotslav in
Poland.

In an ancient Catholic church he was being awarded a doctorate,
an olive branch between the two countries. The discreet ceremony
involved at least eight bishops, some candles, and incantations from
a sturdy choir. A group of reporters stood behind scarlet rope at the
back of the church.

Out of courtesy I thought I should leave the Shout until the very
end, when I assumed everyone would join in. Sadly they did not. So
my lung-bursting yell, 'WHERE IS THE MONEY, CHANCELLOR
KOHL?' must have echoed in that place for a full minute, as he, and
the choir, and all the bishops in their impressive headgear, glared at
me in disgust.

But doing the Shout is great practice. You may have had to travel for a day just to ask that one question. Every word needs judging. There is no second chance. It needs unimpeachable confidence. And if they don't answer? Then your colleagues will probably broadcast just the question, so it had better be good.

One of my first experiences of *Newsnight* came when I was loaned to the programme during a parliamentary recess at Westminster. The editor, Peter Horrocks, sent me off to film a report on whether the rock band Oasis were splitting up. I drove with a camera crew to the north London home of the singer Liam Gallagher, and stood among the pack of reporters outside the front gate.

Nothing happened for a long time. Finally I thought, 'What's to lose?' and with the cameraman I walked through the gate and bounded up the white stone steps to the front door, pressing the entryphone.

An impatient 'HELLO?' came through the speaker.

'It's Jeremy Vine from *Newsnight*,' I said. 'Who's that?'

'This is Liam,' said the unmistakeable Mancunian voice.

'Are you coming out?'

'Am I fuck? It's raining,' he said, and cut the connection.

Gallagher's response made for a short interview: five words, one of which could not be broadcast. The programme bleeped out the swearing, and my reward was having Paxman introduce me on air as 'our new rock correspondent.'

I reflected on it afterwards, and realized I had got the question wrong. With only one shot at it, 'Are you coming out?' had been a mistake. It should have been 'Are you splitting up?'

Questions. When I was a trainee I ended up sat next to a much older reporter called Geoffrey Wareham one day. That drizzly Friday turned out to be his last. He was retiring; taking his BBC pension and going. I couldn't quite believe nothing had been organized to mark the end of a forty-year career, so I offered to take Geoffrey out for pizza.

I felt rather embarrassed that, at twenty-three, I was in charge of the celebrations, which only comprised two ham and mushroom thin crust at Pizza Hut. But Geoffrey made liberating company. He had taken all the BBC had thrown at him and reached sixty-five with apparently no major psychological disorder. Not only that. He told me he was the one who put to James Callaghan the question which led to the then Labour prime minister replying: 'Crisis, what crisis?' in 1979.

'Really?' I said.

'Yes,' replied Geoffrey, 'but he didn't actually say that. I asked him about the crisis, and he said there wasn't one.'

I remembered the famous *Daily Mail* front page because my grandmother dropped it on her breakfast table in Guildford in front of the thirteen-year-old me: the headline, **CRISIS? WHAT CRISIS?** in big blaring letters.

So Callaghan had never said the historic phrase? In that case, all we were left with was Geoffrey's question – but what a question.

We toasted it with garlic bread and he retired.

*

Questions, questions, questions . . . they are at the heart of journalism, and interviewers are obsessed with them. What makes a good one?

In the run-up to the 1997 election, the Conservatives went on a desperate hunt for new initiatives. The country was just pulling clear of a bone-crunching recession, and they produced one of the most bizarre slogans in the history of political advertising, an attempt to claim credit for the recovery in six words: YES IT HURT. YES IT WORKED. In the *Guardian*, the cartoonist Steve Bell lampooned the slogan with his own version: YES IT SMELLS. YES WE FARTED.

So the creaking Tory administration was up against it. The government would produce one last Queen's Speech – the term for the annual launch of the governing party's programme in Parliament. Ministerial aides knew it was all-or-nothing. They wanted the occasion to be turbo-charged. So they told the political staff from

all the newspapers and broadcasters to assemble in a room, perhaps sixty of us in all, for an off-the-record briefing in breach of
parliamentary convention.

Since it is actually not possible to have a private briefing if the
number of reporters goes above one, the whole event would be
leaked spectacularly. But the party chairman Brian Mawhinney was
not to know that as we craned in to hear him. He indiscreetly ran
through the list of new policies, swore us all to secrecy, then said the
aim of the list was to 'smoke Labour out.'

He added, cryptically, 'The thinking behind these policies will
not be lost on astute observers of the political scene.'

A man from *The Times* cleared his throat and asked: 'What about
us?'

That must be a good question, because the room shook with
laughter.

Sometimes questions work by getting a speaker to deny the obvious. The poor man responsible for Saddam Hussein's publicity, the
Iraqi information minister Mohammad Saeed al-Sahhaf, famously
proclaimed there were no American troops anywhere near the capital – 'The infidels are committing suicide by the hundred at the gates
of Baghdad' – just as American tanks came into view behind him.

I watched a different version of the same technique during a
lobby briefing at Downing Street. The political editor of the Press
Association asked Sir Christopher Meyer, the prime minister's official spokesman: 'Does the Prime Minister have any plans to meet
Charles Saatchi?'

Sir Christopher did a good line in synthetic outrage. He rolled his
eyes. 'No, he does not, there are no plans to meet any advertising
"gurus" or however you want to describe them, there are no secret
meetings, no "encounters", no whispered conversations, no quiet
tap on the shoulder, and *no, he is not planning to meet Charles
Saatchi*. Whatever made you think he was?'

'Mr Saatchi just walked past the window,' said the reporter.

Sometimes questions work because they seek a fact. Ask the

shadow minister campaigning for 'more dignity for the elderly, and a better pension' exactly what the weekly pension is for a married couple for this simple reason: *he may not know.* In 2011 the Labour leader Ed Miliband came unstuck when an inspired BBC Scotland reporter, Tim Reid, asked him the simplest of questions about the Scottish Labour leadership candidates.

Reid: Can you name the three of them?

Miliband: There is Tom Harris. Um, er, there is Johann Lamont. Er, and a third candidate who is also going to be putting themself forward.

Reid: He is the frontrunner. Ken Macintosh.

Miliband: Ken Macintosh, yes.

Reid: He is the frontrunner and you can't name him.

Miliband: No. Ken Macintosh is going to be an excellent candidate.

(I love the word 'No' in that last answer. What is it doing there? It is the quiet 'No' of someone who realizes the satnav has just taken his car off Beachy Head.) Reid's ambush may well have been inspired by a man called Andy Hiller, whom I think of as the King of the Factual Question. The Boston-based reporter is renowned for asking politicians questions that cannot be evaded. Unfortunately for George Bush, he did not know this when he sat opposite him in 2000, resulting in the following:

Hiller: Can you name the president of Chechnya?

Bush: No, can you?

Hiller: Can you name the president of Taiwan?

Bush: Yeah, Lee.

Hiller: Can you name the general who is in charge of Pakistan?

Bush: Wait, wait, is this fifty questions?

Hiller: No, it's four questions of four leaders in four hot-spots.

Bush: The new Pakistani general, he's just been elected – not elected, this guy took over office. It appears this guy is going to bring stability to the country and I think that's good news for the subcontinent.

Hiller: Can you name him?

Bush: General. I can name the general. Just general.

Hiller: And the prime minister of India?

Bush: The new prime minister of India is ... no. (Attempts to take the initiative.) Can you name the foreign minister of Mexico?

Hiller: No sir, but I would say to that, I'm not running for president.*

As an interviewer you collect questions. What makes a good question and what makes a bad question? It fascinates me. I have always admired Jeremy Paxman for the interview he started like this:

* The answers (at the time): President Lee Teng-hui of Taiwan, Pakistan's General Pervaiz Musharraf, Chechnya's Aslan Maskhadov and Atal Bihari Vajpayee of India.

'I'm joined by Vivian Linacre, who is president of the British Weights and Measures Association, which is dedicated to keeping the pound, the foot, the inch and the mile. Mr Linacre, haven't you got anything better to do with your time?'

Or his first question to the German ambassador in 1989:

'Good evening. Well, it's not been a very good century, has it?'

And then there was this exchange with Nancy Dell'Olio, former girlfriend of the football manager Sven-Goran Eriksson. She was being asked about the impact of the credit crunch.

Dell'Olio: It should be used much more fantasy to help us. That is I think what we're gonna turn, when I talk about values. I think we need more fantasy, to use our intelligence. I tell you, rules, rules has been over too much. And rules needs to change, so it would be easy to—

Paxman: I'm sorry. I haven't the faintest idea what you're talking about.

But the greatest ever question in a current affairs interview was surely asked by Richard Madeley when *Richard & Judy* booked Bill Clinton as a guest. The former occupant of the White House was promoting his post-presidential memoirs and Madeley decided to draw a parallel between his own acquittal on a shoplifting charge, and Clinton's affair with Monica Lewinsky. I hope you will allow me to take this from memory – I have tried and failed to find a tape of the broadcast. But I well remember the confusion on Clinton's face as Madeley launched in:

'I was once arrested for stealing some wine and I was totally innocent, but it was such a terrible time for me, I came through it, but you must have felt the same when people accused you of having an affair with Monica Lewinsky . . .'

Clinton's face at this point had taken on a waxy appearance.

'... although,' Madeley added, 'of course in that case you had actually done it, whereas I hadn't.'

*

Questions tend to have two halves: the set-up and the knockdown. 'Prime Minister, you asked the nation to holiday in the UK last year. Did you enjoy Tunisia?' is the classic formula. If Madeley/Clinton gets the award for the most brilliantly bewildering combination of first and second half, we must at this point mention a BBC radio interviewer who managed to compose a question with fifteen halves.

The interview was on an arts programme in the fifties where the guest was the Irish short story writer John McGahern. I cannot be sure who the interviewer is, because I just happened on the tape in the BBC's Sound Archive when I was looking for something else. The question is 245 words: an astonishing two minutes and thirty seconds *for a single question*! When I heard it I realized it was an undiscovered gem and ran off a copy to keep. I believe this to be easily the longest question asked since the invention of the microphone, and here I transcribe it, without edits, exactly as it went out.

> *Interviewer:* John, can I take up with you an aspect of your work which has to do with your preoccupation with detail, and has also to do with your characters' detailed responses to experience; what I have in mind here is that you often in your writing, er, depict people engaged in trivial activities, which they carry out with meticulous precision, as for example in *The Barracks* and the short story [inaudible], we have for example policemen who are required to fill in daybooks—
>
> *McGahern (in background):* Um.
>
> — and who are living lives of the most crashing boredom, and you are frighteningly good at depicting this quotidian,

clichéd, repetitive activity, which fascinates you because of its daily futility, the way in which people fritter away the precious days in formal, useless activities of this kind; this seems to me to be in some way related to your consuming interest in all kinds of detail, I noticed for example the vividness – and it seems paradoxical to say vividness, but it is vividness – of your description of the guests in the boarding house, for example, in *Strandhill, the Sea*, you know, the short story about Strandhill; you are achieving the thing that Coleridge is after; wasn't it Coleridge who said, 'If you want to depict a bore you must never be boring'? You seem to me to have a remarkable capacity for depicting bores and the boredom of existence without ever being boring; you are fascinated by cliché in speech and by cliché in behaviour; your policemen, Garda Mullins and the rest of them, they—

McGahern (interrupting): Oh, sure, but that goes back to a different thing. You see, I think that either everything is important or nothing is important.

Interviewer: Yes.

What is going on inside that interviewer's mind? The answer is that he has forgotten the lesson of Chapter Two – *no matter how important you think you are, you aren't* – and he now believes his questions to be more exciting than the answers. To him, they undoubtedly are. I have never asked a single question which has not caused me profound excitement. But everyone else is listening for the answer.

The arts interviewer also broke the first rule of all public speaking, interviewing, conversation, indeed any utterance made in a public space: *elaboration is death.*

Just say it once. Or if possible, even less than once.

*

So how do you interview a prime minister?

Truth is, it depends. Depends on which one, for a start. There are fifty different types of interview for fifty different PMs. You have to brief yourself exhaustively whichever person you are interviewing and prime ministers are no different. And here is a good principle – you may not know as much as they do about everything, but you can know more than they do about something.

Knowing more than them about something is important, because you choose the something when you speak to them.

Interviewees hate the fact that the reporter chooses the terrain. One of the most tempestuous exchanges I ever had was with the late Robin Cook. At the time he was foreign secretary. I was inside his vast suite of rooms in the Foreign Office, asking him about the new International Criminal Court. He had been one of the politicians behind it.

This being *Newsnight*, it was not enough simply to ask him why it was such a great idea. There had to be a catch.

Again and again, I tried: 'What happens if they try to prosecute the UK for sinking the *Belgrano*?'

As I kept on, I could see Cook gently coming to the boil in front of me. His eyes seemed to go all stary. He kept trying to dismiss the question and I kept asking it. Finally we ran out of tape and paused the camera.

He jumped up from his chair. 'What is the point of all these school-boy questions?' He shouted: 'WHAT IS THE BLOODY POINT?'

Now he was going to storm out of his own office. As he reached the door, which was huge, and made him look even smaller, he turned and shouted from the doorway: 'Jeremy – do you not give A FART about foreign dictators?'

With the word 'fart' echoing off the woodwork, Cook exited the room and was hosed down by his spokesman. When he returned, we started the second part of the interview and all was well.

Rule No. 37: *If it's going to be a tricky one, don't run out of tape halfway through.*

Rule No. 38: *Never race a member of the House of Lords.*

In 1997 I was sent to cover the Conservative conference. With the party beaten and in a shambles, the event combined tragedy and hilarity from all angles. William Hague was manning what he later termed 'the nightshift' as Tory leader. Off the leash, his MPs were having just a bit too much fun. One of them, the charming but dangerous Alan Clark, was asked at a fringe meeting what the 'answer to the troubles in Northern Ireland' was. His astonishing response – 'The only solution for dealing with the IRA is to kill six hundred people in one night, let the UN and everyone else make a great scene, and it's over for twenty years' – caused a day of happy news chaos, with Conservative high command having to deny it was official policy. It was that surreal.

It also gave me my loopiest, and one of my last, memories of being a pol-corr at Westminster. I appeared on *Breakfast News* one morning and said, quite reasonably I thought, that the Conservative party had a growing problem with the increasingly elderly profile of its members. At the time the average age was touching sixty-two. For some reason Jeffrey Archer became incandescent about this perceived slight and stormed into the hotel reception where our camera point was. He found himself a broadcast area to hurl a denunciation of me.

Unfortunately the camera was not ours but GMTV's. But Lord Archer was not the sort to worry about issuing his challenge on a rival channel:

'Find me Vine!' he bellowed. 'I'll give him "old". OLD? I'm an Olympic sprinter and I will have him on the beachfront anytime. Two o'clock today. Me and him, and I'll take him down. I'm serious. I'm going to TAKE VINE DOWN.'

I had by this stage crept out of the back door of the hotel in a state of alarm, but the contents of the outburst were relayed to me. Westminster had thrown many tricky situations my way, but surely this was the most awkward. If I did not turn up for the race, Lord Archer could hold a beachfront press-call and do a lap of honour for the reporters. Surely I was not responsible for the hurt feelings of famous novelists, but on the other hand . . .

How could I not take up Jeffrey Archer's challenge? Thinking this was as mad a day's work as I would ever do, I went round the shops in Blackpool that morning and bought training shoes, a white T-shirt and shorts that were slightly too large, so I had to use string as a belt to hold them up. No question of putting even the string on expenses: what would the claim say? At 2 p.m. I was at the beach-front with our camera crew, shivering in shorts and vest on the bitter seafront. At least, if we had this crazy race, and especially if Archer beat me, I would have a lively package for the next morning.

At 2.30 I was still waiting.

Eventually I rang Jeffrey Archer's office. They claimed I had mis-understood the timings, and when I said I would wait, they said (with him clearly there in the background) he was 'too tired'.

'Too tired?' I repeated.

'After making an important speech,' they added.

*

It was during my breakfast with Alastair Campbell that I realized I would have to leave Westminster after the 1997 general election. My place on the Labour battlebus had been booked by the BBC and immediately reports had emerged that Campbell, Blair's head of com-munications, was trying to get me replaced with a different reporter. My speciality, said a diary piece, was 'sketches' and my approach was 'irreverent'. These two words seemed deliberately chosen to cause maximum negative impact with my bosses. A number of articles sug-gested Campbell had gone and told Samir Shah, the head of BBC Westminster, that I would not be welcome on the bus. It probably did not help that Joy Johnson had left to work for Labour. An editorial executive, Anne Sloman, once asked me, 'Why does Joy hate you so much?' – and that was while Joy was my boss! I doubted that joining a party press office had turned her into an admirer.

But Samir did not give way. He had now been joined by Ric Bailey in the management team, and they made for a tough combo. In situations where the BBC feels its independence is being threatened or even questioned, it often finds its own antique collection of knuckledusters. So it was with my seat on the battlebus. I would be on it and would be filing, Ric told me, 'as often as possible.' That was good.

Now I just needed to clear the air with Campbell. We met in the Atrium restaurant on the ground floor of the BBC's offices early one morning.

Having learnt my lesson with Peter Mandelson, I was well aware that with Alastair Campbell I could be friendly, but not friends. In a good mood he was fun; in a bad mood he was Ivan the Terrible, Freddy Krueger and Chopper Harris all rolled into one. He and I had already had a number of arguments, not least during the Blair/Clinton trip to Washington where I had filed a report describing how he had struggled to brief nineteen correspondents spread across the economy section of a busy aeroplane. He believed that my description of him squeezing back and forth past the stewardesses was a breach of lobby rules guaranteeing anonymity for party spokesmen, but I argued they did not apply on commercial airliners. It is never a good idea to win an argument like that.

Campbell was also angry when Blair made a speech entitled 'The Seven Pillars Of A Decent Society' and I had to tell him that there was only enough space in the lunchtime news to mention three pillars.

Still, we sat down and enjoyed our breakfast. He was chummy, discussing football. I reckoned the whole battlebus issue was closed. After all, Alastair Campbell was now charged with guiding Labour into an historic election victory and nothing was in the bag until the votes had been cast, so he really did have bigger fish to fry than me (and, as mentioned, a smaller breakfast). Indeed the mood was warm between us – until the moment I said to him:

'On the battlebus we'll obviously just be looking out for the unexpected.'

'The unexpected?' His face darkened.

It did not seem controversial to me. 'You know, the news. The unscheduled stuff. We report on all the stuff you didn't plan, Alastair.'

Bad move. It is fair to say he became slightly apoplectic. 'No. You report on what Tony is doing. You report on the speeches he makes and the people he meets. *That is your job.*'

'Surely,' I tried weakly, 'news is what you *didn't* expect to happen?'

Campbell was furious. Like a huge boiler gradually starting to thump and bang, he seemed to raise the temperature of the air around me. He stared away into the distance, full of loathing.

And that was pretty much the end of the conversation, which threw me right back to Nick Clarke's wise words at that party conference some years before. Alastair genuinely believed that my job as a reporter was to report the things Tony said. I thought my job was to report all the stuff we weren't expecting. More than that – for him and the others in his trade, politics is what happens between parties. But for reporters, politics is what happens *inside* parties. Politics (I still believe) is the often complex process by which a group of powerful people come to a decision; that journey is called politics. The decision is a policy. What the other party yells while they are doing it is irrelevant.

In the years to come, as he became the single most dominant PR man in political history, Alastair made great play of the way journalists – in his view – 'obsessed with process'. He did not want us to describe or understand how the record player worked, he wanted us only to appreciate the music. Politics was the fluff on the needle; it just got in the way. His aim was nothing short of abolishing the whole pol-corr industry. In his view, a leader called Tony Blair made speeches and took decisions, and Alastair would call us when he needed us to pass them on.

He was wrong, of course. To take one very obvious example, the subterranean insurgency conducted by Gordon Brown for more than ten years was a hugely significant bit of 'process', as all the memoirs from the time make clear.

But our strained breakfast, in the words of the folk singer Catie Curtis, Got Me Wondering. It followed, if Blair won a thumping majority in 1997, that Alastair would clean the fluff off the needle. There might be no real politics for many years after.

I had this worry constantly as I rubbed shoulders with the Labour leader on his election battlebus. One day, passing through Bury, it was just him and me having a cup of tea together. No one else was around but the driver and a couple of junior aides sat in the curtained-off area at the back. I glimpsed a group of residents waving at Blair through the smoked glass in a way that was quite different, as if he was Not Like The Others.

Looking at them, he smiled. Then turned back to me. As we sat across a table from each other, the future prime minister said: 'I like tea.'

'So do I,' was my reply.

I was thinking: *Remain neutral.*

'So you're a Christian, Jeremy, aren't you?'

'Um – well – a struggling one,' I said apologetically.

'Me too,' he smiled. 'I would actually say it's the most important thing in my life.'

Just to make conversation, I asked: 'So do you not feel, Tony, that the big stuff – what you'll do if you get to be prime minister – changing social security, and so on – that it's less important than the small stuff? How you treat your next-door neighbour?'

Given that his next-door neighbour would be Gordon Brown, this was a spectacularly inept analogy.

But Blair answered, 'Oh, completely.' Which was his genius: in a couple of sentences he had bonded with me on everything from tea to God. We sat there for a few minutes, then he politely said he had to finish a speech and left for the back of the bus.

I began to see that a massive victory for Tony Blair would shut down the burgeoning industry which employed political correspondents, because dominance allows a leader to ignore dissent. Without dissent there is no call for the vast array of professional adjectives describing splits and gaffes. We might not even hear how a 'senior backbencher' had attacked this or that policy (backbenchers are, by definition, not senior. They are only described that way when they criticize their own party.) For this pol-corr, and all the others, the war would be over.

So if there was going to be no more work at Westminster, what should I do?

The answer, it turned out, was six thousand miles away.

Chapter Twelve

TWENTY-FOUR AND WE BOWL

I was met at the airport. A friend from college days, Jayne Morgan, kindly looked out for me when I stepped off the plane in Johannesburg. She drove me to the house where I would be temporarily staying, but a producer was waiting there to stop me going through the front door.

Kate Peyton stepped forward, smiled warmly, gave me a kiss on both cheeks and said, 'I was going to help you unpack, but there's been a coup in Zambia.'

In my head I ran through my Zambia facts. Capital: Luanda. No, Lusaka. Famous ex-president: Kenneth Kaunda. Current president: *current president, come on . . .*

For some reason I was only getting the name Frank Zappa, and I knew that couldn't be right.

The distance between the Westminster and Africa correspondent is better measured in aeons than miles. Zambia? *Coup?* Eight days before, I had been doing a piece on Welsh devolution. As I counted my bags off the airport belt (seven), I asked myself the question again and again, once for each bag: how exactly did I end up here in South Africa?

Departing from its usual accidental nature, the Beeb had reached into its political unit after the 1997 election and shifted the orna- ments with care. Working a minimum of seven days a week, some of us might have been close to cracking. Sopel went to Paris, Edwards (who was fluent in French) to *News 24*. I was packed off to a differ- ent continent. The news chief Richard Sambrook sent me a letter wishing me well, ending with three words of advice in scrawled cap- itals: 'DON'T GET KILLED!'

I did not get killed, I got educated. Even on that first day. Kate Peyton took me straight to the bureau past a parade of screaming- pink jacaranda blossoms. Bob Dylan, her hero it turned out, played on the car stereo. In the office I met Milton Nkosi, the Sowetan pro- ducer who would become a lifelong friend. I confessed I 'had very little' on Zambia. He had anticipated that, and produced a pile of freshly mown agency copy.

The president was Frederick Chiluba – not Zappa – and the rebels had taken over the national radio station but nothing else. The army had then surrounded the station and taken it back. End of coup. I would file from a small booth in the bureau that was hard-wired to London. The World Service wanted me live in eight minutes.

I think, looking back, I imported too much of my Westminster approach to Africa in those first days. To me the Zambian coup was another press release to be relayed with as much zing as possible. It was another story needing to be analysed with vim and bounce. So, one hour after arriving in Africa for the first time, I went on the World Service and pronounced magisterially that the incident had clearly been a 'Mickey Mouse coup', where the plotters should have taken control of the army and then the radio station, but had made the fatal mistake of doing them in the wrong order. Chiluba, who I pointed out was only five feet tall, would 'grow in stature' as a result of seeing off this challenge. Now the question across Africa would be, who plotted it?

I am sure my breathless piece made a gripping listen, and it was the kind of lively textual analysis that made British politics so much fun: but at Westminster life and death are normally not in the balance. When Michael Heseltine's coup against Margaret Thatcher failed, he went back to his arboretum to tend a collection of trees. By contrast the Zambian plotters probably had their heads smeared across a wall by the time my broadcast went out. My tone failed to register that reality, and the piece was also factually wrong: the idea that 'Who plotted the coup?' would be asked across a continent where most women spend more than four hours a day carrying water, and the average breadwinner gets by on less than ten dollars a week, was foolish. It was more likely to be asked across Islington.

Eventually unpacked, I had a large house with a swimming pool and an electric fence – and, I already knew, a lot of lessons to learn. Even searching for a home to rent in South Africa was eye-opening. Time and again my wife and I saw palatial properties, but having looked at four or five bedrooms fit for a princess we would then apologetically be shown the quarters for the domestic staff, which were not much better than a toolshed.

From the shadows within one unlit, crumbling outhouse by a well-manicured tennis court I saw three pairs of eyes blinking back at me: the perfect, and most painful, juxtaposition of rich and poor. I murmured to the estate agent that the dog lived in a better kennel, and he whispered back: 'Often the domestics do this to themselves.' Come again? Mandela might be president, but some of the swisher bits of Johannesburg had evidently not yet been informed.

And the security situation was interesting too. Soon after my arrival, someone squeezed through the gate to the driveway at night. They opened the unlocked boot of my car, removing a flak jacket marked 'BBC' and a laptop. When the police arrived they looked at the house and found bars on every window but one. This seemed to amuse them beyond reason, the fact that no one had realized it was pointless having any bars at all if you were going to miss one window out. 'Your laptop saved your life,' said the officer. 'If they didn't find anything in your car, they are through that window and they'd definitely carry weapons.' When I told them the raiders took my flak jacket too, and described it, they split their sides at the idea that someone might raid a bank with 'BBC' stencilled on their back in big letters.

Poor South Africa. In my first year there, with virtually no political violence, there were 25,000 murders in a population of forty million. By contrast, Britain had 750 murders in a population of sixty million. The crime was an inconvenient truth, and no one wanted it told.

After one of our freelance cameramen was woken by intruders in his bedroom who had peeled the slates off his roof and climbed in through the ceiling to avoid the alarms, the Beeb got concerned and insisted we review security.

Milton brought in a man called Robert, a short, white South African with a ponytail and strong accent. He looked carefully at our domestic arrangements and then gave his recommendation:

'Okay, you need sensors in the attic because they're climbing through the roof now. You also need a beam across the front and back doors. That one window without bars – that's crazy. Plus, keep geese.'

'Geese?' I was noting it down.

'Geese in the garden. They make a hell of a racket if someone climbs the fence. You need to up the voltage on the electric fence, don't worry about the legal limit, it's not enforced. Use a different armed response company which is on 24-hour call. You require panic buttons in the bedrooms and a rape gate across your main bedroom door so it can be used as a refuge.

'Finally,' Robert concluded, 'there is a serious risk of hijacking if you drive this model.' We were standing in my driveway and he indicated the leased BMW. 'They call it "Break My Window" in the townships. What I recommend is you put a notice in the windows on both sides, saying DANGER: LIVE SNAKES IN CAR. These people will not take the chance when it comes to snakes.'

After he was gone, Milton took me on one side. 'This man,' he said, 'represents everything that is wrong with my country.'

*

I lived in South Africa with my wife, Janelle. A hyper-intelligent American, she worked for an investment bank. In truth we were growing apart. Or maybe a better way to put it was that she allowed me the space to do all the things the BBC wanted me to do, and in the end the leeway I wished for proved fatal. I was the selfish one. Janelle was gracious and blameless throughout. These days she is a mum and blissfully married to a Canadian entrepreneur. The two of us are now, luckily from my point of view, firm friends.

In three-and-a-bit years in Africa, I would visit eighteen countries and have more adventures than I could ever dream of. Fundamentally I grasped one single unshakeable truth, definitely a Rule, which is that *News is a serious business.* I know, I know – how could I not have understood this at Westminster? The answer is that in a highly developed country, politics is so choreographed, so theatrical, it can feel like a game. The Tory in the lift who got trampled by the wildebeest? Well, he knew the score. The MPs in jail for their expenses? Stretchered off. The Blair/Brown conflict? Terrific spectator sport. But Africa?

Another world.

When we drove to Namibia to look for evidence of the Aids crisis there – in one area, Oshakati, nearly seventy per cent of pregnant women were testing positive – Milton, cameraman Glenn Middleton and I were held up for hours in the office of some local authority functionaries who pottered around saying they had to wait for a fax granting us permission to film and giving the locations of sick people in the vicinity.

The day grew old. If the sun went down, we could not film. What was the delay? We waited and waited. It turned out there would be no fax. The officials did not even have a fax machine. They just did not want us filming. Aids carries a huge stigma, not only for the sufferer but evidently for their local council too. Furious, we told the officials where to get off and left, belting across the oceanic Namibian plains in our jeep.

With no official assistance, how could we find people suffering from an illness nobody would talk about? Sometimes, on the road, I would spool back and forth the title of the classic seventies book on journalism, *Anyone Here Been Raped and Speaks English?*, trying to ensure I was not playing out its caricature of the heartless dolt out of his depth everywhere.

The answer to our question was all around us. In one tiny village we came across two elderly Namibians looking after a small boy. The boy's mother, their daughter, had died of the disease. She had been infected by their father, a trucker who had slept with scores of women on his routes. He was dead too. Their son, a boy of five, was also ill with Aids.

'Can I see him?' I asked.

'Over there,' they said.

I walked round the side of their hut. On a low brick wall sat the young boy. He was staring into the distance with his back to me. The low sun threw red and purple streamers across the sky. I moved round to the side of the boy, but he never turned to look at this lanky westerner with the baseball cap who had suddenly appeared. As I came closer to the front of him I gazed into his features. Sick at five, with no parents and no future to look forward to but pain, his was the drawn face of an adult already. The expression was sheer, blank hopelessness. In the silence, neither of us spoke; taking off my hat, I stood staring at him quietly as the light on his face gently shifted, considering my luck and privilege, and for how much of my life I had missed the point.

We interviewed the boy's grandparents and filed the piece. It was knocked off the news by a row about the Millennium Dome.

*

Gathering news was sometimes so difficult you felt foolish even trying. An editor in London saw some richly worded agency copy about how war had suddenly broken out between Ethiopia and Eritrea at 4.24 one afternoon. The reason was a dispute over a piece of land called the Yirga Triangle.

The outbreak of war tends not to be as precise as that in real life. But the last thing you want to say when you get the call is, 'Oh, don't worry, those two are always declaring war on each other.' A famous cautionary tale in the world of African news was how one British journalist, instructed to go to Rwanda because hundreds of people seemed to be dying, replied: 'Nah, it's not worth it. They hack each other to pieces all the time down there.'

So we set off at high speed to report on the outbreak of the Ethiopian–Eritrean war. With me were the freelance producer Tony Wende and cameraman Byron Blunt. We flew to Nairobi, had a night in a small hotel and started looking for a charter flight further north.

The first airman we found was happy to fly towards Eritrea, but not over it and not into it. He said he was not insured to fly in a war. Fair enough. He took us as far as neighbouring Djibouti, and we spent another night in a smaller hotel.

Day three. In Djibouti the only pilot who would take us to Asmara was originally from the south coast of England. He sported dirty grey stubble, a Bobby Charlton comb-over and a line in casual racism so infuriating we wondered how he had not been murdered by any of the airport staff he enjoyed insulting. He said he would take us, but needed a written assurance from the Eritrean Air Force that they would not bring down his twin-prop plane, 'because it would be just like those twats to do it for fun.'

'Jerk,' whispered Tony.

So we waited for the faxed guarantee from the Eritrean Air Force to arrive at the residence of the Eritrean ambassador to Djibouti. When it finally came, Tony emerged waving it like Neville Chamberlain. The pilot squinted up at the sky. It was too late to fly now, he said, because the light was about to fade and some of his cockpit instruments had broken.

'What do you mean, broken?'

'I'm saying we can't go there because I might not land in the right place.'

'What, after all this?' We gestured at the fax.

'I'm telling you I've got navigational problems and I've got the light about to fade and unless one of you wants to sit beside me with a map on his lap—'

We took off in late afternoon from the pot-holed Djibouti strip, with Tony in the co-pilot's seat and a map of north Africa spread across his knees. He took a few minutes to find the right fold, then started pointing out bits of greenery and town, and what with that and following the sun, and some banking and circling as it started to set, we landed in Asmara without a hitch, without being shot down and without needing any of the lifeless panel instruments.

This was not the end of the journey that had begun with those two lines of wire copy in London. I had always wanted to jump into a taxi and say, 'Take me to the front line' (partly because my colleague Nicola Carslaw told me she yelled 'TAKE ME TO THE REVOLUTION' at an airport cabbie in 1980s Bulgaria, and the fellow actually drove her without any further instruction). But the first taxi driver we tried that command on refused point blank. He told us the war was at least five hours away across a mountain range. Anyway, it would be impossible to film at night.

So to Day Four. There was only one road to the Yirga Triangle. The drive was lurching and sweaty. Byron, a happy-go-lucky hippy who had occasionally expressed disappointment that he had never been shot at while filming, pleaded: 'We must chill out on the front line. We must love the front line.' The car was piled high with camera gear. Tony, at the wheel, was deep in thought. The wire copy had come in on Monday. This was Thursday. It was all taking a lot of time. But at least we were close now.

A mountain later, we saw a sign to Zalambessa, the village where the most recent Ethiopian attack had been driven back. 'Where is the fighting?' Tony shouted from his wound-down window. A group of Eritreans at a corrugated iron Coke kiosk pointed down the route: 'Five miles.' We hurtled on.

Ten minutes later we had to slow up. There was something in our way.

A piece of string had been stretched across the road. Hanging in the centre of it was a large piece of white card saying

WAR: NO PRESS.

Byron said what about driving straight through, it was only a piece of string, but Tony pointed out the Eritreans moving to the roadside ahead of us, waving at us to slow down, two with rifles.

'No further,' they said. 'Turn back.'

'We're here to cover the war.'

'No press. Turn back.'

'But—'

'Go away.'

And that, essentially, was that. For all our ingenuity and technology, we had been stopped by a piece of string. We tried everything to get round it – including an attempt to bribe a local official which almost got us arrested – but time was pressing and we had to get something on tape. So in the end, after a journey that took us three days and most of the length of a continent, we filmed our war from a distance: a lingering shot of a horizon. We spoke to disconsolate soldiers and got pictures in an empty village where skirmishes had happened some days before.

Still we had to file our story of the war we never saw, which meant getting back to Asmara and sending it. The edit equipment was too bulky (and fragile: the worst combination) to be driven over a mountain, and since the only place the story could be filed from was in the capital, another day was lost. Finally the report aired on

Saturday night. The sixth day. We rang the editor, expecting dismay. Instead he told us, 'Thanks. It looked fine.'

It looked fine! Six days slower than wire copy, and nowhere near the action – but it looked fine. We talked about it on the hotel terrace, trying to see a funny side, eventually laughing.

'So what would you call a book about television?' I asked Tony.

'*You Should Have Been Here Yesterday,*' he replied. 'Every story you go on, you get there a day late. It's what I keep being told when I arrive – every single time.'

I told him that if I ever wrote a book on television I would call it *Twenty-Four and We Bowl*, because ... well, let's come to that in a moment.

Television is uniquely vulnerable to inconvenience. Africa is full of it. A lost cable will only stop a newspaper journalist shaving, but it will take a film crew off air for a week. Next time that American cable channel boasts, 'When a story breaks – we're right on it,' feel free to roar with laughter. In fact, when the story happens, their cameraman has just started looking for the key to the clasp that locks the cage that contains the camera that needs the spare battery which is under the tripod whose lid got torn so the airline won't accept it in the hold. He will bring extra tapes, film labels, battery chargers, rolls of masking tape, lapel microphones, another camera lens, the tripod case, assorted cables, a radio receiver for a wireless microphone, and spotlights. One cameraman I know was caught out trying to put up a set of lights during a riot.

Sure, what appears on screen is snappy and sexy. But the first camera operator you see spending half an hour unloading crates of gear from the back of their van will tell a different story, one that would alarm any right-thinking osteopath. Haste may look like speed, but it is not. News moves like lightning; logistics are dead weight. The piece of string that brought us to a juddering halt in Eritrea was proof.

Technical advances have been closing the gap between reporter and viewer, but not the gap between reporter and story. Since I made that trip to Eritrea, laptop equipment has become available that would speed up the editing, and a videophone will allow scratchy images to be sent to the UK without the crew having to go back to Asmara, but nothing has happened to get us to the frontline faster – and no amount of digital technology will get you past a piece of string.

*

We were a happy crew in the Johannesburg bureau. George Alagiah, a reporter of quite astonishing style and class, who was so good I found him intimidating, went back to London to read the news and was replaced by Jane Standley. She was a chain-smoking Africa buff with a more complex personality. Martin Turner, who ran the bureau's budgets and assignments, tried to ensure Jane was happy but he did not always succeed. It did not help that we discovered the bosses had told us both we were the senior correspondent. Milton came into my office one day and said, 'You know, I think maybe the problem is the laughter. You and I are laughing too much.' It was true. In Milton, and the wonderful Kate Peyton, and Glenn and Tony Wende and Martin, and the locals Patience and Connie, I felt surrounded by friends.

And I don't think I had ever felt more professionally fulfilled. At Westminster I thought I had the best job in the world; in Johannesburg I knew I had. Time and time again, I would show up at the bureau on a Monday morning and be bundled straight into a foreign adventure. Stories were like movies but they were so real they would claw at your heart. In Sierra Leone I met youngsters whose hands had been sliced off by the rebels of the RUF. Surging into the capital, Freetown, they cut off the limbs of an estimated 1,500 people. I met Damba and Emma, aged eight and ten, who had each had a hand and forearm hacked off simply because their parents were suspected of voting in a democratic election. Nothing I saw before or since appalled me more.

In Nigeria we raced in a speedboat around the Niger Delta, finding villagers being polluted to death by big oil companies, nearly being kidnapped along the way. In Sudan we trekked to Mile Forty, an outpost for the rebels in the south, and slept on mats under the stars. Mosquitoes must have had the feast of their lives – drugged up with Lariam, I was the only one of the team not to get malaria. In Angola I followed the footballer David Ginola as he took on, with a swagger that was maddening, the anti-landmine campaign of the late Princess of Wales. In Zimbabwe I interviewed Robert Mugabe. In Mozambique the focus was sugar and nuts. In Kenya, elections. Algeria, Islamist terror. Congo, child witches. Uganda, a terrifying religious cult that committed 800 murders. Mali, poverty. Lesotho, war.

If I had ever had a glibness, I lost it in Africa. The reporter of whom Sargie said, 'His scripts are so good, sometimes you wonder if the story even matters' realized there was more to life than having the boss admire your suite of adjectives. And, to quote from our Rules again, news is not a game. In Africa almost every story put lives in the balance. My poetic hero, W. H. Auden, once wrote: 'A phrase goes packed with meaning like a van.' In Africa all stories were freighted like juggernauts. My assignment was to convey as much of the meaning as possible. But in a sense – and it might surprise you that I write this – my job was to become less professional. News was no longer simply material to be crisply cut and spliced for impact, it was human life and it was as raw as life and death can be. I saw my first dead bodies and unquantifiable suffering. I had to find a sensitivity I had never previously allowed or even known of, and above all I had to give time.

Often I encountered people who had never seen a microphone before. It struck me that was the heart of journalism: a scoop was an interview with a struggling mother in Biafra who had not previously spoken into a camera, not some smart-Alec exchange in Westminster with a minister who forgot his lines for a second. And furthermore: that fellow with the Cabinet title was worth not a single penny more than the struggling Biafran. There was even an argument that she should take his space in the bulletin – after all, he talked his rubbish on the air every day of the week, whereas she only had one chance of a sound bite in her entire life.

So you can see, I went native. These were lives we could not barge in and out of. I threw out my Westminster ties and got a watch with no second hand. I tried to go to stories with no preconceptions of what package I wanted at the end: I would simply listen. If we missed our deadline, so what. Africa resists the tyranny of the newsdesk anyway. It is near-impossible to get anywhere on time, and the only interviewee you have booked will have found something better to do with her afternoon. You are forced to wait, and wait ... and as you wait you can listen and learn.

It probably meant I was a crap foreign correspondent. I noticed I became less agile with the material. I struggled to sell stories because I couldn't do that classic reporter thing of lathering up a sexy top line. I couldn't bear to cut someone down to sixteen seconds, so I gave them a minute, so the piece was three, so it didn't run. Everywhere I went I thought I saw poetry: the sign on a burger van in Durban made Milton laugh. What, I asked him, did those Zulu words mean? 'If you are hungry, move closer to me', he translated. Beautiful. Wasn't that worth bulletin space? What about the women who carry water on their heads all day long? Or that lady we saw walking at the roadside in Mozambique with a baby on her back and a full-size bathtub balanced on her head? Can we stop and film that? It was all new to me, so it was all news.

Emphasizing how out of place we all were, we did something res-olutely Anglo-American every week – tenpin bowling. Bureau space was shared with the Australians Ben Wilson and his feisty fiancée Sarah Tilley. Ben worked for ABC and Sarah helped run the office. Each Saturday we would all go out. Producer Mark Orchard and I even had our fingers measured for our own bowling balls.

One Friday evening there was a massacre up north, in KwaZulu-Natal. A local warlord, Sifiso Nkabinde – whom I had interviewed only a month before, and remembered being struck by the garish yellow of his baseball cap – had been shot in the head in a bar. Some of his followers had carried out immediate revenge killings. In the new South Africa, this was an ugly echo of the old.

As the news came in, we convened an emergency meeting in the bureau. Should we go up to KwaZulu-Natal and do the story? London were sleepy, in late Friday mode, batting the decision back to us by asking how important this really was. Hadn't the same sort of thing happened a couple of weeks before, and didn't we decide not to cover it that time?

Stymied, we reckoned the next few hours would make the decision for us.

'Okay. Let's see what happens. If it escalates, if twenty-five or more people are killed overnight, we'll go to KwaZulu-Natal in the morning,' said Martin Turner, the bureau chief.

'But hang on,' someone else responded. 'That'll mean cancelling the bowling tomorrow.'

'Only if it's *twenty-five* or more,' Turner repeated.

At that point Sarah Tilley leapt to her feet, threw out her arms and shouted: 'GREAT! TWENTY-FOUR AND WE BOWL!'

We guffawed with laughter. We probably should have cried.

And I didn't use it as a book title after all.

*

In 1999, into the office on a hot Johannesburg morning, walked a young woman called Cecilia Veloz Roca.

She was half Chilean, half Swedish, aged twenty-five, nearly six foot in her heels. She had been given a placement funded by the EU. No one seemed to know she was coming and there seemed to be nothing we could offer in the way of meaningful work. English was not Veloz Roca's first language, and she was dyslexic, so she was not expecting to write or broadcast. But she was eager. We asked her to pull some tapes for a new obituary of Nelson Mandela, because the most recent one ended with him still in prison.

That went on for a few days. Then she was at a loose end again. So I said, 'How do you fancy filming with the local police?'

I had been wondering for a while how to get access to the force in Johannesburg. A local journalist had told me how a veteran of a Chicago SWAT team came to lecture the cops about how to open fire in public without collateral loss of life. The American had twenty-three years' experience and had been in one shootout. The first policeman he met in Johannesburg had been in uniform for two years, and had been in six.

But going out with the police would involve nights, building relationships, probably not leaving the city for a month. We didn't have the resources for a correspondent to disappear from the rota like that. But now we had our new intern.

She was willing. She fixed up to meet the police chief in Brixton, a dangerous suburb. Not surprisingly, given that Cecilia looked like a supermodel, the chief fell over himself to help. She would need a flak jacket and he said she should be willing to squeeze into whatever small space was available on the back seat of the squad cars. She must carry the smallest camera the market could provide.

It was all agreed.

She disappeared to start the project.

Gradually, tapes piled up in the office. Veloz Roca would leave them in the edit suite and then go home to sleep off the night's filming. We were all haring around with other stuff. No one viewed the tapes. She would come back and add another cassette and see the stack untouched. Soon there was a second pile, also untouched.

One day I saw her put the latest tape on top of it. I got out of my chair and made my way over to them.

*

The material turned out to be sensational. Cecilia had brilliantly shot a whole series of sequences where the police made arrests in as violent a manner as possible. Think Gene Hunt in *Life On Mars,* then double it. In one sequence they pursue a stolen car. They ram the occupants off the road and stub cigarettes out on their heads. The men are heard crying out in pain as they are punched from behind. Police dogs are set on them, even after they are handcuffed. Fists and boots go flying. The material is made all the more incendiary by the fact that all the police in the film are white, and all the suspects are black.

I wondered how they had allowed Cecilia to go in for these close-ups and shoot the violence so unsparingly. Were the officers – terrible thought – showing off to this beautiful woman who had attached herself to them?

Different images were playing out on the bureau's main television set at the time. NATO had started bombing Kosovo. I was being asked to go to Albania. The war on President Milosevic meant there was little room for Africa on the bulletins, and I might not even be around. But I knew I just had to cut a piece from Cecilia's rushes; they were ground-breaking. So I spoke to Sian Kevill, editor of *Newsnight*, and agreed it with her. The film would be fifteen minutes long and it would be ready in a week.

We worked our way through the piles of tapes and cut the best parts together. It was hard leaving out some of the material, because so much was powerful. The film ran on *Newsnight* and all the daily news programmes. On Radio 4, *Today* took an audio version. It was the best scoop the bureau had got for an age, and it was all down to Cecilia. For reasons of safety she did not want to be seen in the piece. The heat was on the police who had been filmed, who might now lose their jobs, and they were not the kind of people you wanted to leave feeling betrayed. Obviously they knew who Veloz Roca was, although hopefully not where she lived. It took us a few extra days to grasp what she had realized immediately: there was going to be serious blowback inside South Africa.

The existence of the film triggered requests from the local newspapers for stills and details. I could see no harm in providing them, but one morning I drove the highway into the city centre and saw a line of billboards tied to the lampposts saying

BBC SENSATION: COPS BEAT SUSPECTS

and I realized we had unleashed forces beyond our control.

The race dimension made it super-combustible. White cops roughing up black citizens? President Mandela was supposed to have put a stop to all of that at least five years ago. It did not help that a lot of whites seemed to think it was exactly the kind of thing they were paying taxes for. A police source was quoted saying he was 'delighted' because the film showed 'we fight fire with fire.'

Now the Beeb was getting it in the neck for being arrogant outsiders undermining the police through sheer ignorance. Peter Mokaba, the tourism minister, claimed our film was a plot by England to stop South Africa getting the World Cup. When I braved a Johannesburg studio to appear on 702 Talk Radio, the presenter described me as 'the man who made the film which is massive across the whole country right now', and I was roasted by so many white callers I kept the tape as a souvenir:

Angry Man: The necessary force has to be applied, and the necessary lessons have to be taught to the criminals, before they will learn that it is not worthwhile going along and hijacking people, and robbing firms, and putting people at gunpoint and doing bank robberies.

Upset Woman: I feel so desperately sorry for our police. There may be corrupt policemen, but by Jove they have an incredibly difficult job.

Furious Man: Quite frankly I think it's justifiable police actions.

Vine: But how can you justify what happened in those pictures?

Furious Man: You can justify it by saying criminals have declared war on society therefore they should not have the protection of society.

A different note was struck by the only black caller.

Worried Man: When the police go out of their way to punish criminals, they are themselves committing crime, and by so doing, it means we need another police force to police on the police.

It all just highlighted what a fascinating, complex society South Africa is. But then came another development: one of the arrested men died. This turned the heat back up for the police. Nelson Mandela got personally involved.

I might not ever have another career moment where I see one of the great icons of the century holding a press conference about a film I have made, so this one occasion was memorable for me: Mandela gathering the local media to speak about our pictures, saying they showed his national police service needed 'faster reform' and there might be 'mental health issues' with some officers.

Then eleven police were personally identified from our footage and suspended. The bureau had a bomb threat. The BBC sent security advisors over who told us there was a 'real risk' to our safety, and I spent a couple of nights in a hotel. But maybe, I consoled myself, we could congratulate ourselves on that rarest journalistic achievement: we had *found something out.* The much-maligned John Birt once said that journalism should 'sizzle and crackle with discovery', and he was so right.

The film won awards. The issue was on and off South African television and radio for weeks. It was probably not quite what the EU bursary scheme intended, but Cecilia Veloz Roca had made her debut in British journalism and brought the house down.

*

Nearly a month after Cecilia's film went out, I had a phone call in the office.

'Is that Mr Vine?' said the hesitant male voice at the other end.

'Speaking.'

'My name is Jean and I would like to tell you my story. But I need to tell you it face-to-face. I promise you will want to hear it.'

Remembering Geoff Grimmer – 'Go down and speak to her' – I picked up my car keys and told Kate Peyton I might not be back for a couple of hours.

Jean Smit was a white man in his mid-twenties. His first name was pronounced *Zhon*, combining the 'J' from the French Jean and the 'on' from the English John. He sat at the coffee-cup-stained dining table in a modest house with a bay window at the front looking down onto a quiet avenue.

'A few weeks ago I was at a party,' he said. 'I was in the centre of Johannesburg and I stopped my car at some lights. There was a knock on the window. It was a guy with a gun. Two of them, both black. They told me to get out.'

With the gun pointing at his face through the car window, he had no choice. He stepped out of the car. Before they climbed in, the man with the gun pointed it at Jean Smit's temple and calmly pulled the trigger.

The gun clicked, but did not fire.

By this stage the other hijacker had climbed into Smit's car. The man with the gun 'shakes the weapon as if it is a can of Coke or something.' He is trying to unjam it and smacks the butt on his palm. Then he holds it to the head of Jean Smit again. He tries to shoot him a second time—

Click.

Now the second man is in the passenger seat. He is shouting for the gunman to hurry. The first man backs off Smit. He climbs into the car. They slam the doors and scream away into the Johannesburg night. Jean Smit is left on the pavement, a nervous wreck.

I look at him closely during this account. I think I might know where the story is going. I can see the anxiety in his face. He talks calmly. But it sounds like it is an effort for him to put the sentences together.

'The cops see the car speeding through the centre,' says Jean. 'And they give chase. And they run the car off the road. *And you are filming what happens next.*'

So the police car which chased Smit's attackers has Cecilia Veloz Roca on the back seat. When they crash, she gets out of the squad car to film the suspects being beaten.

Pointedly Jean Smit says, 'I believe they deserved their treatment for what they did to me.'

He has finished. To understand the story fully, I ask if we can drive to the place where he was carjacked. 'I have no car,' he reminds me, so we use mine. We arrive fifteen minutes later at a nondescript set of lights on a wide road in the centre of Johannesburg.

'So he was standing exactly where I am?' I ask, recording us both.

'Yes, he was standing exactly where you are. But there's only one difference. He had a gun pointed to my head.' Smit demonstrates how he moved. 'I jumped out of the car like this, and the guy still had the gun pointed to my head. He squeezed the trigger once, the gun didn't go off. He shook it, looked at it with a sort of amazed expression for a split second, then squeezed the trigger again. The gun did not go off.'

We are standing there, on the pavement. I turn off my tape machine. He looks me in the eyes.

'So, Mr Vine, I only wanted to ask – face to face – where is your story now?'

He said it politely, without a hint of anger. I said I would at least report his side of things to put the whole episode into context, and the comments above went out on the air. Needless to say, they did not run prominently. Maybe it was too complex a footnote. But I would not ever forget that morning with Jean Smit, and what it told me about the job I do.

Chapter Thirteen

'My Father and My Son'

In South Africa I owned a dog. I bought him for 150 Rand (£15) from a Johannesburg kennels after the break-in at our home. I called him Zola, after Chelsea's best player. I plumped for him as soon as I saw him eagerly romping around in the cage at the pound, rangy, doe-eyed – he was a cross between a Labrador, Dobermann and Pointer, with a glossy black coat that shone in the sun. No scientist with a test tube could have concocted a more handsome balance of breeds. The problem, I would discover, was that Zola was a racist.

Something must have happened to the dog before his previous owners disposed of him aged only sixteen months. He would become furious when he saw any person of colour, no matter whether they were strangers, friends of mine, colleagues, bankers or burglars. South Africa is fifteen per cent white; Zola had it in for the other eighty-five per cent. I bought him thinking we needed a guard dog. But my main preoccupation soon turned to guarding other people from him. One day the armed response company attended a false alarm at our house and Zola pinned the security officers into their small car, slaveringly unimpressed by their uniforms or the guns all four had drawn as they cowered inside.

It sounds like the start of a funny/unfunny story, but it's not. Zola was a fine dog with a bad attitude. When I went running with him in the park each morning, I learnt not to let him off the lead or he would attack the park-keepers. I did everything I could to impress on him that South Africa had changed and he needed to be a part of that change – you can imagine how hysterically this cosmopolitan Brit pleaded – but Zola's view of the world was a reminder of just how entrenched apartheid had been. Even the dogs in the street signed up to it.

However, Zola had one black friend, and they were as close as close can be.

Paulina Mabogale had been employed by a succession of corre-spondents. She was a maid to some, nanny to others, cook to most. She worked harder than anyone I had ever met. Through guilt that I felt every time I glimpsed the perfect crease down the leg of my jeans, I kept begging Paulina to put her feet up. She never did. At some point in the distant past the BBC had paid her wages. The arrangement had been deemed too dangerous, for the obvious PR reasons – 'NOW BEEB REPORTERS HAVE MAIDS' – so these days correspondents employed Paulina privately and paid from their own pockets. Back from a trip to Timbuktu or Kinshasa, Harare or Mogadishu, pulling kit from a battered suitcase, they would find a neatly pressed change of clothes lying on their bed and vegetable soup on the stove.

Just like the view a lot of Brits have of the rest of Europe, Paulina regarded Africa as abroad. 'You are travelling to Africa tomorrow?' she would ask me before I went off somewhere on a story. 'Oh, it is such a long way to go.' More than a housekeeper, Paulina was a friend.

I got terribly close to her. She was in her late forties, not well edu-cated but with a heart of gold. Because my own personal life was in a state of self-invoked disarray, I found myself confiding in her. She had lost the love of her life, Shepherd, in township violence years back. He had been shot in the chest in 1993 by a neighbour with a grudge; at the time Paulina worked for Fergal Keane. Now she was married to Henry. Both of them had had the tough lives ordinary black South Africans grew used to under apartheid and which had not meteorically improved with Mandela. Both of them lived on the property. Henry, who seemed to be drunk a lot, had a truce of sorts with Zola.

Paulina had one huge love above all others – her son, Matthias. But he was elsewhere, and it was Zola who was her daily companion. The two of them would sit out in the sun in the afternoons, at peace with the world. When she cleaned the house he would walk an inch from her, staring at every surface she cleaned. For Zola, Paulina was Queen. His life's duty was to protect her. When a passer-by shouted a flirtatious greeting through the gates, the dog was so keen to eat him he began dribbling.

The arrangement we came to was this. Zola was Paulina's. She would keep him when I left and I would persuade the correspondent who followed me to employ them both.

But there would be a very unfortunate postscript to the story of Zola, which would contain difficult truths for everyone involved.

*

If Africa taught me how real lives do not always fit into the apportioned 1-minute-26-secs of the news package, it also showed me the value of friendship. I had not really made friends at work before, but Milton became one. As did the charming Kate Peyton, who loved her work with heart and soul but always had time to put her feet up and shoot the breeze. She made me a tape of obscure Bob Dylan songs, and I reciprocated with a set of Elvis Costello's less well known.* As one who was committed to Johannesburg, to South

---

* Motel Matches; Shoes Without Heels; Beyond Belief; Tiny Steps; I'm Your Toy; King Horse; White Knuckles; New Amsterdam; Chemistry Class; Waiting For The End Of The World; Alison; Riot Act; Lipstick Vogue; Night Rally; Green Shirt.

Africa, and indeed to all things African, Kate formed a strong bond with Paulina. She and I would often meet, entirely platonically, and worry about the long-serving housekeeper over a drink. Peyton was short, blonde, with sparkling eyes. She belonged to a choir and spent a lot of time doing voluntary work. She had a wonderful sense of humour and a kindness that is rarely in evidence among journalists.

I hope you will forgive me for dwelling on her qualities and the times we shared. It is because on 9 February 2005, Kate had just arrived in Somalia and was in the forecourt of her hotel, getting ready to climb into a taxi. A man fired a single shot in her direction. Kate was hit in the back and slumped across the cab.

In the panicky hours after the shooting, word got to her friends around the world that Kate was sitting up in a hospital bed in Mogadishu and talking, which we all thought meant the wound was not lethal. In fact she never recovered consciousness after the bullet struck her.

Kate and I were both born in 1965. She would have turned forty later that year. The gunman was not caught; there was talk of Al Qaeda. Her death was one of those totally random acts that defy any explanation, and it left a huge hole in many lives.

*

However normal we all tried to make our time in South Africa – with tenpin bowling, walking the dog in the park, movies, squash matches, all the usual journalistic revelry and London-inspired gossip – there were constant reminders that 'normal' was a variable concept in this continent, and sometimes a brutal one.

One day Milton took a call from his wife. Dorcas was at the leaving do for Martin Turner, the bureau chief. Milly and I were elsewhere and could not attend. All he said was 'No, no, no, no,' down the phone.

When I asked him what was wrong, he said a band of local musicians had come to play at Martin's party and suddenly someone noticed that a young boy, the brother of the drummer, was lying dead at the bottom of the swimming pool. No one had seen him knock himself out in the water. By the time they found him, it was too late.

Another day we stood in the bureau watching live pictures of President Clinton arriving in Ghana. There was a crowd surge that could easily have killed the youngsters whose hands he was shaking. One minute waving and laughing, the next Clinton was red-faced, yelling: 'BACK OFF! BACK OFF!'

Watching the TV beside me was the super-experienced South African cameraman Glenn Middleton. His time in Rwanda had darkened his sense of humour, and years previously he had been in the car crash that killed the famous reporter John Harrison.

Watching the footage grimly, Glenn said: 'Hey. If you can't take a joke, don't live in Africa.'

Then there was the time I was working with the producer Sean Salsarola and he tripped, dropping our car keys down a drain. We stood cursing helplessly at the side of the road in Vryburg, a small town, and pretty soon a crowd of mainly white shoppers gathered.

An enormous Afrikaner in regulation khaki shorts and shirt strolled over and took charge. Wheezing as his belt cut into his belly, he and another man pulled the grille off the drain and then he said, in a thick accent – 'Get me a little floppy.'

In a minute an enthusiastic young black boy was being dangled by his ankles head-first into the sewer. The fat man held the boy as you might wield a piece of faulty gardening equipment, yanking the ankles to steer his body.

The lad was thin enough to pluck the keys from the dirty water at the bottom of the drain and was pulled out, smiling, to cheers.

Sean accepted the car keys with relief. But what, we wondered, was a 'little floppy'? Beside us was a tight-faced white lady wearing too much lipstick and a wide-brimmed straw hat with plastic flowers on the brim. When we asked, she explained queasily: it was slang for black person, because 'they go floppy when you shoot them.' Registering our shock, she added: 'I never did that.'

We watched the fat-bottomed farmer climb back into his jeep and slam the door. And this was the era of Mandela.

One afternoon I sat in the bureau watching rain come down in lumps. Water ran away down the roof of the warehouse next to the bureau. Rain was unusual in Johannesburg. Most days the sky was gemstone blue. What happened next was unusual too.

Sian Kevill, the clever and hard-working *Newsnight* editor, rang and asked me to join the show as a presenter. Peter Snow had left some time before, under the regime of Peter Horrocks. The regular presenters were now Jeremy Paxman and Kirsty Wark, but vacant slots on the rota were taken by so many people the programme was starting to look like an airport. 'We need a full-time number three,' she told me, 'to join later this year, replace Peter properly and do all the extra shifts.'

This was, quite literally, the pinnacle of all my ambitions and climax of every student daydream combined, and I should have been thrilled to bits.

For some reason I was not.

I can't really explain why: a premonition? Watching the rain I said, somewhat stupidly, that I would give the offer some thought as it was a Very Big Step. It would mean returning early from Africa – after three years, which I did not want – but *Newsnight* is *Newsnight*. If you are in broadcast news in the UK and someone asks you to present the show that is the undisputed best, there is only one answer.

In retrospect I should have found the other answer, because working on *Newsnight* would trigger a whole series of totally unforeseeable and almost professionally fatal ramifications which I shall describe shortly.

I was still digesting the exciting news, and it was still raining, when the phone went again. This time the voice on the other end was stressed, and closer.

'Jeremy, this is Paulina.'

I asked her what was wrong.

'Matthias is dead,' she said.

Matthias was her son; or, to be more accurate, the son of her sister who had died from cancer, leaving Paulina to bring up Matthias herself. She had spent every cent she had on getting him an education.

I had met him half a dozen times, and now I called the image to mind. Handsome, happy, tall as me, hair in plaits, full of youthful energy. 'This is my darling son,' Paulina had said, bringing him to the house. Her voice was full of pride. South Africa was still a long way from the perfect society, and as a young black man Matthias was bound to have his fair share of frustration. But there was opportunity for him too. I remember feeling buoyed up after our first encounter. I had met the future.

And now he was dead. She told me it was a car crash. I went straight back to the house to see her. The downpour had stopped and we took Zola for a walk together while she shed silent tears. The crash had happened the previous evening. Matthias had been driving from work. Two young male neighbours had hitched a ride with him, as they often did. Somehow his car span off the road in Limpopo, between Polokwane (which used to be called Pietersburg) and Turfloop. The car overturned. Matthias died in hospital. His two friends were killed instantly.

A fortnight later, the funeral was imminent. Paulina had been let down by some of her closest relatives who were expected to pitch in, and she came to me to ask a simple favour.

'Please could you type a tribute to Matthias on your computer?' She would dictate it with my help, she said. Then we needed to print about sixty copies.

'I need you to assist me in finding the words,' she told me.

I said I was happy to. I was the professional, after all.

At this point I was three-quarters of the way through my BBC posting to Johannesburg. By the end I would have visited eighteen African countries and passed through a dozen more. I had covered everything from war in Sudan to the divorce in Cape Town of Earl

Spencer (the only person in Africa whose braces pulled the top edge of his trousers above his stomach). The stories, all kept on discs in my drawer, mounted up and blurred into each other. I must admit to being very proud of that pile of discs, pleased with the vivid soundtracks on them. I still have them today. But I was about to learn the biggest lesson of my posting – Paulina's voice would cut through more clearly than anything I had recorded. The maid had better words than me.

The afternoon we sat at the computer together was scorching hot, the weather back to normal since the day she first rang. Johannesburg, I reckoned, had the perfect climate – no more than a month of real winter, sometimes only a fortnight. Most houses did not have central heating because it was not cold for long enough. Today, in the garden, workmen were digging up a flower border for the landlord. Zola was inside, barking at shadows.

I closed the door of the study, took the chair at the desk and pulled another one over for Paulina. She dictated while I typed.

Dear friends and family,
Thank-you so much for coming today. It is a very sad event for all of us. I am so grateful that you have come to share in this ceremony. Matthias was born in 1972 – he was only twenty-seven when he died.

I will miss him so much, and I have been missing him so much already.

I was very proud of him because, despite all the difficulties of getting started in the world that young people face, he managed to build a wonderful life for himself. I was very proud that he found a job at Thobela FM.

I would like to say thank-you to the BBC people who helped him and encouraged him. He became a journalist because of Milton Nkosi. He was always telling me that he wished to be like Milton.

We can be thankful for Matthias's life because he did so much with it. He was always full of energy and full of ideas. He has two children, a girl and a boy. We must all think of them, and of Machigo, his girlfriend, because this will be a very hard day for her.

To her I would like to say I will help her through her life for as long as I am alive. I will always be here for the children. I would like to thank all the people of Thobela FM because they have said such nice things about Matthias on the air since his death. I have heard them, and it makes me realise how special he was. Thank-you again for coming today to remember Matthias, who I always called my son.

I will miss him because he was always calling me 'mum', and no one is going to call me that any more.

I will always love you, my son. Rest in peace.

During all of this, I never spoke. She turned out not to need any of my words after all. After it was over, with work she felt impelled to do, Paulina silently left the room. I enlarged the font, checked the text, pasted a coloured border onto the outside of the page and printed it out.

That was the sum of my contribution: the font, the typing, the border, the printing.

And that night I sat up in the dining room rereading Paulina's words as tears rolled down my face. The single page I had in my hand was the most powerful piece of writing that had been typed on my computer since I had bought it – and they were not my words. Paulina had spoken in a voice more clear and forceful than mine or that of any of the presidents and prime ministers I had interviewed. What made the tribute so devastating was its truth and simplicity. 'No one is going to call me that any more.'

Paulina could not read and could barely write her own name. And yet she spoke with an authentic voice, and freely. By contrast mine was constricted: I lived in a world where you had to put on a tie to address an audience. When it came to language and feeling, I was the one with all the shortcomings.

The funeral for Matthias went by. It was surely the lowest moment in Paulina's life. But before long, things seemed to have got back to a normal rhythm, or what passed for one. Occasionally I was reminded of the gentle clashing of civilizations. In a misguided attempt to cheer Paulina up, I said I would get her tickets for the blockbuster *Titanic* because I thought she might enjoy the spectacle of it. But when she and Henry returned from the cinema and I asked her how they had liked it, she looked underwhelmed.

'Did you not enjoy it?' I asked.

'No, it was good. Well, it was very ... violent,' she said, embarrassed at having to explain.

'Violent? *Titanic*?' I asked, puzzled. And then an idea occurred to me. 'Paulina, was there a ship in this film?'

She thought about it for a while. Then she said, 'No, I don't think so.'

After questioning her further, I got the full story. She had been late at the cinema, and because her reading skills were hit-and-miss, Paulina had been to a film with roughly the same number of letters in the title, called *Hoodlum*. The movie was about two gangs in 1930s Harlem fighting to control a gambling racket. There was no ship.

Eventually she did get to see *Titanic*, and then all the adventures were over – I had been in Johannesburg for three years and was due to pack up and go to work on *Newsnight*.

*

My time in Africa had started, oddly, with that visit to a court in Cape Town to report on the chaotic divorce of the brother of the late Princess Diana. It was what press hacks call a gangbang, and the courthouse swarmed with reporters flown in from British tabloids who wanted to work Charles Spencer over. The very last story I did in Africa was equally untypical. I had to broadcast from the top of Table Mountain as the new millennium broke.

There was to be a mammoth programme anchored by Michael

Buerk in London, the biggest ever exercise in global satellite hook-ups. Reporters were positioned all over the world.

Cape Town seemed ideal to me. The top of Table Mountain would afford a stupendous view, with fireworks launching from the city below. I would be announcing the dawn of the millennium for the whole of Africa as the sky exploded with pyrotechnics behind me.

Milton, Glenn and I took the cable car to the top with a technician and a pile of gear so large it backed us into a corner of the cabin. I had a sense of mounting excitement, as well as a sense of mounting equipment. Announcing the dawning of the African millennium could well be a career highlight and a fitting way to end my time away from London.

There were only eight things we had not considered:

1) Table Mountain is half a mile high. Fireworks do not go up that far.
2) Midnight is some hours after sundown. All that would be visible behind me was the Atlantic Ocean covered in darkness: i.e. nothing.
3) The forecast was fog. The cloud is so much a fixture of the mountain it is known as the Tablecloth. So I would be standing in fog, in darkness.
4) When you shine a spotlight onto a person who is standing in fog in darkness he looks as if he is trapped inside the steam room at a budget hotel.
5) You cannot see a mountain if you are standing on it.
6) We had arrived in sunshine, wearing summer shirts and light jackets. We had not considered that the temperature on the mountaintop would plummet to near freezing as the night drew in ...
7) ... and that, struck down by man flu, the combination of cold and damp meant I would lose my voice as midnight approached.
8) Or that *Cape Town is in the same time zone as Bethlehem.*

The last – number eight – was a more serious problem than the first seven combined.

Setting up the equipment on top of the mountain, and roping it off from drunken Brits, took all of three hours. By 8 p.m. we were ready to go live, but we were not even acknowledged by the London gallery until 11.30. Now it was bitterly cold and my voice was a squeak. The Bethlehem factor was disastrous. Just as we were expecting to broadcast our fog party, Jeremy Bowen would pop up from the birthplace of Christ and kill us.

At ten to midnight, I was starting to stamp my feet, partly from cold and partly from frustration. 'This is terrible,' I told Milton and Glenn. 'We're not even going to get on the air after all this.'

At that moment, in my earpiece, I heard the director in London.

'Vine!' he said urgently. 'The line to Bethlehem's disappeared. If you hear me shout "NOW", start talking about Nelson Mandela.'

Sometimes stuff they say to you from TV news galleries is so good you want to stop the world and get everyone to write it down. When I was a pol-corr I went to Luton to see John Major visit a car factory. It was a non-event in news terms, but we rang the *One O'Clock News* desk at 12.15 and they said, 'You have to cut us two minutes as fast as possible. You're the lead item at one.'

'The lead?!' I exclaimed.

'We've got no stories,' the producer told me.

We've got no stories ... Twenty-four and we bowl ... If you hear the word 'NOW', start talking about Nelson Mandela ...

It is good for the soul to regularly inspect a personal collection of memorable lines.

I relayed the director's instruction to Milton and Glenn. 'If we hear someone shout "NOW", I have to start talking about Nelson Mandela.'

Milton said that was the standing instruction for all Johannesburg correspondents anyway.

More was to follow on Table Mountain. As I stood on a grassy outcrop jutting over the sheer drop to the city, we heard the Bethlehem broadcast begin and started to grasp that Africa had been knocked off the running order by the Middle East.

But then, in my ear, I heard pandemonium in London and the director shouting:

'WE'VE LOST BETHLEHEM!'

A fraction of a second later, a different voice in the gallery called out: 'NOW!'

I had forgotten the code word, so I stood stock still, blinking.

'NOW, VINE, NOW!'

Oh, right. That was the cue? I started to talk but my voice was gone and all that came out was the high-pitched squeak of a choirboy. 'Nelson Mandela is eighty-one. He was born in Umtata. He spent much of his life in jail, and for twenty-seven years—'

A voice in my ear, calmer this time, interrupted. 'Well done, Jeremy. We got Bethlehem back.'

Were we still on air? Apparently not. I was told afterwards that television viewers in the UK just saw a shot of me standing in what looked like a steam room, then a tape ran of Mr Mandela lighting a candle on Robben Island as I said in a faint fluting voice: 'Nelson Mandela is eighty-one—' at which point the picture crashed to Jeremy Bowen at a festival in Bethlehem and we were never heard from again.

Still, it was all worth it if only for those three words, just as the new millennium broke, which have also been added to my collection of entirely accidental wisdom: *We've lost Bethlehem.* Sometimes, sitting in a church pew and trying to feel spiritual, I wonder if that director in London had accidentally spoken for the entire world. Or my world, at least.

*

During my time in the Africa bureau I had worked with some of the best news staff. They were kind when I was all packed, and laid on a small party with generous speeches. A researcher, Jackie Martens, showed surprising dexterity with a cocktail shaker. Needless to say, all the words from all the speeches are lost in the mists of time. Only one line remains.

As I was leaving for the airport that final night, being driven in Milton's sports car, I wanted to say one last goodbye to Paulina. We had been through so much. 'Hey, Milly, stop for a second,' I said, and ran back to the house through the beam of the head-lights.

Paulina was in the kitchen, cleaning. Now I saw she was crying.

I gave her a hug and told her, again, how much I had enjoyed meeting her and spending time with her.

I felt myself towering over her, almost as if she had been physically shrunk by her sadnesses. Despite her natural diffidence, she smiled warmly.

'It's been a very good thing for me, living here,' I blundered. 'One of the best bits has been meeting you. I'm really sorry I'm going back to Britain.'

She replied: 'You have become my father and my son.'

And that, I reflected as I walked back to the car, takes some beat-ing. You could have a life in journalism and never write a sentence as monumental as that one. Imposing the inverted values of the news world, you would say that the most important words had come from the least important person. The fundamental truth of my three years in Africa had come from the maid.

The rest ... Sudan, Zimbabwe, Botswana, Cape Town, Durban, Nigeria, Namibia, Zambia, Eritrea, Algeria, Sierra Leone, Kenya, Congo ... well, I will have to dig out that pile of discs to remember exactly what happened there.

Paulina has given us the perfect example of the power of the smallest voice. Which I guess, if I had to sum it up, is what the whole of this book is about.

*

Zola: the postscript

A year later, I was told what happened to Zola. While Paulina waited for the next BBC correspondent to arrive, she went briefly to work for a freelance cameraman to earn some extra pennies. Somehow Paulina then moved back to work for my successor (Allan Little, who had returned to the bureau) without bringing Zola immediately. The cameraman casually lent the dog to friends of his, a software analyst and his British wife, but did not consult Paulina. The analyst's wife then decided Zola was hers to keep.

After a while, Paulina mentioned to Allan that it must be time to bring Zola back to be with them. Not knowing anything about the situation, he made enquiries and discovered that the computer man's wife had 'fallen in love' with the dog, was lonely in South Africa and 'could not bear' to part with him.

I went over the painful story with Allan as I wrote this chapter, and he told me: 'Paulina was with me in the car, sitting quietly in the passenger seat, when I said I thought Zola belonged to someone else now. I'll never forget what happened next. She let out a howl of grief and despair that I had never heard before. For the first time in all the years I'd known her, she stood up for herself. I sensed that it was a hard and counter-instinctive thing for her to do. All her life she had been rewarded for being meek, compliant, undemanding, unconcerned with her own welfare or comfort. But now she said, "No – Jeremy Vine gave Zola to me when Matthias died. And I want him back."'

The bureau staff discussed how to deal with the situation. Incredibly, the new 'owners' were not even up for negotiation. They were already in the process of getting the documentation to take the dog back to the UK. So far as they were concerned, Paulina never really had any rights to Zola.

The affair had a big effect on Allan, he says now. Bear in mind he had travelled the world for the BBC on some huge stories. Yet something in what was essentially a microscopic sequence of events – the misappropriation of a pet – spoke to him of a profound injustice.

'This was the moment of epiphany for me. I saw in this episode all the power relationships that defined the country I was living in. I was shocked and ashamed of my own failure to have noticed before,' he says.

Kate Peyton, who was so close to Paulina, was upset. Milton was furious and consulted pro bono lawyers. Getting involved in London, I rather idiotically suggested using our armed response firm to swoop on the dog and recapture it. Milly asked me to ring the software analyst's wife, since she was behind the whole thing.

So I did, from the *Newsnight* office in London, feeling uncertain of my ground.

When she picked up the phone I begged her to see how this looked – rich white westerners cheating a poor African lady out of her most treasured possession, her guardian – but I was accused of hypocrisy because I had left the dog in her care. When I said I was more interested in Paulina's rights than Zola's, I got a tirade of animal rights abuse. I could not persuade the analyst's wife, and the phone call went from bad to worse.

The final straw was when I asked her whether she accepted that Zola's kennel – which I had bought, and given to Paulina – was the maid's by right and should now be returned? 'Of course I accept that. I will give the kennel back to Paulina tomorrow,' the lady said firmly.

'If the kennel, why not the dog?' I asked. Typical *Newsnight* question: unanswerable. The phone clicked. The conversation was over. Zola came back to the UK and Paulina never saw him again.

Not only that, the analyst's wife fell pregnant soon after they arrived in Britain and gave the dog away to a relative in Wales. So the postscript to the story was the biggest slap in the face of all. Allan emailed Kate Peyton about it, sharing his disgust with Paulina's biggest supporter. But Kate set off on her fateful trip to Somalia the day he sent the email. It seems she never saw it.

If you ever wanted a snapshot of how the rights of some people are erased the second they collide with the rights of others, the story of Zola was it. And Allan was right. The ownership dispute was bigger than a dog. It was a matter of principle. And it was also a matter of heartbreak for Paulina Mabogale. That is what normally happens with the smallest voice: it gets ignored and spoken over. Journalism is the art of reversing that. But a whole bureau of reporters could not retrieve a large dog swiped from under their noses.

Could Paulina bear any more loss in a single life? Matthias, Shepherd, Zola, Kate . . . I would never forget how casually Fate visited miseries large and small upon her, and with what dignity she pressed on despite them.

Chapter Fourteen

THE BRIEF LIFE
OF MINI-ME

Where I work, Jeremy Paxman is a kind of god. If you saw him at a bus stop you would take in a diminutive, grey-haired man with a lean figure and possibly not look twice. If you see him in a television studio you know you are watching a giant, one of the four greatest presenters in UK news history, along with Richard Dimbleby, his son David and Robin Day.

The first thing he said to me when I walked into the tiny *Newsnight* presenter's office for the first time since they started printing NEWSNIGHT PRESENTER on my payslip was: 'What on earth are you doing here?' (The accent was on the words 'what', 'earth', 'you', 'doing' and 'here'.) As he asked the question, he gave me the full eyebrow. By then it was too late to avoid the cliff-edge.

*

But let me spool back a few months before I continue the story. In the BBC, if the wind is in the right direction – and if you are slightly

optimistic, a touch egotistical or just totally deluded – you can feel
a guiding hand. I thought I felt it when they gave me that job at
Westminster. I was certain I felt it when I moved to Africa. But sitting in Johannesburg at the tail end of my life-changing spell as a
foreign correspondent, contemplating the *Newsnight* presenter's
chair, I started to worry. No matter how hard I concentrated, I
couldn't feel The Hand.

I wondered if there was some way of finding out whether the
BBC, as opposed to just the editor of *Newsnight*, was moving me.
But who do you call when you want to ring the BBC? In these circumstances you should always contact a deputy head. So I spoke
to Richard Ayre, who served at the right hand of the chief of
news Tony Hall. He had always been friendly, canny, and sometimes hair-raisingly frank. So – should I do this *Newsnight* job,
Richard? Is this a move you want me to make? Ayre hedged, then
said yes. But the hedging sounded more important than the yes.
So I asked him if I could call Tony Hall and talk it over with him
direct.

I was still in the Africa bureau at 7 p.m., sitting in the glow of a
single striplight, when I got through to Hall. He was being chauf-
feured somewhere and the line was not good.

Bear in mind, I was one of 2,500 news staff and he was the boss of
bosses, the *capo di tutti capi*: so I was nervous when he picked up.

'I know about the offer, and yes I think you should do it,' he said.
'The only thing I would say is this: no guarantees.'

'No guarantees?'

'No guarantees that if Jeremy Paxman leaves the programme you
will get the top job.'

Blimey. I honestly had not had that thought process.

I turned the conversation over in my head. Nope. I definitely
couldn't feel The Hand.

And there was another unsettling, even weird, turn of events. The
Guardian picked up the news of my impending arrival on *Newsnight*
and ran a piece which cheered me greatly:

Vine's Newsnight Job Makes Him Paxman's Heir Apparent

Janine Gibson, Media Correspondent
12 July 1999

Jeremy Vine has beaten off competition from some of the BBC's most prominent journalists to co-present Newsnight, a move which insiders predict will see him crowned as Jeremy Paxman's eventual successor.

BBC2's flagship news programme, currently anchored by Paxman and Kirsty Wark, has been trying out a number of potential presenters since the departure of Peter Snow. Vine, at present the BBC's Africa correspondent, will be announced this week as co-presenter of the series after viewers became confused by too many stand-ins.

After audience research about the programme's content and presenters, Vine emerged from the team of stand-ins, including Gordon Brewer and Gavin Essler, to take the job. Mr Brewer, who has often been described as 'the next Paxman' because of the similarity in their presenting styles, will remain a reporter for the programme.

Since Snow's departure, both Paxman and Wark have increased their workload outside of Newsnight, with Paxman also presenting Radio 4's Start the Week and BBC2's University Challenge. A BBC spokesman said: 'Jeremy Vine will join the presenting team to cut out the confusing number of stand-in presenters.'

An insider said: 'Jeremy Paxman signed a new four-year contract last year, but I can envisage a day in the future when Vine is the main presenter of the programme.'

Vine's appointment is also an answer to Newsnight's problem of who to send to anchor the programme from the site of a breaking story. During the Kosovo war, for example, the show was unable to relocate to Kosovo because of the other commitments of Paxman and Wark.

Speaking from Johannesburg, Vine said he was 'delighted' to be joining the team. He will be sole presenter for the next two months while his colleagues are on holiday, and officially joins the rota in November.*

He has been standing in over the summer for Paxman for two years.

The 34-year-old former BBC news trainee, who joined the corporation in 1987, has worked for the Today programme, PM, the Moral Maze, and Radio 5 Live. He spent four years in Westminster as political correspondent, which, he said, proved he could deal with pressure over bias from the political parties.

Reading the piece by Janine was like dying and waking up in heaven. You probably got bored reading it once. I was still excited

* The millennium broadcast would change this slightly.

after the twentieth time. I could not remember ever boasting about my bias-resistance (it would have been a bit odd if I had said, 'I pride myself on completely collapsing under pressure'), but that hardly mattered. The key thing was, as a reporter you never get mentioned in the newspapers unless one of your pieces brings down the director-general, shuts a channel or costs the Beeb a million in damages. So this was a sudden, and thrilling, breaking of the water. Not a single syllable of Janine's article could I have minded. Gloriously, the *Guardian* had even misspelt Gavin Esler's surname.

But a week after it was printed I was rung by Sian Kevill again. She sounded embarrassed. 'Could you try . . . just to – um – when you arrive . . . just not, not have a very high profile?'

This sounded puzzling. 'What do you mean?'

'Well, just not be seen around the office too much. At the start.'

What the hell was going on? If that were not enough, I was called two days later in Johannesburg by Jon Barton. A supremely likeable and intelligent man, he was one of the new super-editors whose job was to handle problems on two or three different shows. *Newsnight* was one of his.

'It's all been a bit difficult, for various reasons,' he said, mystifying me even further. 'But we're going to need you to keep quite a low profile after you get back here.'

'Low profile?' I laughed. 'But *Newsnight* is a networked news programme. How do I keep a low profile if I'm presenting it?'

He bit the bullet. 'Could you try not to be seen in the office if Jeremy Paxman is around.'

Later, a friendly press officer in the TV department would explain it to me. The 'heir apparent' line had caused serious ructions between the programme, the presenter's agent and the press office. Understandably, Paxman's people thought the corporation was briefing against him – the Beeb was sore after ITV flirted with him in the mid-nineties – and they wanted the whole 'heir apparent' idea corrected. Apart from anything else it was a gross discourtesy to

Kirsty Wark, the other presenter. But the BBC could not correct a line that had never been part of any official statement, so the best course of action would just be to render me as invisible as possible.

Invisible? This was going from bad to worse, and it hadn't even started yet.

*

After that first encounter with the other Jeremy – him asking, 'What on earth are you doing here?' and me responding shiftily, 'Just trying to keep my nose clean' – I adopted the Kevill/Barton approach and tried to keep a low profile while presenting *Newsnight*.

But my presence on the show, I could see, might chafe. The manager responsible for my salary (none of the ones previously mentioned) had initially congratulated me on a 'massive move, to a massive show, which will be an absolutely huge break for you.' When, a fortnight later, I told him in an embarrassed tone that I felt my pay should go up to recognize the importance of the programme, he countered: 'Come off it, Jeremy. You are moving into a junior position on a show with a small audience that is aired very late at night.'

I have never been any good at negotiating, and in the end accepted a five-figure sum of which the rise between Johannesburg and *Newsnight* was paid as a non-pensionable bonus. I had no idea what Paxman earned, but one day I joked to a boss that managers should feel pleased every time they saw me, 'because each time I walk into the building I save you five grand.' It may not have been true, but I later heard the inflammatory remark had got back to the other Jeremy. Suddenly invisibility seemed like a sensible career move; I wasn't exactly helping matters.

My reaction to the distant buzz of disturbed hornets was to beaver away maniacally. These days, with Rachel in my life and two lovely kids to give me the sense of proportion I never had back then, I do a good deal less maniacal beavering.

The hard work thing – well, that was me for a long time. Silly, really. At Westminster Joy Johnson once gave me a rocket for coming in at 8 a.m. when I was not expected till noon. 'Do you not read the bloody rota?' she asked, and I replied no, why would I – 'I just come in early and leave late every day.' Hmm. I suspect my family would not tolerate that Jeremy now.

Still, if you are reading this as a budding journalist I will repeat some powerful advice. At a social occasion when I was twenty-three, the tennis commentator Gerald Williams told me: 'You need to work very hard for the next twenty years.' I replied: 'Don't worry, I will,' at which point my girlfriend, sitting next to me, burst into tears and quite rightly dumped me soon after. But that's definitely a Rule – *Work hard.*

However, at a certain point, hard work may not make the difference.

Sometimes you are just in the right place at the right time. It was a bit like that with my Gordon Brown moment on Radio 2. My friend Rageh Omaar became the Scud Stud quite by accident. But Fate is a dual carriageway: on another occasion a collision of wrong time and place will wipe you out.

*

So as 2000 unfolded, I was industriously turning up at *Newsnight* at 9.30 a.m. to be at the morning meeting, leaving the office after the show fourteen hours later, ambling home across the roundabout-for-drunks-disguised-as-a-park that is Shepherds Bush, gladly seizing the opportunity to learn how a person should conduct themselves on the biggest stage.

The first principle of television interviewing is: *Don't look down.* By which I mean, firstly, don't look down at your notes. Hold the gaze of the person opposite you and emit total certainty (presenters and goalkeepers have much in common). If you show doubt, the entire illusion collapses. On the motorways they have signs saying 'TIREDNESS KILLS'. In a TV studio it is any form of uncertainty, including even one bead of perspiration.

But more important than that, don't look down from the great height at which you are perched; don't think about how far you could fall, how you will be remembered in 150 years if you suddenly vomit, or blurt an obscenity.

It sounds ridiculous, but I was talking about this absolutely primal presenter-fear to my workmate Emily Maitlis just before the 2010 general election. We had a shared moment of escalating anticipation as we waited for first sight of the exit polls. I was doing the 3D graphics extravaganza and Maitlis had a high-tech touchscreen.

'It's electrifying, isn't it?' I said as we looked around the huge election studio, as vast as an Olympic velodrome.

'What's your biggest fear?' she asked.

'I don't know.'

'Mine is that I'll suddenly shout the word "c***" to the whole nation,' she confided.

'Come to think of it, I think that's mine as well,' I agreed. It really was. There is something above-and-beyond awful about the C-word. 'That would be the most horrible thing you could ever imagine.'

'We would never recover,' Emily confirmed.

At that moment, as we stood there lost in our thoughts and fears, the election editor Craig Oliver walked over. 'Right, I have the exit polls, and they're tight,' he said. 'The Conservatives are close but they may not be close enough.'

We craned in to hear him. Craig is softly spoken, which adds to the drama.

'The key phrase I want you to remember is "on the cusp". Okay? *Cusp.*'

Cu-sp. Cusp.

'Um – how about . . . knife-edge?' I suggested.

*

If there was any tension between the two Jeremys, I did not notice it at the start. I did my job and tried not to be photographed falling out of too many nightclubs (as if). My personal life was a rented bedsit in Shepherds Bush, surrounded by translucent curtains and takeaway cartons; the television was hidden behind unopened boxes containing possessions shipped back from Johannesburg. When you put half of everything you own into cardboard boxes you realize how little it means. Anyway, I had *Newsnight*. All I had was all I ever wanted.

And it was extraordinary, coming in to see the rota by the office door and reading a sequence for the week along the lines of:

WARK PAXMAN VINE PAXMAN WARK

or

VINE VINE PAXMAN PAXMAN WARK

or sometimes

WARK PAXMAN PAXMAN PAXMAN WARK

and once

VINE VINE VINE VINE VINE
VINE VINE VINE VINE VINE
VINE VINE VINE

The last a record-breaking thirteen in a row when Jeremy had a hacking cough and Kirsty was away. Mark Lawson promises me that I excitedly told him at the time:

'Paxman has pneumonia, Mark. There are only eighteen antibiotics available for pneumonia. *They have tried fourteen already.*' Doubtless my eyes blazed with youthful ambition as I said it . . . if I ever did.

Why do I say it was extraordinary, seeing that rota? Because Paxman and Wark are broadcasting royalty and there I was, wearing cheap shoes, sandwiched between them. Plus, television does not recognize the complexity of a pecking order. The #1 presenter of *Newsnight* is the one in the chair when you switch on the programme. That was good for the new kid.

And luck was with me on a couple of occasions. My seniors were both off when Tony Blair agreed, at short notice, to be thrown questions by voters in a school (against my better judgement, I asked the Prime Minister the question: 'And if literacy is not improved for under-fives, as you have promised, will you resign?' Blair just laughed.) Then I travelled to Austria to do an exclusive with the far-right politician Jörg Haider about his Nazi past. Completely engrossing. I was solo in the studio for big-ticket specials on BSE and the NHS, and anchored from all over the world: Harare, Washington, Jerusalem. I volunteered for everything and with no home life apart from a faulty toaster I was hugely flexible.

Bit by bit, I gained confidence in a daunting arena. I felt I was keeping the ball out of the net; maybe even scoring. I really cannot describe the feeling when you hear the BBC2 continuity announcer say, 'Next, *Newsnight*, with Jeremy Vine' – that's you, mate – then all that martial music rolls out of the studio speakers and the lights go up and in the chair it really is you and you can discreetly pinch your inner thigh and be sure of it.

Newsnight was magnificent, but not perfect. In New Hampshire to report on the run-up to the American presidential election of 2000, James Stephenson and I ended up watching Al Gore speak to a small audience in a school. Gore drew laughter when someone passed him a scrap of paper. He inhaled deeply and said: 'Well, this is a first for me in public life. Would the owner of car registration PG7 88FJ ... would the owner please move it as you are blocking a throughway.' He laughed. The audience joined in. James and I started laughing heartily too – until we discovered it was our vehicle, the *Newsnight* hire car, which had been towed.

When the former Archbishop of Canterbury Robert Runcie died, John Biffen was booked to talk about their lifelong friendship in the studio. Biffen, a senior Conservative MP, was always very concerned to ensure he received a payment for every single interview he did – something I had found incredible at Westminster – so it may be that the initial conversation with the producer was more about his fee than what he had to say, because when he appeared in the studio and I asked what sort of person Dr Runcie was in private, Biffen proudly told the *Newsnight* audience:

'I have no idea, because I never knew him.'

Still, I loved the show. And I worked hard. But that would not affect the outcome. Looking back I think the tipping point was the day the *Sunday Telegraph* printed a far-too-generous profile of me, saying I was the coming man in current affairs. I was pictured standing in front of a vast picture of the world, head tipped back as if I owned it. There was more 'heir apparent', as I remember. Certainly my hair was apparent. And the tone of the piece might just have turned a distant resentment into something more flinty. Because the next thing that happened was that the roof fell in.

*

Less than a year after the *Guardian*'s laudatory piece about my appointment, its sister paper the *Observer* published the following in its diary. It was strikingly different in tone.

Media Diary, 12 Mar 2000

A bitchy tale of two Jeremys

Because Jeremy 'Paxo' Paxman is the most talented male broadcaster in Britain, by a country mile, we would prefer to think of him as having no taint on his character.

So, can it be true that Sian Kevill, editor of Newsnight, has had to slap Jeremy's wrists for being beastly to the new boy? The allegations, false we are sure, are that Mr Paxman has been referring to the other Jeremy, Jeremy Vine, as 'mini-me' and holding up his little finger, no doubt to indicate the junior stature.

Tsk, tsk, except, of course, that it may be a bit disconcerting to be followed around by someone mirroring your mannerisms and appearance.

Reading it was like hearing a hacksaw edging into bone. As soon as I saw this piece – the first published reference to Paxman's 'mini-me' – I knew I was in trouble. The problem was, it was brilliant. *The Spy Who Shagged Me* was in the cinemas and Austin Powers was a perfect reference point.

Not for a second did I suspect that Paxman himself was behind it; as a god of the small screen, he did not need to stoop. The difficulty with my arriving on *Newsnight* – and my premonition of doom in Johannesburg should have led me in this direction far, far earlier – was simply that *I was also called Jeremy*. Why had I not spotted this? Why had Human Resources not flagged that *there is already one Jeremy* on *Newsnight*? I was the guest who arrives at the wedding in the same dress as the mother of the bride. Except I couldn't carry it off so well: I was so conscious of not being soft cop to Paxo's hardman that I had deliberately gone the other way, interviewing people with such ferocity that I often looked as if someone had parked a ride-on mower on my foot. Gordon Brewer, the 'next Paxman', had had the same difficulty, I remembered. His anger was so thermal he would tremble like a faulty chip pan. *Newsnight* presenters were snookered either way. Too gentle and people said, 'Not a patch on Pax.' Too tough and you were charged with mimicry. Lose-lose.

From that moment on, in every single item that was written about *Newsnight* or its third presenter, I was ... yup, *mini-me*. I was even mini-me when the London *Standard* did a piece in their property section about a house I had looked at. Mini-me went from *Private Eye* to the *Mail* to *The Times* to the *FT* – the *FT*! – and all the way back again. I have never seen a simple set of six letters with an off-centre hyphen reprinted in so many fonts and sizes and colours.

When a tube train I was on stopped in a tunnel, with carriages packed full of Liverpool fans on their way to a Chelsea game, some recognized me and started singing lustily: 'PAXMAN'S NUMBER TWO, PAXMAN'S NUMBER TWO.' The entire carriage joined in.

One night, attending the Royal Television Society Awards, I squeezed into a crowded lift. A drunk man with sweat on his forehead eyed me beadily. 'I may never get the chansh agin,' he slurred in a pantomime Glaswegian accent as I and the rest of the lift wondered what was coming. 'But I want to shay, *yew* are bloody *showing* that other prick what's what. Bloody showing Jeremy what's what.' I felt a surge of relief until he added: 'And I bloody loved your fourteen-questions routine wi' Michael Howard.'

I spoke to Mark Ogle, the TV press officer who had warned me initially about the trouble caused by the 'heir apparent' line. 'Can we not try to change this narrative somehow?'

'I don't think so,' he said bluntly.

'Well how long do I have to put up with it for?'

'Until you die.'

Now, looking back, the whole thing seems strangely wonderful. At worst it was a gentle bit of playground bullying, and richly deserved. It mattered too much to me at the time because at the time it was all I had.

So what did I do? I kept working, as if that would make it go away. I observed Paxman keenly and realized that, turning fifty, far from being on the fade, the guy was close to the top of his game. Watching hopefully for signs that he might scale down or scale out, I saw none. He was clever; he was even funny. He knew the stuff that really makes people laugh out loud is on the most serious programmes, and when the camera cut to his face during an interview he pulled expressions of such theatrical disgust you thought he had spent the day doing callisthenics on his cheeks and eyebrows.

But Jeremy also had that classic journalist thing, simultaneously seeing the big picture and the fragment of loose mosaic. Like Humphrys, Paxo could zero in on The One Question That Could Not Be Answered. Producers often bring you piles of stuff: their job is to miss nothing. The great presenter's skill, I reckoned, was the converse – throwing most of it away. An editor who worked with Jeremy for years, Karen O'Connor, once pointed at him pacing the presenter's cubicle and told me quietly: 'He sometimes spends the whole afternoon just thinking up one question.' Your average presenter thinks up fifteen. That is why they are average.

*

One day they pulled out the *Newsnight* set to prepare for broadcast and discovered it had been vandalized. Someone had sprayed that very rude word on it (the one Emily was worried about). The four letters were aerosoled in bright yellow across the programme's signature blue, unmissable along the side of the desk that faced the camera.

I was due to be in the chair that night. The editors were made aware of the difficulty. It would simply not be possible for the programme to start as normal, and for us to hope viewers did not notice that I was sitting at a desk with the word C*** in huge capitals across the front of it. The set was erected from storage every day because the studio was shared with *Breakfast News* and *Newsround*, so the rapid respray operation that was now needed put the entire system under pressure.

A few days later I was chatting about it to a near neighbour, the journalist Matthew Norman. He went on to mention the story in his diary in the *Guardian*. It was a nothing reference, just a couple of sentences. But the *Mirror* editor Piers Morgan saw the diary piece and gave the story a full page the next day, under the headline:

WHO DAUBED ****
ON PAXMAN'S DESK?

BBC chiefs hunt paint spray joker

April 14 2001
TOM NEWTON DUNN

TV interrogator Jeremy Paxman's famous Newsnight desk has been daubed with a four-letter word.

The aerosol attack spelt out the word c*** in bold letters.

The message was spotted before the nightly BBC programme went on air.

Now furious BBC bosses are hunting the culprit.

But 50-year-old Paxman has clashed with so many politicians and other public figures that the list of suspects is huge.

The obscene message is thought to have been sprayed late at night after programme workers had gone home.

Technicians quickly painted it over when it was spotted.

Paxman was in bed with flu at his country retreat in Oxfordshire yesterday.

But his long-term partner, TV producer Elizabeth Clough, revealed that he had seen the funny side of the spray attack, which was revealed by The Guardian Diary.

She said last night: 'Jeremy is well aware of what was written on the desk. But I don't think his response was anything I could pass on. It wasn't printable.'

A BBC spokeswoman said last night: 'As a prank, someone did scrawl an inappropriate word on Newsnight's set.'

PRIME SUSPECTS

ALASTAIR CAMPBELL
Odds: 2-1
Tony Blair's Press Secretary, known for his foul language and bitterness towards

enemies, had a run-in with Paxo, refusing to be interviewed for fear of being 'made to look like a criminal'. Paxo said this was 'crap'.

MICHAEL HOWARD
Odds: 10-1
Paxo gave the former Tory Home Secretary one of the most famous TV grillings of all time, asking the same question 14 times. Howard's reputation never recovered from that 1997 interview about a prisons row.

JEREMY VINE
Odds: 25-1
As Newsnight's junior presenter, Vine shamelessly replicates Paxman's sneering and abrupt interviewing style. Insiders say he wants the top job of chief inquisitor but Paxo is refusing to budge.

I suppose I should have been grateful I wasn't the favourite. At this juncture I started keeping a note of my time on *Newsnight* as I (wrongly, as it turned out) thought it could only end in tears, probably with me leaving the Beeb altogether. These days, looking at what I wrote down, it seems laughable more than anything.

For example, would Sherlock Holmes have been able to solve *The Riddle of the Missing Coat Hangers?*

I needed to put a coat hanger in the office so I could hang up my jacket in the daytime. Naturally I brought in a cheap wire one. But every time I left it on the coat-stand, I would return for the following shift and find it had been thrown away. Was there a misunderstanding with the cleaners? So I bought an upmarket, non-disposable hanger from John Lewis. This too was thrown away during my days off shift. Next I went to Debenhams and bought the most expensive hanger I could find. I stuck a label on it saying JEREMY VINE. It vanished. Was there some malign force in the office

which felt I had no right to mark out any territory? Jeremy himself
was above suspicion; did he have a stooge who resented me? I fell
back on hiding a wire coat hanger in a cupboard belonging to *The
World Tonight.*

And then there was *The Mystery of the Disappearing Publicity
Shots* (the press office launched an inquiry and found they had been
dropped down the back of a cabinet), and *The Conundrum of the
Family Photos.* For which I shall simply reprint what I wrote at the
time:

15 Sept 2002

First a picture of Justin Webb's twins [which I had put on the
presenter's office wall] disappears ... Second, there was the
whole business of my coat hangers being thrown away, so I now
keep my coat hanger hidden in a cupboard ... and my press
office photos, taken in the *Newsnight* studio, being found down
the back of a cupboard.

So that brings us up to now. My wedding was September
14th and I thought, no one would take down a wedding photo
would they? And I stuck one up on the wall next to the very
sweet pics of JP's kids. Not too close; in close proximity, but
with at least four inches in between. Small pic of me and
LARGE pics of Jeremy's children: which have been on wall for at
least two years. Today I come in and, lo, the wedding picture of
me and Rachel is <u>still on the wall!</u>

Then I notice the space to the right. The pictures of Jeremy's
kids have been taken down.

*

Certainly Jeremy would not have stooped to hiding photos or throwing away coat hangers. His attention had been distracted, anyway, by
the unlikely decision to give Nicky Campbell a clutch of presenting
shifts. It had been some sort of contractual fix but caused such

tumult on the programme that the executive Steve Mitchell had to explain it at a programme meeting. When he said Campbell was a broadcaster with a different kind of voice, the veteran reporter David Sells shot back: 'So is Donald Duck!' What with Nicky's swift cameo, and the decision to drop the back end of *Newsnight* in Scotland to allow for a separate programme from Glasgow, the Paxman/Vine static was masked by other infuriations.

But it kept reasserting itself – in my own mind at least. At an end-of-year party a producer, Allie Wharf, who prided herself on a close relationship with the main man and was so frank she thought tact was a type of carpet, drunkenly pinned me to the wall and told me: 'As long as Paxman is on *Newsnight* you are fucked.'

I rolled my eyes. What other response was possible? And I found myself thinking, sadly, as everyone got louder and drunker around me: This is the way all careers end. A wrong turning, sudden impact, and you're gone.

Chapter Fifteen

HAVING DOUBTS

Everyone has doubts. But for a journalist, doubt is a career. Their job is to doubt – hang a giant inflatable question mark over everything – so they tend to be a bit good at it. I think I probably do doubt a little too well. Maybe turn it inwards a touch too often.

Some doubts are minor: did we really cut the best clip out of that interview? But some are monumental. Why am I doing this? What is the *point*? Is it entirely vacuous, thrashing yourself to collect material that, if you're a broadcaster, literally gets thrown to the four winds?

During the 1997 election campaign, while supposedly assigned to the Blair bus, I was told to break away for two days to follow a man who was dressed as a chicken. He was an actor the Conservatives had hired. They had instructed him to wear a large chicken suit, follow Blair around and disrupt his public appearances.

The Tories wanted the idea to lodge with voters that Blair had – watch closely for the joke here – chickened out of a TV debate. It all got a bit lively. As soon as the chicken appeared, Labour aides would form a doughnut around it, jostle the actor and try to pull off his chicken-head. Alastair Campbell confided to me that he intended to lure the actor into the battlebus and get Blair to 'turn' the chicken, because **TORY CHICKEN COMES OUT FOR LABOUR** would be the headline of the campaign. It never happened.

But for forty-eight hours, while nominally a political reporter following the most exciting election for years, I was actually on the trail of a man dressed as a farmyard animal. It was Radio 5 live's fault. They thought a profile of the chicken would liven up the election. When he flew north to Glasgow (by plane), I lost him in the airport. My mood was entirely humourless when I asked an assistant at the ticket counter, 'Silly question, but have you seen a man dressed as a chicken come this way?'

She was obviously having a bad day too, because she remained deadpan as she turned wearily towards a colleague four desks down and called:

'John, have we had a chicken through check-in?'

I failed to get the interview, or even the name of the actor, although I did once see him in a business lounge with the chicken-head resting on the lap of Eric Pickles, the senior Tory accompanying him. The actor looked so fed up he might have needed medical, or even veterinary, attention.

Later, in a catch-up with other reporters, we were all laughing about whether there are some jobs even an out-of-work actor should turn down.

'Can there be any job lower, more humiliating, more demeaning, than having to dress as a chicken and try to prance around behind Blair?' asked a woman from one of the papers.

'Yep,' I said. 'Being the person who has to report on the man dressed as a chicken who prances around behind Blair. That's me for the last two days.'

Doubt. It is the enemy of enthusiasm, which is a real problem because enthusiasm is the single most important quality for anyone going into the media.

A while back a lad off a media studies course came in to watch my show on Radio 2. He was nineteen and we had been told he was the best in class. I invited him into my studio, and he sat opposite me wearing headphones as I set about a minister (who was down the line, at Westminster) with some energy.

Afterwards, putting on a record and feeling a little self-satisfied with how the interview had gone, I asked the student what he thought of it. 'Oh, sorry, I wasn't really listening,' he said in a voice that so sagged with boredom I am afraid I had to gently ask him to leave.

Enthusiasm is precious. But it is also a delicate flower. I clung onto mine despite the playground bullying on *Newsnight*, though it was a close-run thing. Years back, on the *Today* programme, a producer called Marie shouted across the office: 'Who did the piece linking vitamins and intelligence?' and three of us raised our hands. The day I filed the report I had thought I was discovering something; as I looked at the raised hands I realized I was merely repeating it. When you do a story for the third time, it is probably a good moment to consider your position in the universe. I left *Today* not long after.

So journalists are professional doubters, but they rely on enthusiasm, which is destroyed by doubt. Squaring this triangle is not easy.

One sign things are going wrong is when scepticism curdles into cynicism. Journalists need to be sceptical – to question everything – but a cynic is a sceptic in a crash helmet. The cynic is not receptive. He throws his rotten fruit first, then asks questions after it has landed. Somebody once said a Conservative is just a Liberal who's been mugged. Well, a cynic is just a sceptic who has done the same story three times.

I both love and hate the tale of the room with a hundred people in it that is hit by an earthquake. Ninety-eight people panic. The ninety-ninth jumps onto a table and tries to direct the crowd toward the exits: that's the politician. The last person stands at the back of the room and hurls abuse at the one on the table. That's the journalist.

Sometimes you can even become cynical about cynicism. When Princess Diana announced she was withdrawing from public life, the *Mirror*'s headline was so gloriously shameless I copied it down:

WE'LL LEAVE YOU ALONE DI
See pages 2, 3, 5, 6, 7, 9, 10, 11, 12, 13, 24 and 25

Similarly, and just as much fun (although not for those involved), the broadsheet *Daily Telegraph* spread the adultery of the Chief of Defence Staff Sir Peter Harding across half its front page and all of page three. There were full-length photos of Sir Peter's mistress Lady Bienvenida Buck (great name) and accounts of the affair from every conceivable angle. Then came the high-minded editorial halfway through the paper:

> As for this story, its personal details are best left unrepeated.

For the satirists these are easy pickings. Chris Morris and Armando Iannucci invented a fake news agency called Smokehammer. After 9/11, during a period in which the former Beatle George Harrison died, Smokehammer uploaded the following to its website: 'The British defence secretary Geoff Hoon has asked the Taliban at Tora Bora to stop firing back, out of respect for George Harrison.' Some American radio stations found the report credible enough to run unchecked.

But journalists have *real* material crossing their desks which begs for a response just as cynical. 'A report out today claims visitor numbers to libraries have halved, and predicts that if the trend continues there will be no visitors to libraries in twenty years' – the only place for that report is the fireplace, but it got published instead of burnt. 'A report out today says the running speed of women is increasing faster than the running speed of men, so in fifty years women will be able to run faster than men' – again, the fireplace. Those two stories were based on the seriously mistaken assumption that all trends continue forever in a straight line. And yes, they did actually get on the news.

Another example of a heap of cynicism-fertilizer is anything where an organization claims to have discovered something that, strangely, helps its own cause. The Hopper's Disease Research Society will always tell you that a study has found research into Hopper's Disease is chronically underfunded. Always. Swap 'Hopper's Disease' for any other illness and the result is the same. When did we last hear a report saying a survey by a charity called Help the Elderly had found the care of old people was taking *too much* NHS funding? It may or may not be, but since when did we expect Help the Elderly to be a neutral voice? Yet somehow this stuff ends up on the news. It is enough to make you dread the call of the alarm clock on a Monday.

*

At the conference of editors I mentioned earlier, a fellow from the *Kent Messenger* series of newspapers stood up and made a speech that contained a gobsmacking line of argument.

'We discovered,' he said proudly, 'that if we print pictures of babies, it sells papers – because people want to see their own baby in the news.

'We then discovered that, the more baby photos we print, the more copies we sell.

'So we held a baby competition and covered the paper in pictures of babies. Sales went through the roof,' he beamed, 'which goes to show that—'

I was on tenterhooks.

'—all news is local.'

Just as I was thinking about this, he reached his triumphant conclusion.

'News is about me.'

He actually said that. I was hosting the session, so chances are some people might have wondered why I nearly fell off my chair. Up until that moment, I had more or less assumed that everyone agreed journalism was a process through which we find out about *other* lives – and the further information travels, the more valuable it is. The editor was saying the opposite on both counts: that news is a way of finding out about *our* lives, and the most precious information travels no distance at all.

If in doubt, ask your mother. I read his baby quote to mine on a bank holiday weekend. 'Is that true, Mum?' I asked. 'That news is about me?'

'Well of course it is,' she replied without hesitation. 'Our house is full of pictures of us. We don't have pictures of people we don't know. And watch, if you ever pass round a set of photographs, all people ever do is look for the ones they're in.'

In this globalized world, where we can swap text messages in seconds with friends on the other side of the planet, where a stock crash in Japan wipes out pensions in London and a cartoon in Denmark starts a riot in Gaza, we seem to be developing a heightened sense of neighbourhood. The Czech Republic splits from Slovakia. Wales has its own Assembly. As we have gone global, so we have become more local. News is a picture of your own baby.

But if that is the case, then there is no need for journalism at all.

*

For me there was a particular day. I was walking up Wood Lane towards TV Centre. The sun was out. And I caught myself having the thought that kills journalists: *We have already done that story*.

It was not the vitamins-and-intelligence piece again. This particular September day I would be hosting *Newsnight* for the main event of the TUC conference: the speech by the prime minister, Tony Blair. The newspapers had given us a fairly good idea of what Mr Blair was going to say. The unions would get 'fairness, not favours' from his government. The only problem is that he had made the speech before. The line first emerged during the TUC conference four years earlier. He promised fairness not favours then. He had definitely promised fairness not favours on other occasions. We were getting perilously close to our count of three.

So when I got to the *Newsnight* office I was having one of those moments of self-doubt. What are we all doing here? Can't we buck the system, cancel the news and do something else? The running order said no: it already had 'Kearney/TUC' as the top item, the formidable Martha K being down in Brighton already.

We talked about interviews. I got a sandwich for lunch. And then, at around 1.45 p.m. as I sat watching a feed of news channels on the pocket television on the desk, the top right corner of the screen started to show a skyscraper in New York, with black smoke pouring from the top of it.

Chapter Sixteen

9/11 AND 10/15

The live pictures of the World Trade Center on 11 September 2001 did not attract much of our attention at first. As the fire flickered in the corner quadrant of the mini-television in the presenter's cubicle, one of the duty editors arrived to talk about the stories we would be doing besides the TUC. He told me not to worry because 'the sprinklers will come on in a minute', and when someone said the crash into the first tower looked serious, he declared with total conviction, 'Nah, that's just a light aircraft.'

Strange how certainty and ignorance are often close buddies. The *Newsnight* team all had half an eye to their TV sets when the second plane, United Airlines Flight 175, hit the South Tower at 2.03 p.m. UK time. There was a gasp across the office. People stood up and looked around. 'My God,' I said to no one in particular, 'come and look at this.'

Within seconds, *Newsnight*'s diplomatic editor Mark Urban was at the door of the presenter's office where we were now all gathered. He only said two words: 'Al Qaeda.' At the time the words were not on the lips of most people. In fact very few watching TV that day would even have heard of Al Qaeda; Bin Laden was not yet the poster child for global terror. Credit to Urban.

Jeremy Sr was fishing in Ireland. The managers clearly had to get him back for what now seemed like it would be the biggest show in *Newsnight*'s history. All I wanted was to know if I was definitely *not* doing the show; or might I be? It would be a blow, having to return to my flat to watch my own programme because the story that had broken was just too big. But of course it wasn't really my programme.

The extraordinary rendition of the other Jeremy from Ireland would apparently not be easy. It was a difficult moment for the editor, George Entwistle: with the wisdom of Solomon he said, 'Give me till 5 p.m. to try and get Paxman back. If I can't, you do the show and no one else.' That seemed fair on everyone.

It was strange, looking back, how long the TUC stayed in the programme menu. At the conference Blair spoke briefly about the attacks only. But we were glued to the idea of 'fairness, not favours' for at least an hour. It dropped to the second item; then the fifth. It hung on as a brief package in the running order until the towers completely collapsed and buried it. That is the human condition, I guess. We get wedded to Plan A without realizing.

In the States a congressman called the attack 'our second Pearl Harbor', just as the clock ticked past five. Okay, I will admit now, somewhat shamefacedly: I was watching that clock for the wrong reasons – but maybe reasons you will understand. This was *the* day to front a television current affairs programme. To front *Newsnight*, in particular, the evening of the biggest news event in decades.

It also fulfilled our classical definition of news from the earlier chapter. The attacks on the twin towers and the Pentagon, not forgetting the heroic downing by passengers of a fourth plane on its way east, were unscheduled and shocking in a way that even the fall of the Berlin Wall was not. The events were, without question, a disruption of the norm.

Among the studio guests were James Rubin (formerly of the US State Department) and the ex-PM of Israel, Ehud Barak. The broadcast crackled with energy. But the most memorable moment

for me was a live interview with Stephen Evans, our New York correspondent, who had been on the ground floor of the South Tower
when the first plane went into the North Tower. 'There was a bang,
and the building literally moved,' he said. People shouted at each
other to get out. Then a second explosion. Office workers jumped
from windows at the top of the skyscrapers to avoid being inciner-
ated; not a single person survived on any floor above the level
where the jets struck. Those who heard the bodies of the jumpers
strike the New York asphalt a hundred storeys below would never
forget the sound. Steve's personal shock, so crisply conveyed, was
also a nation's.

The programme ended. The other Jeremy was on his way back. I
was sent to America.

*

Despite everything that happened, to this day I vividly remember
the walk to work that morning. The sun was shining on Wood Lane
on 11/9/01 – which we now call 9/11 – and I was deciding that news
was getting too predictable.

September 11 did not only cause this inexperienced presenter to
rethink. During the nineties the name of the supposedly brilliant
American academic Francis Fukuyama had been on everyone's lips,
especially down at Westminster while I worked there: he had written
an essay called 'The End of History' in 1989 which had been seen by
the US president at the time, George Bush Sr.

It argued that history – in the sense of great, world-shaking
events – was over. Fukuyama predicted the collapse of commu-
nism in eastern Europe and said the story from now on would be of
countries gradually becoming liberal democracies. There were
echoes of this in a book published later by Thomas L. Friedman, an
academic who invented the 'Golden Arches Theory of Conflict
Prevention', arguing that no two countries with a branch of
McDonald's in their capital cities would declare war on each other.

His theory was almost immediately destroyed by the actions of NATO and Serbia.*

Bush Sr had seen the Fukuyama paper in 1989. The Berlin Wall came down a few months later, seeming to prove the thesis, and the academic became the world's philosopher-king for more than a decade. While I was a pol-corr, clever MPs at Westminster like George Walden went on and on about Fukuyama.

Then 9/11 proved him completely and utterly wrong.

In the *Newsnight* office that day, George Entwistle had the single most valuable insight. I have always thought this moment shows what makes an editor. He told a meeting held barely twenty minutes after the second plane went in: 'We have moved out of the world of Francis Fukuyama, and into the world of Samuel Huntington.'

I nodded sagely, then later quietly googled Huntington, of whom I am afraid I had never heard. He had written a book called *The Clash of Civilizations*. Entwistle had nailed it. Huntington's book, which said conflict between the West and Islam would shape our world, did indeed become famous in the years to come. Even as *The End of History* hit the bargain bins.

A year later I would interview Fukuyama. Instead of the tidy, sparkling man I had seen in photos, he looked as if he had stepped out of a hurricane (though I suppose it could just have been the overnight flight from Washington). 'Do you admit that you were wrong about the End of History,' I asked, 'given what happened on 9/11?'

No, he said hesitantly. History had ended, but 'some countries are still in it.'

As I mentioned earlier, a hearty distaste for experts can be life-enhancing.

*

* Since NATO bombed Serbia, there have also been wars between Israel and Lebanon (2006), and conflict between Georgia and Russia over South Ossetia (2008). All have branches of McDonald's.

We slept at a B&B outside Stansted for two days. Flights into the States had been stopped by the attack. Eventually a jet packed full of journalists – nicknamed 'Ego One' – flew from the UK to a small airport just outside Toronto, which at least was the right continent. There were no hire cars. The Canadian cab driver we hailed was surprised when we said, 'Manhattan.'

In the event he took us to the Canadian–US border, where we resolved to get a lift. The tension between current affairs and hard news was perfectly expressed when we started dropping hints that we had no transport. The BBC newsmen Ben Brown and George Alagiah commiserated politely. The team from *Channel 4 News* intervened and offered us a ride. During the trip, squished into their rented saloon car, we were overtaken by a roomy SUV with, ahem, two rather well-known BBC colleagues in the back. They sat high up in the glow of top-of-the-range interior lighting and we could not help but notice the suggestion of ample available seating. Competition between outlets is fiercer, clearly, when you work for the same organization; current affairs programmes understand each other.

The producer Rachel Thompson found us a vantage point high up on a rusted fire escape from which the gape in New York's skyline was visible. Our cables ran down all the hundreds of metal stairs to a TV production company. I anchored *Newsnight* from what seemed, at the time, to be the axle around which the world was grinding.

Then we headed west, supposedly to find out 'what middle America is thinking.' As if you could, by going a hundred miles into Pennsylvania for two days. But actually, the experience was special. In the early evening, hearing loud music through our car windows, we stopped at a bar in the middle-class town of Lock Haven. It turned out a teenage punk band called Milton were playing. The guitarist was a young man called Adam Franz. When his father Keith arrived to collect him, we said who we were and, with the air of desperation that only a *Newsnight* deadline creates, angled an invitation to Sunday lunch.

We spent the following day in an idyll. The Franz family had friends, the Pribbles, who owned a spot by the Susquehanna River where they spent bright weekends. The Pribble and Franz youngsters threw footballs. In the shade the adults – Keith and Karen Franz, Randy and Barbara Pribble – barbecued and drank beer. The scene was immaculately placid, almost as if Hollywood had created it, but the fire and dust of 9/11 had still swept through. Watching their kids, the mums and dads shared some of their deepest fears about their future: would there be a war? Would their children have to fight? Was America changed forever?

It stayed with me: that contrast. The sunshine sparkling on the river, and the fear.

*

Five weeks later I was back in America – not 9/11 now, but 10/15 – and this time I travelled with another exceptionally clued-up producer, called Claudia Milne. The initial impact of the attacks had barely faded. We found a vantage point where we could look down on Ground Zero, and it was still on fire below the surface. Incredibly, more than a month after the attack, I watched smoke still belching out from the ruins.

There was, also, a once-in-a-lifetime experience of the worst kind. Claudia used her American connections to get permission for us to accompany a man back to his apartment. The block was known as 125 Cedars. He had not been allowed access to it since the day of the attacks. We went up the silent stairs of the brownstone building, which stood right alongside where the twin towers had been.

The man did not know what to expect when he turned the key in the door. And we could never have guessed what we would find, either – shoes. More than thirty individual shoes, mostly trainers, littering the apartment floor. The place was a mess. The windows were blown out. A computer lay on its side on the carpet. All the books had been whooshed off the shelves. But *shoes*?

We worked it out, thanks to our friend. American city workers often commute wearing trainers, then change into heels or more formal footwear when they get to the office. So when the towers fell, thousands of spare shoes inside were sprayed over the area. For some reason this fellow's apartment had more than its share. The sight was so bizarre, so unsettling, we forgot to film it – the first and last time that has ever happened to me.

Lying on the floor was a shard of that distinctive World Trade Center steel, shaped like a dagger. I put it in my bag to take home, then saw all the reasons I shouldn't – the post-9/11 security measures would definitely cover bringing jagged shards of metal onto planes, and anyway, this piece of metal was the property of New York City. Maybe the thought was irrational, but taking a piece of the building where so many people had died felt akin to looting. I took it back out of my bag and replaced it carefully on the floor.

We walked onto the roof of the apartment block. It was covered in dust. From on high we could gaze down at the smouldering ruins below, a mess of concrete and metal in forty different shades of grey covering the area of several football pitches.

Then I saw a backpack by my feet. Bending down, I gingerly unzipped it and opened the bag. Someone's lunch was inside. A sandwich and a chocolate bar, sealed in a small Tupperware box.

*

In some ways the trip five weeks later was more emotionally powerful than the one straight after. Americans had digested the full force of the impact, yet the clear-up was only just beginning. As we walked to our hotel one afternoon, a wide-eyed man in a filthy T-shirt stopped us, almost hysterical. He was on his way back from Ground Zero.

'We've just had the most incredible moment down there. Incredible luck – we found this torso. And the guy's cellphone had penetrated the torso, it was lodged inside his chest wall. And we got it out and turned it on and it was still working. So we could identify him!'

He spoke at ninety miles an hour, tearful, thrilled, talking to himself as much as to us. I said, 'Great, great,' caught up in his fervour. Although the man had stopped us because he saw our camera, he decided against being filmed. He was so traumatized I was not sure it would have been right to interview him anyway.

On another street corner Claudia pointed at a tall fellow in a hat. 'Hey – that's Spalding Gray,' she said. If you are getting the impression by this stage that some of the people on *Newsnight* were outrageously smart, I'm glad, because that impression is correct.

I wasn't sure who Spalding Gray was. '*Swimming to Cambodia*,' was Claudia's answer as we speeded up and caught him. 'Mr Gray, we would love to interview you about what it's been like, living the last month in this city,' she told him carefully.

The face that turned to us was woven with uncertainty and pain. 'I'd – rather not, I think,' he said. 'I'm so sorry.'

That was our micro-moment with Spalding Rockwell Gray; writer, actor, pioneer of pared-down theatrical monologues, depressive, artist, a man whose books I had never read and who was found dead in New York's East River three years later.

*

Daily life in the US was affected on every level by 9/11. Air travel in particular. A month later, a newspaper reported that passengers on a domestic flight heard the pilot make this announcement:

'*Ladies and gentlemen, thank you for flying with us today. The doors have now closed so there is no way off this plane. If you have a bomb, you are already in control. If anyone does try to hijack this plane we must all act together. Stand up and throw whatever you can at them, hard objects if you can, and aim at their heads. They will not be able to hijack this plane if we all act together.*'

Amid the hysteria, the Japanese branch of Germany's Triumph

Group said it was developing a metal-free bra (available in white, orange and blue) so businesswomen could pass quickly through airport metal detectors without setting them off. Another firm, Precision Aerodynamics, began marketing the Emergency Building Escape Parachute System: parachutes for high-rise office workers costing almost $1,000 each.

Back in London, *Newsnight* got angles from all over the globe. There was plenty of anti-US sentiment and, of course, massive anger would be fuelled by the wars that followed. But that was for the future. For now we were simply looking into the crater.

During that second trip it seemed the life of everyone we met had been changed in some way. The Pentagon, at the time the biggest building in the world, was so huge that when we drove there for an interview we could not see where the third plane had gone in. Even as we glanced out of every window in every corridor we were rushed down, we still could not tell.

Our appointment there was with Paul Wolfowitz, the hawkish deputy defence secretary whose moment had come, and who coined the term 'asymmetrical warfare' to describe what had happened. But the selling point of the current affairs show is that it has time to tell the human story, and once again this was about the power of the smallest voice.

It belonged to the husband of Stacey Farrelly, whom we met in her house in New Jersey. We set up our camera with as little fuss as possible as she pulled out a well-thumbed album showing photos of her and Joseph.

New Jersey is the home state not only of *The Sopranos* but also Springsteen, of course. Bruce had rung Stacey personally to offer his condolences. Joe Farrelly, a firefighter, had left home the night before the eleventh, and never came back.

Stacey appreciated the personal call from Springsteen – 'He's real. He cares. He's from round here. Bruce would never forget his people' – but no one would expect even that to take the edge off her loss. Her husband shone out of the family photos like a living presence.

Then she pulled out the note he had left her before he went on shift. This is what Joe Farrelly wrote to his wife and laid on their bed, heading off for work on what he thought would be a completely routine day:

Dear Stace
I can't begin to tell you how much I love you.
Words are inadequate. Already I can't wait to get
home. Hope you had a good time today.
   Love you, Joe

Chapter Seventeen

THE MAD MINUTE

After a while in the Beeb, people start to realize they are having unique experiences. At that point the crowd parts. There are those who think they are having unique experiences because they *are* unique, and those who realize they are having unique experiences because they are lucky.

The second group actually has some of the best people in it. John Simpson and John Humphrys modestly joke about how, while working as reporters amidst the richness of the BBC experience, they always expected to be 'found out' – a boss would quietly walk over, tap them on the shoulder and thumb knowingly at the door. Without needing an explanation, they would pick up their briefcases and tramp out of the building for the last time.

The producer on the *Newsnight* Van with me, Isobel Eaton, said much the same one day. 'Do you ever have that thing – where someone catches your eye in the office – and that understanding passes between you?'

'No – what?'

'That if you weren't being paid to do all this you would do it for free, and no one must ever know that, and the two of you have just found each other out.'

*

The headline on page three of the *Mail on Sunday* seemed to take up a third of an acre: **NEWSNIGHT'S VINE FINDS LOVE IN A VAN**. Across an entire page the article told how, during the 2001 election campaign, I had got familiar with a reporter in Newcastle called Rachel Schofield, and described how we had used the *Newsnight* Volkswagen for secret encounters.

When the BBC press officer rang to warn me about the story on the Friday I told him it was fifty per cent true – the van had not been used for any such purpose, but yes: Rachel and I were an item, having met when I hosted the North East Press Awards a full year earlier.

His advice was wonderful. 'Don't try to get the van taken out. If they kill the van they'll just replace it with something worse.'

It is what you call benign fiction – stuff people make up because they know nobody will mind.

Next the newspaper rang with an audacious request. Could they do a photo with Rachel?

'Absolutely not,' she said. 'Why would I?'

The answer was so devilishly cunning you almost have to admire them for it. The newspaper came back to the press office saying: 'Well, in that case we will have to print the only photo we have of Rachel, which is the one from her BBC pass.'

It may not even have been true, but threatening a woman with mass-market publication of her staff photo is like producing a Polaris missile during a conversation with a traffic warden.

'Do they want me topless, or fully naked?' was Rachel's reply.

In the end, inaccuracies aside, the piece made for a fairly happy read; not least because, for the first time in an age, there was no reference to me as the stunted stepbrother of Paxo. Were we turning a corner?

Meanwhile Cecilia Veloz Roca, of Johannesburg police fame,

arrived in the *Newsnight* office. She had capitalized on her scoop by securing a promise that she would do some investigative work. Her mild dyslexia and language issues (Swedish and Spanish being her first two) meant she had to get a strict assurance from the editor: on no account would she be asked to write script straight into the autocue, especially not under time pressure.

Needless to say, one night it happened. The producer on duty, a slightly hysterical type, did not know about the editor's assurance. 'Cecilia, can you write the newsbelt please?'

'But I—'

'I haven't got time to hear an excuse! PLEASE!' he urged. 'We're under pressure, Cecilia. It's nearly nine. There's no one else.'

The newsbelt is the swift roundup of other stories which lasts about ninety seconds. The office was quiet. Everyone was in edit suites cutting films or checking graphics. Towards the moment of broadcast the *Newsnight* office is emptier than you would imagine. Staff are elsewhere. Except, on this occasion, Cecilia.

But she was resourceful. Her boyfriend was an investment banker in Johannesburg whom I shall call Geoff. Half an hour later she rang him. Email was not universal in South Africa back then, and Geoff did not have access to it at home, so she told him: 'I have written a script for the newsbelt. I need you to rewrite it for me and check it. Please get into work now.'

It was past 11 p.m. in South Africa. Geoff climbed into his sports car and drove at a tilt to the office. He opened the email and spent half an hour rapidly knocking the script into shape. Then he sent it back to London, it was loaded into the autocue . . .

. . . and Kirsty Wark read it live on air to a million viewers: *the newsbelt written by an investment banker in Johannesburg.*

But the best moment was yet to come. After the programme, long past midnight in South Africa, Geoff rang Cecilia.

'Well – how did it go?' he asked, keen to hear.

'Great. Yeah, it looked good. They changed some things,' she said casually, 'but—'

Geoff interrupted with the line that shows that inside every single person is a performer waiting to jump out.

'Hang on a second, Cecilia. Wait. Go back a moment. You said *they changed things*?'

*

In 2001, despite the entertaining local difficulties on *Newsnight*, I decided that I was still lucky. Most nights the show had an audience into seven figures, which seems staggering now. When I quietly – okay, obsessively – tallied the ratings over six months to see how much the audience was boosted on nights when JP was in the chair, I was surprised to find it wasn't: I was ahead by the width of a cigarette paper. I reckoned it was just the way the stories had fallen – I had fronted the 9/11 edition and somehow survived a loopy coast-to-coast election trip in the famous van, which the other Jeremy had even been heard to praise. I chaired a grinding Tory leadership hustings with Kenneth Clarke and Iain Duncan Smith. When Peter Mandelson suddenly quit, that was my night too. And I was also lucky because ... well, even without the involvement of a stray Volkswagen, I had fallen in love with Miss Schofield.

Although I still occasionally worried that I was not built to last on *Newsnight* so long as I was the second Jeremy – Allie Wharf's brutal version of that sentiment was probably not far off the truth – I sensed I had come through the initiation, at least; the ceremonies had been more testing than joining the Hell's Angels. But why shouldn't they be? If, at thirty-five, because you are lucky or unique, you are accorded the unbelievable privilege of a staff position where you are taught how to do televised interviewing on the best live show there is – alongside Wark and Paxman, two of the very best there have ever been – only a fool would expect plain sailing. In broadcasting, the only unforgivable sin is to be smug. There was no danger of that; I had never thought I was unique.

In 1989 the chairman of British Rail, Sir Bob Reid, was asked why he had not resigned, given that he was against privatization and the Conservative government had announced it was going ahead.

His reply was inspirational.

'If you're in a pantomime, you might as well stay to the end.'

Very often in the BBC, when things have been a slog or gone off the rails completely, I have brought that quote to mind. The organization has a compelling, serious purpose, especially in news, where the sense of seriousness is almighty; but crazy stuff still happens. The Beeb is a bit like a football team that plays exactly as directed for the bulk of every game, but at some point always has one completely insane passage of play – a mad minute – in which the team run around screaming and try to score in their own net as often as possible.

Countless managers have promised to sort out the problems caused by that crazy sixty seconds. All have failed and been shown the door, never realizing that the other eighty-nine minutes are what the BBC is all about. The mad minute with all the own goals is just a bonus.

The crazy stuff can give you the best time you have ever had in your life. It can also catch you broadsides and destroy a day, a week, or an entire career. And at such moments you simply have to face the bathroom mirror and repeat Sir Bob:

'I might as well stay to the end.'

The death of the Queen Mother in 2002 was a news event where the Beeb got attacked for supposedly getting it all wrong. It was one of the most rehearsed news stories in broadcast history, the BBC having conducted preparations for *fifteen years* in advance of the day – that did not matter. Somehow the wheels came off. The newscaster Peter Sissons famously wore an unduly light-hearted tie, at least according to the newspapers (burgundy, not black); they also accused him of asking an indelicate question of a woman who had been at the Queen Mother's deathbed. Sissons later pointed out that the rehearsals all concentrated on the immediate moment of the announcement, not what to do in the long hours after.

At the time, Greg Dyke was the still fairly new DG. He was a populist who clearly hated being seen as a New Labour type (he had once given money to Tony Blair's leadership campaign), but he had already been in trouble for cancelling the broadcast of a hundredth birthday pageant for the Queen Mother. So now the accusation that the BBC was riding roughshod over the black-tie tradition as part of some centre-left conspiracy, although ludicrous, really stung him. When buttocks are clenched at senior levels in the BBC, that's a lot of clenching. A tense atmosphere prevailed in the run-up to the QM's funeral: a desperate desire Not To Get It Wrong Again.

I was in Jerusalem. On a separate story, and a little unsighted on the politics back in London. Israeli tanks had gone back into the occupied territories. Our story was the lead on *Newsnight*. This is the note I made at the time:

6 March 2002

The death of the Queen Mother – the after-effects at least – nearly take us off the air in Jerusalem. We are preparing to lead the programme with momentous events here: the Israeli army has reoccupied the West Bank and everywhere is tense and dangerous. But with two hours to go before our broadcast I receive a message from London – 'You must wear a black tie.'

I explain it will be difficult to find one and it also will mean ditching my light suit and (open-necked) denim shirt. 'No matter,' they say, '*find one*.'

Not wanting to be moved down the running order, we ring them back and say, somewhat optimistically, 'You can count on the tie.'

But then they impose a second level of madness. 'You can't lead the programme even if you have a black tie, because it would not be appropriate to wear one in the Middle East.' As I splutter some ineffective protest through my astonishment, the deputy editor comes on the line. 'Kirsty will open the programme. She will do the headlines about Jerusalem, then hand to you. *She has a black dress.* We bought it for her today.'

By this stage we have lost about 45 minutes of vital editing time. I ring the head of television on his mobile. 'Isn't this crazy? Kirsty starting the programme in London with the news from where we are, because she has darker clothes?'

He is reasonable. 'Okay. Wear a black tie and you're the lead.'

There is only one hitch – still no black tie. With half an hour before our broadcast nobody in the bureau can find one. Our cameraman goes into the streets of Jerusalem at past ten British time. He screeches back 20 minutes later. He has found me a tie from a waiter at a nearby hotel. It is black – it's also a clip-on. We agree that if, while we are live, it falls off my collar, it would mean the collapse of BBC News for a generation. Luckily the clip doesn't give.

Later we discovered the Dep. Ed. of *Newsnight* had messaged the Jerusalem bureau chief Simon Wilson with the question, 'If Jeremy wears a black tie on the air from there, will it cause offence to Jews or Muslims?'

*

Greg Dyke had different ideas for the Beeb. His forerunner John Birt had extolled a culture of High Seriousness, where meetings were rammed with specialists and the *Nine O'Clock News* team sounded like the cast of *The Omen* (with a Damien, a Lucian, a Balen and a Damazer). But Dyke came from the opposite pole: he was most worried that we had ended up super-serving the high end of the audience and not giving the vast bulk of licence fee-payers enough to enjoy. Current affairs, the jewel in Birt's crown, was denounced as obscure and inaccessible. Held up high were the self-defeating words of an editor of *Panorama* who had said that so long as the show fulfilled its Birtian remit, 'it doesn't matter if only five people watch it.' The programme was shunted to Sundays.

People who had won awards in the past were described by Dyke as 'Bafta bastards'. Andrew Marr became political editor and caught the moment: the vogue was for news delivered accessibly, with zing, zip and chutzpah. Marr remains the greatest exponent of the live correspondent interview – the 'two-way' – the BBC has ever seen.

The corporate pendulum is on a cycle lasting ten to fifteen years: it swings from authority to access, and back, and forth. In the authority phase, experts dominate. Hard news is the coal in the furnace. In the access phase, Davina McCall is asked to present a documentary on the history of the Stone of Scone because her surname sounds a bit Scottish. The focus shifts to entertainment. Access, authority, access, authority – back and forth it goes over the years, the arc breathtakingly wide, but rarely does anyone even admit there is a pendulum. Instead they pretend we are close to the end destination of a journey that is linear.*

With Greg Dyke in the ascendant, news buzzed with vague possibilities. For example, the embryonic digital channel BBC3 asked me to host a satirical current affairs pilot called *The State We're In*. Although it was never commissioned, the willingness of bosses to have me cross the corridor from *Newsnight* (hyper-serious) to *TSWI* (hyper-silly) suggested freshly elasticated thinking. It was a new world for me: having always been a head-down news person – the owner of only two suits – suddenly I was assigned a lady called Sue to give me a fashion makeover. I wrote down an account of what happened one afternoon while we were together:

20 March 2002

A wonderful collision with Kate Adie yesterday drives home generational differences in a BBC that's been stretched by the G-force of all this sudden change.

* Credit to Mark Thompson for saying once that the Beeb occasionally gets 'old-style religion', meaning it goes back to those high-end values. It was a rare moment, a DG pointing out the pendulum.

I'm trying on a selection of shirts for a satire show on the new BBC3, currently BBC Choice until it gets its licence.

Past the glass-fronted office comes Kate Adie, MFC (most famous correspondent). The sassy, likeable young dresser who's bought the shirts looks on nervously as Kate stops, frowns, enters the room.

'You can't wear pink,' Adie says. 'You look very, very dodgy.'

'And as for that one' – the hapless dresser is holding up another shirt. 'FOR GOD'S SAKE. That looks like a bloody deckchair at Frinton. PUT IT AWAY.'

Collapse of dresser. Victory to the BBC Old Guard. White shirt, blue tie?

It was not the only moment a new wardrobe was needed. One of the strangest musical items ever performed by the newsreaders on the BBC *Children in Need* charity night was a skit on the *Rocky Horror Picture Show,* where I had to play the part of the transvestite Frank-N-Furter in a live song-and-dance routine.

Hidden by a fifteen-foot panel at the back of the stage, having taken up my position shortly after Alice Cooper had cleared the area, I remember thinking I might have been better suited to accountancy. The BBC traineeship had never covered this: the panel suddenly pulling back to reveal me to a whooping studio audience in a lace-up leather corset, fishnet stockings and pink high heels. To my right I saw Michael Buerk beckoning, wearing his newsreader's jacket and swinging his hips in a pair of what looked like silk boxer shorts. He was possibly having the same thought about accountancy (or maybe the Post Office). The routine included Jeremy Bowen, Sophie Raworth and Andrew Marr in leather skirts. Our song, 'Sweet Transvestite', went out live to an audience of millions, and was so utterly bizarre that I still get asked about it today.

Then another peculiar opportunity presented itself. And this really was out of left field. Radio 2 asked me if I would cover the holidays of Jimmy Young. He was at the time eighty, and although I did not know it then, his bosses had been alarmed by an interview he had given in which he said it was his ambition to die at the micro-phone, with his final words being: 'I put it to you, Prime Minister . . .'

Convinced that news people would only thrive under Dyke if they showed willing, I said yes.

The mad minute was about to begin.

Chapter Eighteen

No More Pipe
and Slippers

On the second shelf down from the ceiling in the office of the controller of Radio 2 stood a bronze bust of one of his most distinguished presenters. The head-and-shoulders sculpture, which had a higher eyeline than the controller even when he raised himself from his desk, suggested a certain permanence; rightly, since Jimmy Young had been at the BBC for thirty-five years, for twenty-nine of them doing the same show.

But the controller could match the presenter for size. Jim Moir was one of a handful of people on the production side of the Beeb who achieved legendary status while still employed by the corporation. He was quite the most extraordinary executive I have ever had dealings with.

Not that his career had been smooth. In the era before John Birt arrived, Moir had been Head of Variety for BBC Television: a force in the land, king of all he surveyed, the man smoking the big cigar when Morecambe and Wise and Jimmy Savile were in, or just past, their heyday. He was the kind of executive whom performers love, because he loved performers – a rare breed that includes bosses like Peter Fincham, Michael Grade, Bill Cotton and precious few others.

'Let me have men about me that are fat – sleek-headed men, and such as sleep a'nights,' said Shakespeare's Caesar. The line captured Jim perfectly. But he was caught on the wrong tectonic plate by the arrival of John Birt, who liked his executives lean and hungry. Moir struggled to fit in. He angered some of his colleagues by unilaterally bringing Bruce Forsyth back for another go at *The Generation Game.* He missed the alternative comedy wave because he was not much interested in people swearing at Margaret Thatcher. And there was also the meeting where, with female executives present, he announced: 'It is time to put our cocks on the table and bring out the tape measures.'

Out of fashion and apparently out of time, he was winched from his beloved TV job and given the dual role of Executive for Royal Liaison and Deputy Head of Corporate Affairs. If ever there was a job title that broke the *FT* rule (see page 57), that was it.

This reminds me of my worst social gaffe in the Beeb. Ever. I was telling the story of Jim Moir to Nick Vaughan-Barratt, the executive responsible for Outside Broadcasts. 'Yeah, he was taken out of TV and given the job you do before you get the sack,' I told him somewhat indelicately. 'I think it was Royal Liaison Officer.'

'Blimey,' said Vaughan-Barratt, alarmed. 'That's my job now.'

For Moir, it might easily have been the early bath. Thankfully, it was not to be that way.

*

TV is all about novelty; radio is about familiarity. So radio listeners hate big changes. Station chiefs often think if the change is the right one, listeners will buy it – think again. If the change is big, listeners will hate it. Doesn't matter if it's right or wrong.

The Beeb has learnt this lesson many times. Radio 4 once had a boss called James Boyle who flashed his scalpel over the schedule with a little too much surgical fervour and not enough deference to the most conservative radio audience in the world: there were, to quote Oscar Wilde, riots in Grosvenor Square. I don't know James, but his friends say the senior executives who supported the whole project on paper dropped him overboard when they saw the first puff of gunsmoke. Life is unfair. Boyle had announced publicly that it was time for big changes at Radio 4. The biggest one turned out to be that it lost its controller. He took early retirement.

Radio 1 had its own Big Bang. The Smashie & Nicey generation – DJs like Simon Bates, Dave Lee Travis and Mike Read, who had the jobs on a virtual freehold – were all jettisoned at once. It may have been the right strategy. Yet there was the smack of Ernst Röhm about it; the massacre left the audience spattered with blood. Matthew Bannister, the controller, came under the most extreme pressure. The *Sun* even ran a regular graphic showing the slump in listeners, captioned 'Sliding Down The Bannister'. The station was destabilized for years, and only got back on its feet under Andy Parfitt and an entirely new generation.

In the early nineties there was ominous concern about Radio 2. Funnily enough I remember the mood very precisely because, working down at Westminster at the time, if I ever asked an MP what trick the Beeb was missing, they would always say the same thing:

'Sell off Radio 2. What *is* the point of it?'

And no one could really answer the question. You could almost sense John Birt sitting at his giant hardwood desk, clicking his stress balls*and worrying about what the solution was. It was not as if you could find huge weak links in the chain – Wogan was the maestro at breakfast, and other broadcasters like John Dunn and Gloria Hunniford were still at or near their peaks. But the station as a whole was – here comes that word again – vanilla.

---

* A former executive who kindly read this chapter through for me corrected an important point: 'John Birt never had stress balls.'

The controller was Frances Line. Her music formula was officially summed up in three words: 'melody, excellence, familiarity'. Unofficially that meant Ella Fitzgerald and Mantovani, with Bryan Adams regarded as edgy. The policy was applied rigorously across the network: the producer of the music quiz *Pop Score*, Phil Swern, was rebuked when one of the questions in the quiz revolved around a fifteen-second clip of Status Quo; the controller told him personally that the music was 'too noisy', and even a fifteen-second burst should not have been played. Another producer was given a dressing-down for playing 'Get Off Of My Cloud' by the Rolling Stones at the start of her programme. The objection was sustained even when the producer protested that her show was *Sounds of the Sixties*.

Radio 2 also lacked a narrative. When a station does not create a narrative for itself, others will oblige. The network was duly christened 'pipe and slippers' listening. Three devastating words that said comfort, safety and a pensionable, even dying audience. Some especially cruel souls even threw in the C-word (cardigans).

In a bid to throw its critics off the scent, Radio 2 brought in a confusing new music policy known as 'Wurlitzer and zither'. This required every third record to be slightly eccentric, possibly containing unusual instruments. Of course it made things worse. 'You would be listening to Frank Sinatra,' one producer told me, 'then up would pop a male voice choir.' The station became the aural equivalent of a jumble sale, with a definite ban on loud jumpers.

Frances Line was well liked, a figure from a bygone BBC. Her intentions were good and her manner was courteous. She treated her broadcasters with respect for the most part, although the buck stopped with her when the eminent David Jacobs, the voice of lunchtimes, learnt he had been dropped from his show from an item in the one o'clock news just before he went on air. He commented immediately after, 'Well – that might have come as a shock to you – but not half as much as it did to me,' adding: 'I think I need a large brandy.' The drink was duly brought to the studio, which triggered all kinds of unpleasantnesses that were far from the perfect way to escort a man with five decades in broadcasting to a weekly evening show. Another presenter was summoned to Line's office and handed a letter firing him but was politely asked not to open it in her presence. Ken Bruce – unquestionably in the pantheon of great DJs – was gracelessly moved to a night-time show, and then, after an audience outcry, back to daytime. So the network was trying to find a new position, but it was like watching a game of Twister in a nursing home.

Which is why, in the nineties, the station was giving the top brass a headache and starting to peak on the meter at Westminster.

But the issue was a tricky one. How do you find an answer for a radio station when you're not even sure what the question is?

What was required was a velvet revolution. It needed keyhole surgery rather than a Night of the Long Knives. The whole Radio 2 narrative had to be changed without the upheavals that had crashed Radios 1 and 4.

It was either a job for an exceptional executive, or an undertaker; there were plenty of people who believed the station was in a more terminal condition than its audience. The job of controller was advertised. Three candidates applied. None was inspiring. In his memoirs John Birt portrays his next step as a visionary one – he sent for Jim Moir. But it seems to have been his key radio lieutenant, Liz Forgan, who pressed him to bring Moir in from the cold. Jim had no radio experience whatsoever, and had shown no interest in the job. But Forgan had found him an entertaining presence at meetings.

It is quite possible that Birt saw two possibilities here, and savoured them both. Outside chance? Moir could pull off a miracle. But much more likely, the combination of washed-up manager and washed-out network would conveniently sink them both.

*

If you are a presenter, and you enter a room with Jim Moir, you leave six inches taller.

It may all be baloney; it doesn't matter. The first time I met him he threw his arms out wide and said, in his sonorous, almost operatic bass: 'You may just be the greatest news voice we have ever discovered.' I mentioned 5 live had offered me a show. He replied: 'Why would you open in Huddersfield when you can play the Palladium?'

But I am getting a little ahead of myself. When Jim Moir arrived at Radio 2 in 1996 we had never met and it would be some years before we did. He told his new colleagues, 'A controller should make changes like a porcupine makes love – carefully.' He was determined not to do what James Boyle had done. By putting up in lights the case for huge upheavals, Boyle had only forearmed his enemies. So Moir went softly. He was helped by Terry Wogan's strength at breakfast, which he immediately decided could remain a staple. But the rest was up for grabs.

Ed Stewart was the first to go, replaced by the phenomenal Steve Wright. Listening to Steve is like hearing a cannon fired out of the radio. Brash, funny, one of the industry's greatest innovators, Wright was less pipe and slippers, more Day-Glo Bermuda shorts and spinning bow tie. Ed went gently to Sundays.

With every change, there was a period of consolidation. There would be no Big Bang, but a powerful flare was sent up when Moir brought Johnnie Walker in at 5 p.m. on weekdays. The avuncular John Dunn, an elegant and courteous man who wanted to retire to his home in Majorca, was giving way to a graduate of 1960s pirate radio: authentic, evergreen, iconic. Ken Bruce's morning slot was nailed to the floor. Moir recognized his class.

The station was changing only as fast as the audience allowed it to. But now for the big one. Moir made the inspirational choice of bringing Jonathan Ross in to do a Saturday morning show. The events that followed some years later should not detract from what was, at the time, the key moment of change for Radio 2.

Sometimes a radio show will catch the imagination: Kenny Everett on Capital, Chris Evans on BBC London, and now, Ross on 2. It was so much the opposite of the Frances Line fare that everyone sat up and paid notice. Melody, excellence, familiarity? *Wurlitzer and zither?* No. Ross was rock and roll, the jack-in-the-box, only slightly under control; always surprising; funny; wild; brilliant in his choice of music (Bowie every show) and, even better, was having a personal comeback facilitated by the renaissance of the radio station, so the two forces worked off and magnified each other.

One day Dermot Murnaghan was Ross's guest. It transpired they lived in roughly the same part of London. 'Let's swap phone numbers,' said the very straight Dermot, and they duly did. After he had gone, but still on air, Ross told his sidekick he had 'left a couple of digits out' of the number he gave Murnaghan. Brilliant. Who else would ever say something as subversive as that?

And still the audience did not take flight. The opposite. People began to say, 'Did you hear Radio 2 recently . . .?' and follow up with some story that usually involved mention of Ross. His show, Moir told me later, was 'the gateway' for new listeners. It gave them 'permission to listen'.

In some ways the genius of what Moir did was to give the impression of seismic change while retaining much of the old station. Wogan was vital in this. The breakfast show is fifty per cent of any radio network; Moir was only operating on the other fifty. With his olde-world charm ('You and I must share a lamb chop!'), his political incorrectness (in front of me, to the unmarried newsreader Fran Godfrey: 'What a loss you were to the world of red-blooded men'), not to mention his BBC operating skills . . . well, he was formidable. And while Messrs Boyle and Bannister had crushed their fingers in the lid, Moir played Radio 2 like a grand piano.

But he had not quite finished his remastering of the station. There was one more big daytime show he wanted to overhaul, and with all the diplomatic skills in the world there was no way of being sure it could be done tidily.

Every day Moir was reminded of the task by the bronze bust that gazed imperiously down at him from the shelf opposite his desk. And every day he decided he could wait just a little longer to take action.

Chapter Nineteen

THE LAST
ABSOLUTE MONARCH
IN THE WORLD

It was actually several years before I got the friendly phone call from a producer at Radio 2. Jim Moir's natural caution, his hatred of sacking people, the desire to avoid being Boyled-on-the-Bannister, all meant he operated as gingerly as the escape committee at Colditz. He knew that even crawling towards that lunchtime show on his stomach might set off the searchlights and klaxons.

There was a second reason for the delay. Two separate crises had erupted at the station (I had only dimly noticed them from the office in Africa). One of the dangers of rebuilding a radio network for slightly younger people is that you can get slightly younger persons' problems: Radio 2 had a scandal over on-air drunkenness and, more seriously, cocaine. Illegal drugs had not been on the menu for John Dunn, that was for sure. It would have created chaos to try to displace Jimmy with brushfires elsewhere.

Oh, and there was even a third reason for delay. There was no obvious successor to R2's lunchtime deity. Moir's deputy, Lesley Douglas, wanted Nicky Campbell. But although Jim Moir had met Nicky (famously telling him, 'Only you can move between Gordon Brown and Golden Brown'), he was apparently unpersuaded.

None of which I was remotely aware of – or would have cared much about – when, in 2001, Young's producer Phil Jones rang me and casually asked if I could cover one of his holidays. People cover other people's holidays all the time: it usually means nothing. Besides, from my vantage point on *Newsnight* I had worked out a whole new bag of Rules, chief of which was this one, valuable enough to have a whole page to itself . . .

The stand-in never gets the show.

... Yep, I'm afraid that is a Rule. The least likely person to be the next chief presenter of any programme is the person currently on the rota in the secondary or holiday cover role. By becoming Jeremy and Kirsty's junior, I had effectively cancelled myself out as their possible replacement, something I had been rather slow to grasp.

So to me, popping up as cover for JY (which incidentally Nicky Campbell wisely never did) only meant I was ruling myself out from ever taking over his slot too. Not that there was a vacancy. So far as I knew, there wasn't.

I was completely unaware of the teetering bust.

*

Jimmy Young and I had never met. To this day I still have not met him, which is a shame. All I knew back then was that JY had been the Robbie Williams of his day, topping the charts with songs like 'Unchained Melody' and 'So Young'. His autobiography records how

> I was flavour of the year. Top theatres were clamouring for my services. In Derby fans threw red roses onto the stage and police had to be called out to control the crowds ... the euphoria also led to me landing a starring role in my first pantomime.

But the year was 1955. Along came Elvis and killed his singing career stone dead. Jimmy smartly relaunched himself as a DJ, first on Radio 1, then 2. More through a series of accidents than design, he brought current affairs into his popular daily shows and created a formula – pop records and prime ministers – that somehow captured the heart of the BBC's purpose as it had loftily been described, long ago, in words attributed to Lord Reith: 'To give the public something better than what they now think they like.'

Young so successfully captured the zeitgeist that Pink Floyd's opening line in the song 'One Of These Days' – where Nick Mason growls, 'One of these days I'm going to cut you into little pieces' –

was rumoured to be a veiled threat against the presenter for talking too much. On stage, Floyd would play a random collage of Jimmy's words and phrases when they performed it.

He also captured the imagination of politicians. The first thing I noticed when I went to prepare for my opening appearance as JY's stand-in at Western House in Great Portland Street, London, was that the wall of his tatty production office was jammed with photos of every famous political leader in recent world history. They were all black-and-white, if not sepia. Young had not only interviewed Mrs Thatcher fourteen times. He seemed to have spoken to everyone else as well.

There is something joyous about doing news in a non-news setting. Radio 2 is basically an entertainment network, so the news guests have to join a queue behind showbiz stars and musicians. In a truly beautiful moment, the King of Norway appeared in reception. The receptionist rang upstairs to inform Jimmy's producers, then pressed her palm to the telephone mouthpiece and asked the royal visitor: 'Excuse me. Sorry. Where did you say you were king of again?'

And it made me laugh a little, arriving in the Radio 2 production office. I was going to be playing records on the radio just as I did for that fleeting segment on Kenny Everett's show in 1978. In the quarter-century since, I had done newspapers, journalism, newscasting, writing, even war reporting – everything but play music. And I love music.

Doing the show as holiday relief for the first time was like going back in time. The *Jimmy Young Programme* had pre-dated the radio phone-in, and also somehow overtaken it. A long time ago, during an interview with Geoffrey Howe, an angry member of the public had called the BBC switchboard who put her through to the production office. As the interview with Howe chugged on, the listener berated a producer about him. The producer noted the comments and then – here is the stroke of genius – *she brought them through to the studio.*

At that point Young said, 'Well, I have just been handed what I gather is a note of an angry call we've had downstairs,' and read it to Howe. With some discomfort, he responded. Thus was the *Jimmy Young Programme* audience-participation format born, light years ahead of its time. And it never really changed. Phone-ins arrived separately, on other stations – no caller's voice would ever be heard on JY. For a while it sounded old-fashioned compared to the likes of LBC, just having a presenter read those comments off scraps of paper; but then suddenly, in the nineties, the world was full of text and email and every presenter was reading audience comments off small pieces of paper.

The production office remained old-fashioned. The numbers for contacts were still kept on a card index system. One day I flicked through those dog-eared cards. AUDREY WHITING, SUNDAY MIRROR was manually typed on one, alongside 'Journalist specialising in the Royal Family'. Listed were the dates Whiting had appeared on the show: March 1978, June 1982, March 1986. Disconcertingly, at the top of the card someone had written: 'May be DEAD'.*

But JY was still hugely relevant. He had been first; then last; then first again. Even as an eighty-something, by the time Radio 2 rang me, the veteran was sounding as significant as ever. His voice was an actor's and had lost none of its power. To repeat a somewhat bawdy description of the late American senator Lloyd Bentsen, his balls clanked.

The first holiday week went fine. Actually it was a lot of fun. I brought in some of my own CDs – *The Queen Is Dead* by the Smiths, *Life's a Riot with Spy vs Spy* by Billy Bragg, Carole King's *Tapestry*, *The Lamb Lies Down on Broadway* by Genesis, *Parklife* by Blur (I know this sounds like an odd combination) – and embraced the music as much as the interviewing. The listener comments were a revelation: rarely were we exposed to anything so raw and real on

* In fact Audrey Whiting was still alive when I saw this card. She died seven years later, on 6 January 2009.

Newsnight. It would never become a full-time job; so what? A long line of people had stood in. One, Susannah Simons, did Young's holiday relief a full fifteen years earlier and confided to me that she thought back then that she had timed it about right for his retirement. For now, for me, it was just a week of Jimmy's annual leave, a chance to get out from under the broiling lights of television while he relaxed in the sun in Florida. So far as I was concerned, Jimmy was eighty, had done thirty-five years behind a BBC microphone, and would still be broadcasting at the age of a hundred.

That is what a lot of presenters think, by the way – they think they will go on forever. Which, more than anything else, is the tragedy of the presenter's career; and it is a tragedy that is only magnified by greatness.

*

Besides, I was having fun on *Newsnight* now. The programme was still my main – in fact only – job. Most of the time I was back in that hygienic open-plan office in Television Centre, prepping interviews for the evening's broadcast or rushing out of the building and back with film crews to grab interviewees who could be reached in an afternoon.

The editor George Entwistle had skilfully managed the Jeremy/Jeremy situation in such a way that any imagined tension with Paxo had dissipated, or was moot; so I reckoned. I was engaged to be married to the beautiful Rachel. I was out of the sad bedsit and into a happy terrace in Hammersmith. And *Newsnight* was not just an enthralling learning curve for this presenter. It kept me on the road with a camera, too.

It also got me back to Africa one more time.

With producer Mary Wilkinson I went to Swaziland. The mountainous kingdom, landlocked by South Africa and Mozambique, is one of the poorest countries on the planet. It also has one of the highest Aids rates.

How bad is it? Well, in 2000 life expectancy was sixty-one. By 2009 the average Swazi lived to the age of thirty-two.

When we went there, near the start of that sickening downward curve, half of all pregnant women were already HIV-positive. Traditional Swazi culture dictates that women should have many children – five is the expected number – and men should have multiple partners. It is understandable, in that it's supposed to enlarge the population and spread life. But it does the exact opposite.

I was telling the world affairs editor John Simpson how we had seen a sign on a church which read: JESUS IS COMING. SWAZIS ARE NOT READY. 'Those poor bastards,' he sighed, with feeling.

Our film was about the King of Swaziland, who seemed unaffected by the disaster unfolding in his country. True, he had reintroduced a chastity rite, *umcwasho*, which banned sex for any Swazi virgin under fifty for five years from September 2001 (imagine a politician proposing that one in Britain). But he then violated his own decree by taking a teenager as his sixth wife.

As one of the last absolute monarchs in the world, with the power to hire and fire the entire government as well as the country's judges, King Mswati III did not exactly face opposition. His father, King Sobhuza II, had been on the Swazi throne for eighty-two years and nine months – the longest reign by any monarch in history – and had passed the time by taking seventy wives who bore him two hundred and ten children. Possibly Mswati III felt he was living a life of royal restraint by comparison. But he was brazen enough to continue the tradition of the annual Reed Dance, where young maidens from all over the country disported themselves for their monarch. We had to film it.

So in a field near the capital, we arrived to shoot several thousand topless young Swazi women who congregated to try to catch the eye of the King. Some assignments are harder than others. Despite the gaiety, there was a heavy-duty undertow: if the Sherborne-educated monarch chose a virgin or two, they would become his seventh (and eighth) wives. Given that abstinence and monogamy were two defences against HIV, the King was not exactly getting with the pro-gramme.

It was one of those days. Sun, scenery, fantastic colleagues (Mark McCauley on camera, Steve Rapley editing) and a combination of beauty and sadness: the Aids rate so disastrous, and the treatment so non-existent, that many of the hyper-excited young women pressing in on us to be interviewed will now be dead from the disease.

The King held a news conference. We were amazed to see that the Swazi journalists had to stand up when he entered the room – and then get down *on their knees* in front of him when he started to speak. I thought of Alastair Campbell for some reason.

A friend, Alex, rang. 'I can't speak,' I whispered, 'because I am with the King of Swaziland.' I heard him roar with laughter as I muted the handset.

Mswati III was, of course, charming to us when he gave us our interview (the pulling power of the BBC worldwide is extraordi-nary). His explanation of the reason he required a harem was a lengthy lecture on tradition. When I asked him why he also needed a private jet costing the same as his country's entire healthcare system, he said any decision to buy it would be made after consul-tation with ministers which had not yet happened; of course he got his plane, not long after we boarded ours. Clearly monarchs aren't monarchs unless they treat themselves occasionally. And as for absolute monarchs . . .

The story summed up the joy of the reporter's life. Away from the urgent trill of the office phone, off the news beat, just exploring. Breaking ground. Being paid to have adventures: that is journalism. To the gentleman who told us in an earlier chapter that 'News is a picture of your own baby', I would have put my foot down and replied that it is actually a picture of Swazi babies. Real news is as far as possible and as different as possible from our own lives.

But Radio 2 was very different. There were not many mentions of obscure African kings around the nation's parish pump.

I came back to fill for JY a second time, then a third, still unaware of what was going on backstage. And I was amazed by the way the team took their cue almost entirely from the audience. The story about a paedophile babysitter triggered a response from mums that was full of primal fear. Smoking, speeding and swearing came up again and again. The closest we got to a foreign story was an item on immigration.

Dog attacks, hanging, soldiers with kit shortages, pensions, mortgages, discourtesy, health and safety, the weather, the Euro. Profound stories on sexuality, religion, race: but always done from the perspective of listener experience. Professors of this-or-that were frowned on. An expert in ladders was someone who had fallen off one. It was what editors used to call 'news you can use', and it was an agenda driven at us by the audience rather than the other way round. Plus, of course, there was the music.

It started to dawn on me: *The audience have better stories than we do.*

From Swaziland to the Smiths. If the news world were built as a city, *Newsnight* to Radio 2 would be an impossible jump between the tops of the two tallest buildings in the neighbourhood.

*

I had made friends with an agent. Alex Armitage of Noel Gay – the one who rang during King Mswati – had a theatrical pedigree. His grandfather had written 'The Sun Has Got His Hat On'. But Alex was branching into the world of news. As a BBC staff person there was not much I could offer him, but there was a lot he could offer me. He saw the problem on *Newsnight*. And he saw the opportunity on Radio 2.

Alex was an old friend of Jim Moir. One day he rang me with what sounded like a direct question from Moir himself: 'If you were to be offered Jimmy Young's show, what would the answer be?'

'Blimey,' I said. 'Is that for real?'

'I think it is for real,' said Alex. 'Jimmy may be leaving Radio 2.'

'Does Jimmy know that?'

'Not exactly, no.'

'Well – I ...' *The last absolute monarch in the world*, I thought. Here was that rare breed, a presenter more powerful than his own executives. 'Yes, of course.' Nothing wrong with being interested.

One day I finished sitting in for Jimmy and the phone went. It was Jim Moir himself. 'I have been in a car heading' – he paused – 'north. And so I have been listening to you for the last two hours. And I have only this to say to you, young Jeremy. Be patient and we will reach our destination.'

I still did not believe it. Jimmy came from an era when the talent owned the stage. Presenters of my generation wake up and go to bed believing they will imminently be sacked. We understand the importance of humiliation. But earlier generations never seemed even to buy the concept of executives – they had managers, of course, but their job was simply to pay heating and lighting bills and make sure the microphones were connected and programme schedules got to the *Radio Times*. Early talent was so powerful in part because the birth of TV and radio gave the first wave of presenters a vice-like grip on unimaginably big audiences. An early-generation broadcaster who got the sack would plead, 'Why not another year?' whereas a nineties-era presenter would respond: 'Why not *last* year?'

There was no intimation whatsoever that Jimmy was planning to leave, or even that he suspected he was planning to leave. I was on *Newsnight*. He was still at the crease, day after day, slogging fours and sixes on a show that really did not sound tired at all.

Looking back, I suppose he might have read some of the signs. On one occasion he had crossed the street to greet Jim Moir. When the controller saw Young, Moir pressed his handkerchief to his face and uttered muffled words about a heavy cold before rushing off.

The editor Phil Jones was full of loyal praise. JY's feel for the audience was 'incredible', he said. His preparation was meticulous – since Jimmy Young's background was singing on a stage, before each programme he would stand in the studio and practise reading out loud the questions the producers had written for him. Those questions were scripted and read so precisely they would even contain phrases such as: 'Ah, but you see ...' or 'Right, well now I want to change tack a little ...' but somehow the presenter made them sound spontaneous and conversational.

And when Jimmy was on form, he was the best. Soon after I arrived at Westminster the corridors had buzzed with a knockdown, drag-out interview John Major had done on Radio 2, where he completely walked into the punch: 'People respected Mrs Thatcher,' Young told Major, 'but they laugh at you.' There had been talk that Major was going on JY to get an easy ride – afterwards Alastair Campbell said, 'Whichever BBC source suggested Jimmy Young is a soft interviewer clearly knows nothing about interviewing, and even less about Jimmy Young.'

One day he interviewed Tony Blair. As always he followed the scripted questions to the letter until he suddenly looked up at him and said: 'Do you know, Prime Minister, your last answer was very interesting, because I counted and you used the word "if" no fewer than eleven times.'

Blair was utterly stumped.

Still, something was up. At the back end of 2001 the controller's deputy, Lesley Douglas, asked me for coffee in the Heights Hotel bar as part of what I guess was a gentle introduction to the station. Like Moir, she exuded a larger-than-lifeness and had a different kind of brain to the typical news animal. Her phone buzzed with a text from Bruce Springsteen's guitarist. Lesley liked her stars as loud and ritzy as possible, so I must have seemed a bit like a postman coming for a job as a lion-tamer. But she was into presenters and understood how their minds worked and how to motivate them. She dealt in primary colours and bold brushstrokes. Later she would be accused of not having enough grip on the details; the professional tragedy which would befall her because of a two-second outburst that came to be known as 'Ross–Brand' was still some years down the track.

So here we all were. The upstart *Newsnight* presenter with a need for direction. The controller and his deputy with a job to do. The agent. The producer. And the octogenarian national treasure, one of the last absolute presenters in the world, who must have sensed shapes shifting beyond the window. It was a bit like that moment of unbearable tension in the Agatha Christie, where everyone takes their places just before the murder happens.

None of us could have predicted that it would be the behaviour of another person entirely that would start the action.

Chapter Twenty

THE PRICE OF
LAMB CHOPS

Nicky Campbell was watching events at Radio 2 with, I think, some concern. So far as the 5 live host was concerned, his pedigree as DJ-turned-journo made him a shoo-in for the job. On paper he was certainly correct. Plus, Lesley Douglas had made it clear to Campbell that he was her choice. For him the situation was just perfect. He could wait it out on 5 live and, at a suitable moment, almost certainly one chosen by Jimmy himself, the crown would simply drop into his lap.

Not only a very flexible broadcaster, Nicky was also part of a revolution. Traditionally, news presenters were chosen from the ranks of distinguished correspondents who had been there, done it and got the T-shirt. The BBC core used to give people like me a very clear message that, if they wanted to present news at the top level, they had to get their shoes dusty around the world and preferably hear gunfire. Krishnan Guru-Murthy had counselled me in the nineties, 'You need bottom.' Krish subsequently grew, journalistically speaking, quite a large one. Horrocks, Sambrook, Entwistle, Damazer, Ayre, Mitchell,

Mosey, Marsh, Thompson, Cramer, Boaden, Hall – name any in that long line of turbo-editors stretching back through the years and they would probably have told a reporter like me to stay on the road for as long as possible. Foreign and political news were particularly recommended for cultivating a stupendous rear end.

So when I arrived back from Africa I was pulled up short. Nicky Campbell now appeared to be the leading news presenter – he had even been given those shifts fronting *Newsnight* – and he had got there via Radio 1 and a game show called *Wheel of Fortune*.

In minding about this, I was being old-fashioned and a bit of a clot. The BBC was simply doing what it does best: changing. The change had all come about because the pendulum we mentioned had swung to the access quadrant under Greg Dyke. I suspect that Dyke absolutely loved the fact that he was blitzing all that high-minded Birtian ideology and completely rebooting the notion of the news CV. And no question, Campbell had personality and talent. Now that his abilities were being recognized on a broader stage, there was even talk that Dyke wanted him to replace David Dimbleby on *Question Time*.

Come to think of it, I reckon Greg Dyke probably felt threatened by traditional news types. In any multi-genre broadcasting organization, the only bunch of people more frightening than the news team are the comedy department.

How painful it must have been for Greg that, in the end, the mis-broadcast of a single news story is what did for him.

*

Anyway. As well as being a highly adaptable broadcaster, Nicky Campbell is smart. He could see what was happening across the pond at R2. Jim Moir's doubts had coagulated and blocked him. Moir had been heard to say, 'Nicky is white bread; we need wholemeal.' I had simply fallen through the ceiling at the perfect moment.

So Nicky did a surprising thing. He gave an interview in the *Daily*

Telegraph where he announced he was turning down Jimmy Young's job because he would rather stay at 5 live. He must have caught the reporter on an off-day, because nothing he said was subjected to any scepticism whatsoever. I just happened to open the paper one morning and saw this:

I WAS OFFERED THE JIMMY YOUNG SLOT BUT TURNED IT DOWN

NICKY CAMPBELL *tells Nigel Reynolds why the veteran's job is safe, for now*

JIMMY YOUNG, the most famous and mellifluous voice on BBC Radio 2, can sleep sounder tonight – and perhaps for a few more nights to come.

Nicky Campbell, the best-known voice of Radio 5 live, has turned down an offer that would have had him switching stations and replacing Young.

After being assiduously courted behind Young's back, Campbell sent an email to Jim Moir, Radio 2's controller, at around 6pm yesterday, thanking him for his interest but telling him that, after a long hard think, he prefers to carry on presenting his Radio 5 morning show 'at the cutting edge of current affairs,' as he puts it, to moving to 'the green pastures' of Radio 2 . . .

Young himself, a broadcaster of more than 50 years' standing whose contract runs out in March, has said that he wants to die with his microphone on and will not be budged. Consistently the Radio 2

line has been that he will not be 'sacked', and that nobody has been offered his job.

But, speaking yesterday, Campbell, a 40-year-old Scot who started as a DJ at Capital Radio, then Radio 1, testified otherwise.

'They first came to me 18 months ago and asked me if I would consider moving. I said I would, and we have been talking ever since.

'They wanted me to take my show over to Radio 2, and they have formally offered me the job. Everything has been discussed except the salary. They said that was the one thing they couldn't talk about until I said yes.'

The courtship has been intense. Campbell says Moir and his deputy, Lesley Douglas, have visited him at his home in Balham, south London, and there have been talks over champagne in out-of-the-way hotels and restaurants.

1st Nov 2001

Nicky went on to say the problem with the Radio 2 job was that he would have to play music – and he was a journalist. 'I'm a news junkie and [on 5 live] I don't have to stop the show suddenly to play a record by Phil Collins,' he said. The next line of the interview was devastating of Radio 2 in a way that seemed almost accidental:

> 'Since September 11, particularly, I thought: my God, there I'd be interviewing politicians or generals, but then if I had to slip off to play The Carpenters, I'd be pulling my hair out.'

He could be forgiven for not noticing that Moir's new playlist policy had resulted in far fewer outings for 'We've Only Just Begun'. Nigel Reynolds then added that Radio 2 was seen as 'a backwater' in the BBC (others thought it was Europe's most listened-to station) and that moving there might prevent Campbell taking over *Panorama* or *Newsnight*. Nicky continued: 'Some people I consulted said that I was the natural heir to Jimmy Young. But it has also been indicated to me by people high up that things like *Panorama* would be less available to me. Some BBC executives said to me: "Aren't you a bit young to retire?"'

He would be renewing his existing contract at 5 live, he explained. 'It's just fiddling about with a few zeros.' And then the most brutal quote of the lot:

> 'Jimmy Young is an institution and absolutely brilliant, but his show is still a bit about the price of lamb chops. The programme is Radio 2's gesture to current affairs. It's not at the cutting edge of current affairs.'

The piece concluded by saying that either Jimmy Young could be kept on, or the job could be offered to Jeremy Vine, 'who is thought to be number two on the list'.

I remember reading it in a café early one morning and not noticing the coffee had missed my mouth and gone down my trousers. As I got back up off the floor my phone went. It was Lesley.

'Have you bloody seen it?'

'Yup.'

She came out with a fabulous range of expletives, some of which were only available in her home town of Sunderland. Then she apologized to me, which was gracious if unnecessary. None of it was her fault.

My friend Mark Lawson – the BBC arts man and *Guardian* columnist – rang next and told me it was 'disastrous for you because you cannot take the job. He has completely poisoned it. If you take it, you will look like the second choice.'

I replied, 'Can you please not sugarcoat it?'

The worst thing about the whole situation from Radio 2's point of view was that Jimmy now knew for a fact that his bosses were moving against him, and he suddenly looked like the injured party. So now he was able to fight back. Those shapes outside the window were not imaginary.

Jimmy hired lawyers and a renowned public relations officer – as he had every right to. They must have hit the ground running, for the very next day the *Daily Mail* had a huge banner across the top of its front page, in a bigger typeface than the name of the newspaper, which screamed: **SAVE JIMMY YOUNG**. People as far apart as Roy Hattersley and Richard Littlejohn converged to assist his cause. There was an Early Day Motion in the House of Commons calling on Radio 2 to change its plans.

For Moir this was a nightmare. All his careful manoeuvring had been shot to bits. It was the first and only time I ever saw him lack self-assurance. He asked me to do the job, assuring me that Nicky Campbell had never been offered it and the whole thing had been a huge misunderstanding (it may have been, it may not – it hardly matters now). Nicky had blundered but I could see why he had done what he did. These things do happen. He has had many successes since.

To add to the sense of farce, the *Times* columnist David Aaronovitch now weighed in. He was on the list of people who had sat in during JY's holidays at some point – which by this stage must have included half the population of the UK – and his column in the *Independent* was published under the headline: **WHY I SHOULD REPLACE JIMMY YOUNG.**

Aaronovitch – a former BBC executive with a kind manner and enormous brain, who had been a Birtian fundamentalist but then lost his way – had been hugely miffed that someone (in fact Moir) had briefed that he was 'more Hampstead than Hampshire'. This is what he wrote:

On radio, at any rate, I think I am a decent broadcaster with an acceptable voice. And – on my day – I can be better than good. So when Matthew Bannister, the former BBC head of radio, writes in The Times that Young's 'successor has the formidable challenge of replacing a true broadcasting institution', I feel I can do this. Not by ditching the Young format, but by evolving it.

So why won't it happen? Because I am too highbrow. I am a pointy-head. I cannot commune with the common weal. My natural habitat is the Oxford common room, the minimalist kitchen or the Tuscan farmhouse. This, at least, is how I interpret the words of a 'Radio 2 insider' who said (with reference to me) that the station 'must reach out to Hampshire, not just Hampstead'.

After reading the column Moir guffawed: 'I don't know if that was a resignation letter or a job application.'

Jimmy struck back powerfully. He told the papers that the talk of replacing him 'is indeed speculation as I am not intending to retire. My ratings are higher than ever and I have increased my audience considerably over the past year. I am flattered that my success has made so many people desperate to get my job, but I have no plans to leave it.'

And then this, an open challenge to his bosses:

'Unless of course, in the ageist pursuit of youth, someone decides to ignore my record-breaking ratings and fire me.'

We were well into the Mad Minute now. Jimmy was going to fight, as he had every right to. A senior figure at Radio 2 confided that he would be getting a knighthood which would 'help sort everything out' – but it did the opposite. This is the *Daily Mail*'s exclusive which broke the news of the honour (my italics are to draw attention to the glories of the fifth paragraph):

THE ACCOLADE is a stunning recognition ... after a year in which Young was deeply hurt and unsettled by a BBC move to 'retire' him.

Thousands of listeners complained and a question was tabled in Parliament after Radio 5 presenter Nicky Campbell claimed he had been offered Young's job.

The Daily Mail also launched a campaign to keep him at the microphone.

The BBC, severely embarrassed, told Young they wanted him to stay and invited him to name his own terms. He is understood to be holding out for a long run of at least two years. His current 12-month contract expires in March.

Radio 2 controller Jim Moir sought and was given the blessing of Director-General Greg Dyke to 'save Jimmy Young'.

The impending knighthood will make resolving the dispute a top priority for both men. Young maintained a dignified silence throughout the controversy, saying only that he thanked all of his supporters. In the past he has expressed a wish to die with his headphones on.

If anything, the richly deserved knighthood – tactlessly described by the BBC staff magazine *Ariel* as 'a crowning moment towards the end of a distinguished career' – only made JY more determined to face down his bosses.

It seemed that everyone involved had been damaged: not only Jimmy, but Nicky, and me, and Jim Moir and Lesley. And the audience, crucially: a favourite piece of furniture was not just being removed from their living room, it was being chopped into pieces to get it through the door.

Things settled down. With lawyers involved and – I gather – not a huge amount of good feeling, in 2002 Jimmy agreed to move to a Sunday show at the year end.

During all of this, I got an email at home which made me sit bolt upright.

From Jeremy Paxman's personal address to mine? But when I clicked to open it, I saw just a random series of letters and numbers: *Gazqq2=orn37621 g/h**idc345.*

I replied, 'Jeremy – got your email but can't understand it. Do you want to re-send?'

My fellow *Newsnight* presenter wrote, 'No, sorry, it's a virus that got into my computer and sent garbage to everyone in my address book. Apologies.'

He then added:

> I hear you've been offered Jimmy Young's job. Can I be
> your agent?

Sensing the opportunity for a smart reply in an all-too-rare moment of light-hearted communication between us, I fired back:

> You can be my agent Jeremy if you give up all your
> other jobs.

I sat there feeling a little too pleased at my joke, and then the email icon buzzed again. Jeremy Paxman had written:

> I can't think handling your career would take up too
> much of my time.

To firm up the arrangement, Alex Armitage and Moir had a meeting which lasted a whole morning under which it was agreed I would leave *Newsnight* (incidentally quitting the staff of the BBC – gulp), and sign a two-year contract to work at Radio 2 for a daily rate paid gross. Thus was a job-for-life exchanged with the fragile existence of the freelance. The personnel department would soon send me a letter saying, with typically casual cruelty: 'We are sorry to hear you have decided to leave the BBC.' But I never had any doubt it had to be done.

After agreeing the terms Moir, a staunch Catholic, surprised Alex by walking him at first not to a restaurant, but to a church. 'Let us go into this place and give thanks,' Moir said as they crossed the threshold, 'for we have done a wonderful thing.'

*

But it was still, officially at least, a secret. Somehow the trauma of the Mad Minute had left the controller reluctant to say anything in public ever again about his lunchtime legend. So through 2002 I worked on *Newsnight*, aware that I was going off to radio, but unable to tell anyone.

The *Newsnight* editor clearly needed to know. I gave George Entwistle the whole story one day, exactly as I have just described it to you. There were moments where we could barely speak for laughing. Obviously he needed to find a successor – someone else willing to have their head turned to pumpkin mash for a couple of years – but an executive in another part of the building leaked to the *Guardian* that I would be replaced by Andrew Neil.

For me, Andrew has been the revelation presenter of the past decade, but at the time his *Sunday Times* associations were still fresh and so the news caused some small turbulence on *Newsnight*. Entwistle held a staff meeting to explain the situation – I would be leaving in a few months; whoever replaced me had not yet been selected.

Afterwards, an understanding dawned.

I said to George, 'Do you realize what happened there? You just made the announcement that Radio 2 have been trying not to make for about a year.'

So I picked up the phone to Moir and explained. The *Newsnight* editor had told the whole team I was going to Radio 2. These people were journalists. They live to spread news. This, surely, was not a secret any more.

There was a moment where I could almost hear his mind turn. Finally the great Radio 2 controller's voice boomed back down the line.

'We have laid down a barrage. We must now make our way carefully through it.'

I was duly photographed with Moir the following day. The deal was announced to as little fanfare as possible. JY did not publicly complain, although he would later decide against going to the Sunday show he had been offered and open a whole new front on the BBC because of what he called its 'brutality'.

For now, it was almost as if everyone involved in the drama was too exhausted to fight any more.

*

For the next few months I was showing up for my *Newsnight* shifts just as the iconic JY, by now an 81-year-old knight, worked out his own notice. Still the two of us never met. A 44-year gap in the age of two presenters is more than a generational change. I left Sir Jimmy a bottle of red wine one day, with a note suggesting a late lunch and politely stressing my admiration. He sent me a courteous handwritten reply declining: 'I gave up lunching about forty years ago, which is just as well because, as no doubt you will discover, lunching is impossible anyway.' I couldn't read the tone. Hurt? Probably. Angry? Certainly. Angry with me? But this had all been very random from my point of view.

And that is one Rule to emerge from all of this. *A career at the Beeb is actually just a series of accidents.* There is no Hand, I decided. There never was.

As the time got closer, I was told to report at Radio 2 for rehearsals. One day I got there slightly early, and keenly texted Phil Jones. 'Shall I come up? I could meet JY.' That day's live show was just ending.

'Could you please wait on street until he is gone. Best to keep a low profile at the mo, thanks,' Phil replied.

Low profile? Where had I heard that before? I stood on the street outside Radio 2, a warm mobile in my pocket, feeling happier and luckier than I had ever felt in my life.

But it must have been so hard for the great Sir Jimmy to prepare for the departure he had fought against for so long. One morning, a few months before the end of 2002, the production staff heard a yell in the office and found that Jimmy had fallen to the floor in agony. His hip had broken. Not his original hip, but the replacement he had had installed some years before. He was in great pain.

They rushed over. 'We'll get you an ambulance straightaway.'

The BBC nurse was summoned. Then Jim Moir, full of reassurance. 'We will organize the best care. Even now the ambulance is on its way.'

But Sir Jimmy's question was not about the paramedics.

'Who'll do my programme?'

'Ken Bruce can extend his,' said Moir.

From the floor Sir Jimmy replied: 'It's his big moment.'

Now that's a star.

Chapter Twenty-One

MADE IN HEAVEN

On 14 September 2002, I married my beloved Rachel. Perhaps we should have parked the *Newsnight* Van outside the church in Tipton St John, Devon – so many people had reminded me how I 'found love in the van' that I had actually begun to believe the story myself. It was a beautiful sunny day without a single cloud in the sky. The South Africans I had worked with – Milton Nkosi and his wife Dorcas, Tony Wende, Glenn Middleton – came to rural Devon, which was a thrill. Milton did the reading. Rachel put her arm round me at the altar, and my mum cried.

Back at *Newsnight*, I was in the final weeks. With programme departures there is a BBC tradition. A sudden cash crisis is blamed for the fact that you cannot have a leaving party, the news is broken to the departer apologetically, and then somehow the party happens anyway. When the economics boffin Evan Davis had left the programme a year earlier I was told there could be no leaving party for him unless it was held in my home – the idea sold to me on the basis that 'you've just bought it, you have no furniture, and you can combine it with a housewarming' – so the event was indeed held there and Evan and I bought the beer and wine ourselves. *Newsnight* scraped together the cash to provide some tomato soup.

My own leaving party was an even more threadbare affair than Evan's. Again there had been a sudden cash crisis, caused (as before) by News Stories We Had Not Been Expecting; I won't return to the theme of previous chapters and point out there is no other type of news story. Still, if the War on Terror had a higher claim on the *Newsnight* budget than my leaving do, that at least was a sign the system was working properly.

A celebration area was booked – for a freezing winter night – in a pub garden in north London. The lone outdoor heater was faulty.

It was the only leaving party I have ever been to where people put on their coats *after* arriving. When we had gathered, a farewell video was shown on a screen rigged up beside a tree which the pub regulars could see through a window.

God knows what they made of what was on that tape. The rather unkind theme was that to become a Radio 2 presenter you needed to wear an ill-fitting toupée. So when Jeremy Paxman appeared in my *Newsnight* leaving video, shot in the studio and broadcast to that pub garden, he wore the most preposterous piece of brown carpet on his head and made a series of hilarious announcements about my career (or lack of it).

At this point you have to imagine the scene from the point of view of the average pub customer. You go to your local for a drink on a Friday and you sit on a bench by the window. Nothing out of the ordinary is happening. You are talking to a friend but you begin to notice that – despite it being a freezing December night – a group of animated people, some young, some middle-aged, have insisted on socializing outside. You see a couple of them busying themselves over the positioning of a suspended TV screen which is powered through the use of two extension cables. Your gaze is drawn to that screen. The people outside suddenly stop talking to each other as the monitor flickers into life.

And as you – the pub regular – watch that screen yourself, you see the country's greatest current affairs presenter appear in the *Newsnight* studio wearing a wig the size of Belgium.

Standing with my colleagues, I watched and laughed. Behind Paxo, a *Newsnight* graph purported to show how my insatiable ambition had grown and grown until I was now eighty-one. Incidentally, there was not a shred of bad feeling that I could detect. Jeremy had called in personally on my last shift to wish me well, which I appreciated.

George Entwistle made a sweet speech in which he quoted embarrassing love scenes from a comic novel about the Church of England which I had written about a thousand years earlier, and then I had to say something. I thought I was looking at nervous faces for a second, almost as if my colleagues expected me to erupt into denunciations in the style of one of those nightmare wedding speeches; and then I checked, and realized that what I could see in their expressions was sympathy.

Standing there at my own leaving party – setting a new record as the youngest presenter ever to depart *Newsnight* – I thought of Sargie: *You want to be the oldest.*

I thanked everyone and said my time with the greatest current affairs show had been full of surprises, recounting the night the computers dramatically flashed up 'ENTWISTLE DEAD' ten minutes into the programme. We thought it meant *Newsnight* had lost its editor; in fact The Who had lost their bassist. Oh, and also how we had to reshoot a piece-to-camera while filming with the *Newsnight* Van in the Scottish Highlands. The cameraman Frank Considine had tutted as he reviewed the first take, and said: 'Nope, sorry, we can't use that Jeremy. As I panned the camera, my copy of the *AA Good Hotel Guide* came into view on the dashboard.'

And then I was gone. The job I had always coveted, and I left at thirty-seven. Like a plane coming in at too acute an angle, glancing off stormcloud, overshooting the runway. My replacement was Gavin Esler.

*

So the road that led to Radio 2 was, if I can borrow a phrase from four of its heroes, long and winding.

That Christmas I began to clock just how big the new job would be. *Newsnight* was *Newsnight*, but even its top dog had to share the stage with other breeds. The same, for that matter, with *5 live Breakfast*. But the presenter of the Radio 2 lunchtime show had their name in the neon. *The Jimmy Young Programme. The Jeremy Vine Show.* Clues to just how much expectation was building around the change came in a slew of articles about Sir Jimmy, about the station, about whether it could survive his departure, about whether I was adaptable enough to move through different weight classes – like a boxer trimming from heavyweight to welterweight.

The *Independent* quoted a 'news insider' saying, 'This is a big gamble for him. He didn't like working alongside Paxman, and he knew if he stayed on *Newsnight* he would always be in his shadow. But you wonder if he's not walking out of the frying pan into the fire by taking over the Jimmy Young slot.'

Free of the BBC's embrace, JY became freshly indignant. He helped draw attention to the changing of the guard by suggesting the licence fee should be abolished because of the 'brutal' way he had been treated; his intervention raised the stakes, and my nervousness. In the newspapers he seemed determined to wage war on his former boss. 'Their efforts to fire me started five years ago with the arrival of a new controller, Jim Moir,' he wrote in the *Sunday Express*. 'He made it clear, in a friendly manner over a nice lunch, that part of his brief was to find the next generation of Radio 2 broadcasters.' I could hardly imagine a line better designed to turn millions of listeners against the replacement. No wonder Jimmy had an aversion to lunches.

After the article appeared Moir rang me, all reassurance. 'There will be what we call audience churn. We will be strong. All I say to you Jeremy is, "Be warm." We need *warmth* more than anything.' He laced the word with meaning. It was good advice. That particular iron was not in the caddy's bag on *Newsnight*.

Another indication of how serious this all was: Moir had been about to retire, and his retirement had been delayed by at least a year so he could manage the new show. Oh, and one more – among dozens of articles were some profiles of me. Information in them, I discovered, always comes as a shock to the profiled person, even though it is their own life that is being described. One piece in the *Independent* revealed that in the eighties I had been 'barred from the *Today* programme's in-house rock band for being too clean-cut', which was more devastating than anything else I read. Most of the articles asked whether Paxo's number two could become Radio 2's number one. I wish I could have answered with any conviction.

Just before the new programme started, the BBC marketing department spent a humungous sum putting large images of me in a grey jumper across what seemed like – and may even have been, in an advertising recession – at least fifteen per cent of the billboards in the entire country. That's an incredible feeling, driving past huge pictures of a person and continually being surprised that the person is you. The slogan they added to the poster was one of the worst in the history of advertising: SOUND ISSUES. But the sheer scale of the billboard campaign hammered it home once again. This was big.

It all added to the sense that I had been spun off the *Newsnight* swivel chair into a position where the spotlight was even more unsparing. And I was not at all sure the Beeb was ready for Moir's 'audience churn.' I was beginning to think so much had been invested that if we dropped a single listener I would go out of the same window as JY.

At the time, under Dyke, the BBC was discovering its winner's instinct, which critics called a commercial edge – a series of disasters, internal and external, would see it pull back in due course. For now, the corporation was happy doubling and tripling the stakes so long as it came out on top.

I tried to put it out of my mind. Not very successfully. Because it was Sunday, 5 January 2003. And I was due on the air the very next day.

*

The winding road led to a door marked STUDIO J1. I approached, knees knocking, that Monday and decided the name of the room was the first positive omen. Studio J2 or J3 would have been a little too painful.

A cold, dark morning in an upper floor of Broadcasting House. *You saw the red flags at the airport . . .*

With my souvenir letter from Human Resources warming a trouser pocket – 'We are sorry to hear you have decided to leave the BBC' – and Jimmy's gallery of world leaders staring down at us bitterly from their black-and-white world, the producers prepped me briskly on the items.

Finally, alongside Phil Jones I went through the studio door holding a sheaf of scripts and some spare CDs. Thirty minutes to go.

I blinked and rubbed my eyes when I saw the playlist. The Radio 2 computer told me the historic first record was Morrissey: 'The More You Ignore Me, The Closer I Get'. Would you play that? Don't get me wrong, I love Morrissey. But as a wind-up merchant for sixty-somethings there was no singer more effective. It was a sign of the change that Radio 2 had undergone that it had programmed me an opening disc I felt was a little too cool for school. There would be plenty of time to play 'Going Underground', 'This Charming Man' and 'Another Girl, Another Planet'. And even 'Leave The Capitol' by The Fall (okay, just the once). Vinyl labelled Dylan and Van Morrison was already stacked high in the record-changer of my mind. But the first song on the first show?

I substituted Morrissey's sinister stalker-manifesto with the anthemic 'Thunder Road' by Bruce Springsteen. Partly because it contains the line, 'So you're scared and you're thinking that maybe we ain't so young any more' . . . a reference, I was sure, to my illustrious predecessor. But mainly because it is one of the greatest – maybe *the* greatest – rock songs ever written or performed. It was never a hit single. But it is cinematographic. The first seven words: 'The screen door slams; Mary's dress sways', blimey, even typing them on this page has brought me out in goosebumps. How did

Springsteen do that, instantly give us an image that is about escape (the door), sex (the dress), then join the two together by having the gust from that impetuous door-slam move her skirts? And how did he come up with the line, 'All the redemption I can offer is beneath this dirty hood'? Or 'I've got this guitar, and I've learnt how to make it talk'? I had been to see the Boss in concert half a dozen times and he had never done a duff show.

The duff show. Now there was a frightening thought. This was Day One for me, and I knew exactly how the system worked: the critics listen once, to the debut. If it goes wrong, if anything goes wrong, they fall upon you like wolves. By the end there is nothing left but your teeth. That's a Rule: *If a programme launch fails on a Monday, there is no Tuesday, Wednesday, Thursday or Friday.* You might as well spend the rest of the week in bed, order Prozac and change your name by deed poll.

On the other hand, if the critical notices say the first show was fine or even just passable, off the writers go to kill someone else until your first disaster brings them back. We would have one of those, but not just yet.

My first-day nerves were not helped by the arrival of the Queen of Radio, Jenny Abramsky. Behind her came Jim Moir, who was unable to enter any room without a flourish. For some reason I remembered that Moir had been the key executive behind *Little and Large*.

Jenny was another manager with a place in the BBC pantheon of greats. Her barely concealed disgust at the entire business of television only made her a more awesome figure to staff in radio. When a colleague told her that he saw a small sign on the wall of a hotel room saying THE RADIO IS NOW CONTROLLED THROUGH THE TELEVISION, Abramsky apparently resolved to stop that ever happening inside the BBC.

She made up for a lack of height with an extraordinary air of command. She did not do small talk, and always walked in a straight line so others had to move aside. She would probably have walked over the top of a desk if the alternative was to go round it. I found her truly terrifying – I can say this now that retirement has softened her – but I realized over the years that her loyalty was phenomenal. I doubt that she ate and drank as normal people do. She lived on a pure diet of radio.

Fifteen minutes to go. Jenny moved through from the control room to talk to me.

'Why are you wearing a suit, Jeremy?'

I didn't know, so I said desperately: 'I don't know, I don't know.'

'It's not *Newsnight*.'

'I know.' I just felt it was a special occasion. My dad always said you wore a suit on special occasions.

Moir poked his head round the door:

'Warmth.'

At this point Jenny opens her mouth, but whatever she is starting to say is cut in two by a deafening burst of gangsta rap.

'MO MURDER, MO MURDER FOR THE ROC EMPIRE, YA'LL WON'T SURFACE YA'LL NERVOUS KNOWIN THEM GUNS ON FULL SERVICE, READY TO FIRE, ONE BODY, TWO BODY, THREE BODY FOUR—'

Moir and Abramsky flinch and glance at each other. I can see they're thinking, *We've hired a guy who wears a suit and plays rap music.*

I explain: 'They're looking for violent rap lyrics next door. We want to play them to the Home Secretary. We're speaking to him about gun culture. Ten seconds and no more. It's not the first record. That's ...'

Twelve o'clock. Bang on.

Red light.

Showing that all the stand-in shifts I had done during Jimmy's holidays counted for nothing compared to this one, Ken Bruce says:

'Now, for the very first time, we say hello to Jeremy Vine.'

'Can I have more time?' I asked. 'Because I'm not ready.'

Ken laughed, for which I remain grateful. I threw to the news-room for a brief summary and then said, in a voice trembling with fear: 'For the first record on the first show, there really wasn't that much of a choice', and hit the CD play button, and, saints be praised—

The screen door slams
Mary's dress sways

It struck me that if the first CD had failed to start, or jumped during the chorus, or the knackered-looking player had skipped to 'Nebraska', there would probably have to be multiple resignations. They didn't. Even now, when I hear that record, it takes me right back to the first show and the most significant single instant of my working life: hitting a play button, hearing a piano and entering a different world.

Later someone told me my former colleagues had the programme pumping out of a speaker in the *Newsnight* office for the first ten minutes, just to be sure I had landed safely.

*

Things took off after the Boss.

The home secretary David Blunkett arrived, back from illness and giving us his only interview of the day. I welcome him, he welcomes me: 'You have a hard act to follow, Jeremy.' *Oooooch* ... and there's the third rail, a near-mention of the godlike presence who had occupied the studio for so long. Blunkett had attended one of Sir Jimmy's parties and the *Guardian* would say the following day that there had been 'a little frostiness' in his tone towards me; I did not pick it up, I must say.

We play the burst of rap. I attribute it to 'Jay Zed', which of course should be *Jay-Zee*, destroying at a stroke our attempts to capture the 16–20 market. Blunkett condemns the music, although thankfully leaves the rest of the playlist unscathed. On we go.

Isobel Eaton, veteran of the *Newsnight* Van, was on the team. She had booked a Welsh comedian friend of hers to speak about being overweight. Ruth Jones would later be the *Little Britain* barmaid and star of *Gavin & Stacey*, but today she was on to talk about her weight problem: 'Right now I can't cross my legs.'

The bulletins follow up Blunkett; the *Sun* leads on him the next day; that's a start.

The first review is encouraging, though the headline is not: **JV TAKES JY'S SEAT AND THE FIRST PROTEST COMES AFTER 14 MINUTES** – a reference to some invigorating comment on the website. Others are friendly. On reflection I think that is because journalists love to flip the narrative. Their favourite kind of story is 'Millionaire Reduced to Begging for Small Change', or 'Downing Street Spokesman Faces Jail' – the most dramatic example I ever saw was 'Superman Paralysed' but they also go for the upside when it suits them, as in 'Bloke Who Was Useless on *Newsnight* Turns Out to Fit in Quite Well on Radio 2'. *The Times* gave us a generous four stars. And I was also criticized by Roy Hattersley, which suggested we were doing something right.

Wednesday.

We want to put occasional phone callers through, a modest innovation on a show where no listener's voice has ever been heard before. Yet the studio switchboard seems to lock if there is more than one every ten minutes. 'I'm joined by Keith – no, sorry, he's not there – well, let's try Maria – er, okay, that doesn't sound good – right, Dennis. Hello Dennis? No Dennis? Here are the Red Hot Chili Peppers.'

And the great thing is, you can always go to a record. *Newsnight* is West Point for aspiring interviewers, but on TV a missing graphic or broken satellite link is studio death. My very first in-the-chair presenter appearance on *Newsnight* had been as cover for Peter Snow, who was in America for the 1994 presidential elections. I was a pol-corr being used for the most menial task: they told me I just had to sit in the studio in London in case the line from the States went down, 'which it won't.'

Of course it did. Live on BBC2. So having been watching Snowie in Washington I suddenly catch my own face in the monitors, frown, straighten up, look at the main camera in mounting panic and say:

'The American elections are—'

At which point Peter Snow instantly reappears in Washington. A four-word debut.

With radio you don't get that kind of nonsense. On Radio 2, music is woven through everything. There is no such thing as a technical fault, just another record.

The papers tried to quarrel with this and that, which is their job. The *Independent* sweetly wrote after my opening show: 'The programme was not seamless', pointing out that I had announced a record by The King and then played 'the wrong Elvis' by accident – Costello not Presley. The criticism prompted the nicest thing I have ever seen written about me. One of the paper's readers understood what had happened completely and came to my defence in the next day's letters page:

I must take issue with Robert Hanks when he states that 'at one point JV announced a record by "The King", only to have the wrong Elvis, Costello, turn up.' This was not a mistake. It was the defining moment of the programme where Vine put down his marker that he was talking to my generation, not Jimmy Young's.

Thank-you, Joe Blair in Reading, you lovely person, wherever you are now, for sending a shiver up my spine.

Where the music was concerned, we seemed to be pushing at an open door. On Thursday Isobel walked into the studio looking worried. I dipped the speakers.

Isobel explained, 'You've played the Flaming Lips two days running. Um, isn't this a bit of an acquired taste?' Yes, I say, it may be, but the choice wasn't mine. 'Yoshimi Battles The Pink Robots' is scheduled for constant rotation on this week's playlist, and a computer printout tells me we must play it. We roar with glee; I jump up, grab the printout and wave it above my head, like an order paper in the hands of a backbencher greeting the sudden election of his party.

Sensing that Moir's marathon revamp of Radio 2, which had looked close to impossible, was now near to completion – akin to stripping and rebuilding a car while it is still hurtling down the motorway – newspapers began to profile the controller. **PLUCKY JIM**, read a headline about him in the *Independent.* A reporter, Vincent Graff, interviewed Moir in his office. He looked about and rather cleverly asked the controller where that bronze bust of Jimmy Young was.

'Didn't you used to have one in here?'

Without missing a beat, Moir replied, 'It has gone to the great art store of the BBC. It will no doubt be on public display in due course.'

*

Relaunching the show, our main aim at the outset was simply to show that we were serious about journalism and serious about news. Two Cabinet ministers in a week; a debate about the legalization of heroin and cocaine involving the mother of a young addict who died; Jonathan Aitken on sentencing; and, stealing the show, Matilda, a nine-year-old who came into the studio to complain that her school had stopped children playing in the snow, for health and safety reasons.

The first programme ended. Then the first week. Jimmy had said on his retirement that he had to do without producers for most of his years in the chair – I actually don't think he meant it, and I had the opposite feeling. Without Phil and Isobel and our tight team of twenty-somethings, there would not have been a show at all. But there was. The papers had given it a tick in pencil. Sixteen years after joining the Beeb, my name was in the neon. And it felt so bloody brilliant.

*

Jim Moir stayed on for the year that followed. But the whole rupture over Sir Jimmy never really went away. One day the presenter popped up on *Sky News* to publicize a lecture tour he was embarking on. 'I accept they can fire me,' he told the interviewer, 'but not that they can fire me without even a conversation explaining why. They never sat me down for a glass of whisky and said, "Sorry, Jimmy, you have to go and this is why."'

Thirty seconds after the broadcast Moir walked in, full of bonhomie, but also looking hurt, I thought. He casually asked if I had been watching Sky at all.

'Yep,' I said.

'What did you think of it?'

I said I thought it was the same thing we've heard before, about the whisky.

'There was a whisky,' he said sorrowfully. 'It's just that the whisky was not drunk at a particular time or place.'

I really felt for Moir. His remastering of the station had been so skilful and so cautious, and he approached danger wearing as much protective gear as the soldiers in *The Hurt Locker*. But even the best bomb disposal expert will sometimes hear a ticking he does not recognize, and know events have moved out of his control.

Now you will think me crazy. The mention of Sir Jimmy's lecture tour made me think – well, why not? It would be my one chance to see the great man in action. And maybe to get just a little closer to understanding what had given this ex-crooner of other people's ballads such a powerful, personal hold over an audience of millions. Since he was averse to meeting me, I decided I should discreetly go to one of the stops on his theatre tour and sit at the back.

I chose the Derngate Theatre in Northampton. Mark Lawson lived nearby and we could go with our partners. Phil Jones and his wife Cathy came too. The problem was that I feared that if I was recognized by members of the audience I could be lynched. So, with some serious misgivings, I wore a beret and a false moustache.

'I hope I don't stand out,' I said to Phil and Mark on the way in. I could see them trying not to giggle (Phil said afterwards: 'You might as well have worn a sombrero. You were the most conspicuous person there.') Once inside the theatre we took our seats as far back as possible and I buried myself behind Lawson's imposing frame.

The experience was an education. Sir Jimmy was surrounded by a hard core of devotees who hung on his every word. He went painstakingly through his life, at one point uttering the line: 'If we could go back to where we were ten minutes ago, which was November 1930.' He was asked by the interviewer what had terminated his active service. Perhaps all presenters suffer bouts of acute existentialism, for he replied: 'The Second World War ended when I got a fistula up my bottom.'

Then the question of how he had survived for so long. 'I am one of the few presenters who can sight-read,' he said, meaning he could take a script and make his reading of it sound spontaneous. 'I took over Steve Race's show because poor Steve had to work off a script.'

I shrank into my seat as a posse of Northamptonians denounced what they variously called his 'understudy', 'substitute', or 'replacement'. But he was gracious throughout, and never referred to me by name at all. When an elderly lady in a smart dress suit stood up and asked, 'Can't you get your stand-in to be less aggressive?' Sir Jimmy replied with one of the most delicious non-sequiturs I have ever heard:

'Well, in my day, contracts used to be seven weeks.'

I crept out behind Mark Lawson in my moustache and felt I had maybe understood a tiny part of Sir Jimmy Young's enduring appeal: old-fashioned courtesy and a straightforwardness, almost a plainness of approach. He was the opposite of the smart Alecs thrown up by the in-house training schemes of the BBC for so many years, many of whom had been educated beyond their intelligence. Jimmy was just a totally ordinary, honest bloke, the least pretentious person you could ever imagine, with strong core values that people latched onto. And his audience adored him for it.

*

Ten months after I started at the station, Moir was close to finally retiring. There was a big dinner for him at the very swish Reform Club. He and Wogan made speeches for each other that left the rest of us feeling like gooseberries. Then Moir stood to address his guests. 'I sent a car for Nicky Campbell,' he said, 'but sadly it missed.'

Emotionally he thanked the station's staff, and concluded dramatically:

'If I am raised high, it is because I was stood on the shoulder of giants.'

Not long after, the listening figures suffered an inexplicable dip across the entire station. Here is what I wrote when I saw the soon-to-be-former-greatest-controller.

> *23 October 2003*
>
> Jim Moir today bounces in, with the listening figures – his last set – down across the station. He throws his arms out: 'It doesn't matter fuck all because I'm leaving!'
>
> And adds, with hand motion as if holding playing cards: 'I know when to twist, and I know when to stick.'

The BBC misses its Moirs. He was a figure from a different age, sure. He had reportedly resisted the idea of firing several of Radio 2's longest-serving personnel, declaring: 'The secret of a great army is that it carries its wounded.' Although the process briefly became ghastly, he had set the network on a different course, given it relevance and confidence – made it a fun place again – without, crucially, frightening off the existing audience. The contradictions inherent in Moir's approach were summed up when the station adopted the laughable advertising slogan, WHERE DIFFERENT WORKS. But the phrase, much-lampooned by Terry in the mornings, actually just emphasized the intricacy of Moir's needlework.

Although Sir Jimmy left Radio 2 under the shadow of some pretty heavy clouds, he recently came back to the station to be interviewed about his career by his old friend Ken Bruce. The programme was fascinating and the interview was brilliantly done by Ken. Jimmy's perspective was historic, his memories as clear as ever. Now aged over ninety, I think he has forgiven the radio station for what must have seemed like rather clumsy handling of his retirement – to put it mildly. I keep hoping I might have the chance to meet him, to swap thoughts about the best job in the world. It still amazes me that he did it for so long and maintained such energy in the chair, even into his eighties. The Beeb being tight on money, he would probably be amused to learn that I spent the first five years wearing his old headphones. There is only one word for him: star.

In 2011, Jimmy was inducted into the Radio Academy's Hall of Fame. A significant honour. He couldn't make the ceremony in Salford, so Phil Jones – his editor and mine, of course – was asked to collect the award. Phil asked me to help him write the short acceptance speech. I remember sitting at my desk wondering how on earth you sum up such a fruitful life in two or three paragraphs. In the end this is what I sent him:

> Television is impact, radio is intimate. TV is all about creating a splash, radio is all about forming a relationship. So in radio, one of the hallmarks of greatness is longevity. The truly great presenter doesn't just do one good show, he does ten thousand.
>
> The joy of working in radio is that if you're very, very good, you might just get the chance to do the ten thousand. Jimmy did. And by the end – which as everyone here knows, wasn't easy for him or the station – he was as familiar to his audience, and as loved, as their favourite piece of furniture. He was that much a part of their lives. They'd gone through nearly five decades together. Imagine: presenting a daily news show, live on the radio five days a week, at the age of eighty-one.
>
> Sometimes it takes a while to understand greatness. I was Jimmy's editor – I guess we were all too taken up with the daily chaos of getting the show on air to see it at the time. Even the mighty, all-knowing Radio Academy took ten years to see it! But

it's a thrill for all of us on Radio 2, and I know for Jimmy, that *his gift for forming a relationship with his listeners* has been recognized like this. There is no doubt that JY is in the pantheon of great broadcasters. He will be delighted that you think so too. And I am honoured to accept this on his behalf.

*

Radio 2 had set me on a different course. I started on some projects for BBC1 – a series in daytime called *Jeremy Vine Meets . . .* was launched with rock stars in the chair (Sting, Debbie Harry, Lionel Richie, Bob Geldof and Elvis Costello, who managed not to panic when he realized he had walked into a room with a fan). A second series moved to actors (Jeremy Irons, Amanda Redman, Rupert Everett). Another BBC1 show, *Pageturners*, sat me between book club members and breakthrough writers like Lionel Shriver. I took over *Points of View* from Sir Terry and was staggered when the fiftieth anniversary programme forced me to look at the lineage: Robinson, Took, Robinson, Wogan, Vine. *Eggheads*, surely one of the cleverest game show concepts ever invented, became a fun way to spend three weeks a year: we have twenty days to film eighty editions. Presenting *Panorama* would come later.

There was more excitement at home, and more to learn. Rachel gave birth to two daughters – Martha in 2004 and Anna in 2006. Both perfect to me. Both beautiful. Years earlier I had gorged myself on the conventional BBC wisdom that, to become three-dimensional, a journalist had to be shot at. Now I realized it was more educational to be vomited on. Covering your sleeping baby is as mind-broadening as covering a war. Much as I admire the globe-trotting conflict correspondents, who should probably write 'I HAVE SEEN MORE LIFE THAN YOU' across their foreheads in felt tip, fatherhood made me wonder whether a mum who had spent ten years out of the newsroom to bring up three kids could claim to be just as battle-hardened.

I guess I began to grasp what life is really all about: Martha, Anna, Rachel. Working counter to my DNA, I gave up *The Politics Show* as it was taking too much family time on Sundays (Sargie would have made much of the fact that Jon Sopel took it over).

But Radio 2 gave other kinds of joy. And things changed on the station as well. When Jim Moir finally retired, his deputy was elevated to station queen. Lesley Douglas was committed to the same trajectory, but she wanted to move faster. In fact, much faster. There was going to be more fun, more change, more of everything. The station would become even bigger and even better. What none of us realized is that when you stamp on the accelerator, you can't always see what lies ahead.

Chapter Twenty-Two

HARD LISTENING

My grandmother – the one who gave me the atlas in Chapter Four – was profoundly deaf. My father, her son, begged her to get the latest hearing aid. The technology was now weapons-grade, he told her. The device would cost £700 but it would work.

She refused, telling him: 'There's nothing worth hearing at that money.'

Journalism is about listening. About believing that things are worth hearing. In 1988, while a trainee, I had something very odd happen to me. I was sitting in the radio newsroom preparing to listen to the Mansion House speech of the Chancellor. Nigel Lawson is now best known for being Nigella's dad and inventing a masochistic diet regime – she cooks rich puddings while he writes books on how to avoid eating them – but at the time he was working alongside Margaret Thatcher, presiding over an economic boom that sent house prices rocketing and brought in Harry Enfield's Loadsamoney generation.

To my surprise, sitting there with no work to do but wait, when I turned the headphone control to channel 30 on the ringmain the line was already up. So, I could hear Lawson in conversation with whoever was sitting next to him at the dinner. He would speak publicly later; this was just private chat. Wrong of me, I know, but not many 23-year-old news trainees would resist eavesdropping as they sat there in official Broadcasting House headphones.

'This year's Budget may not be necessary,' the Chancellor bragged to the whinnying lady beside him. 'I may not even have a Budget. I think I shall just announce in a few minutes that everything is going so well there doesn't need to be one.'

The significance of these remarks was not lost on me a year later. Interest rates rocketed, house prices crashed, the *Daily Mail* printed a famous front page headline **THIS BANKRUPT CHANCELLOR**, and poor old Lawson lost his job. The self-confidence of that private conversation was blown to pieces.

Broadcasting does that. Life does that. In 1972 Ephraim McLean, an early pioneer of IT systems, said that any new venture goes through seven stages: unwarranted enthusiasm, uncritical acceptance, growing concern, unmitigated disaster, search for the guilty, punishment of the innocent and the promotion of the uninvolved. If I made a mistake when I joined Radio 2, it was to think everything was now set fair and that history had ended.

All presenters look for the truest on-air iteration of themselves, their broadcast self, the chair that fits their bottom: think Sir Robin on *Question Time*, Sue Lawley on *Nationwide*, Lauren Laverne on 6 Music, Chiles and Bleakley on *The One Show*, Parky on *Parkinson*, Humphrys on *Today*, or the great Magnus Magnusson on *Mastermind*. If you are a very lucky presenter, you get to try out different chairs until one fits.

Radio 2 was unquestionably the perfect seat for me, and being named Speech Broadcaster of the Year* allowed me to publicly acknowledge my luck in having the job come free when it did. But ventures have stages. Arriving there would not be the end of the story.

---

* At the Sony Awards in 2005 and 2011. The Gordon Brown moment also won Interview of the Year in 2010, although I've always thought that trophy should be on his mantelpiece.

Meanwhile, around me, some titanic figures would strike icebergs of their own.

*

The thing that surprised me on Radio 2 was the discovery that the audience was now broadcasting, and I had become the listener. As I wrote way back on page thirty-something, the audience have better stories than we do. Heavy-duty news and current affairs shows often give the impression they are handing tablets down from the mountaintop. By contrast, the joy of a daily radio show with all the interaction that modern technology makes possible is that communication is two-way, and totally informal. A caller does not need a lighting rig to take part; just a telephone. We say what we think the news is, then the listener tells us what's really happening.

Sometimes the tone struck is intimate beyond belief. Take this comment emailed in by a woman called Carolyn during an item on adoption. A life was summed up in four paragraphs:

> *In 1965 I was raped and found out I was pregnant. After an arduous 72-hour labour, I gave birth to a girl. I was allowed to look after her for the two weeks when I was in hospital but social services arranged for her to be adopted. I didn't have a say in the matter.*
>
> *I was given a chance to say goodbye. I whispered in her ear, 'One day, come back to me my darling,' and then she was gone – nobody spoke of it again.*
>
> *Later in life, I married and had two daughters. In 1997, my daughter who was adopted made contact and wanted to meet. We exchanged reams of letters, lots of photos and phone calls, and then when we all met it was wonderful.*
>
> *Since then she has given me 2 grandsons. We meet whenever we can and all keep in touch. There can be a happy-ever-after, despite all the heartbreak and pain.*

Or what about Cathy Wilson, ex-wife of Peter Tobin? The serial killer murdered at least three young women while brutalizing his Cathy, and she came into the studio to talk about her feelings when police dug up the sandpit in Margate he had built for their three-year-old, Daniel.

He had not exactly been a good father, she said, and building that seemed like one of the few affectionate things he had done for his son. Now she knew his real purpose. The forensics team found two of his victims underneath it.

When the footballer Gary Speed committed suicide, a listener called Paul Neal rang us from Dawlish in Devon. His brother had also been called Gary. His brother also had two young children. And, like Speed, he was forty-two when he took his life for no apparent reason. Gary Neal had parked his van with a lawnmower running in the back. On the programme, Paul spoke of how the family were just left trying to work out why.

'I ask myself that question every day and it will haunt me for life. I keep thinking, "If only he had phoned me", and on the records on his mobile it looked like he had tried but had no signal. The cruellest thing of all is the sense of anger at what he has done to his family and children. I would rather have had a letter to explain it. I don't know if I will ever accept his decision or if his kids will forgive him.'

*

But the ability to hear what your audience is saying can be a curse as well as a blessing. In my first year on Radio 2, I would stay in the office until 7 p.m. some days replying to every single email. Often there were a hundred I thought needed a personal response. My wife wondered why work stopped at 2 p.m. and she didn't see me till eight. A passionate affair with Sally Traffic? No, with the listeners. Where people were really furious and had left a phone number, I would ring them personally. The exchange usually went something like this:

'Hi, is that Derek?'

'Yep.'

'Derek, it's Jeremy Vine here. I just wanted to say thank-you for the email you sent today—'

'Ah.'

'—which says I am a left-wing idiot with no idea of how the world works who should be locked in a freezer till Christmas. I was only calling to assure you, I really don't have any politics myself, because—'

'Right. Well, Jeremy, you see, I actually wrote that email when I was very upset with the wife. She'd been out in our car, and there's this bend . . .'

We often became friendly and stayed in touch. But replying to so many messages was exhausting and probably unhealthy, and in the end I had to rein back my obsession. One sign it had gone too far was when I rang a particularly angry listener in Northumbria. After I had said my piece – probably a contrite promise to do better – Wilf responded, 'But that's exactly what you told me last time you called. In fact, both times.'

The dear old BBC, which you can probably tell by now I love beyond all reason, is the target of a million times more emotion: a combustible cocktail of adoration and loathing. I regularly have conversations about this with one of my, ahem, senior relatives. Let's call her Eleanor. She complains there is virtually nothing for her to watch on TV. The last fusillade came while she was engrossed in a very high-end documentary on BBC4 about the daughter of Sir Thomas More. I made the slightly inflammatory comment that the programme, which I saw Eleanor was enjoying, 'is the best explanation I have yet seen for the riots.' A young person who had paid the licence fee would switch on BBC4 in 2011, I argued, see their money had not bought them a programme of any interest whatsoever, and go out looting.

She retorted, gloriously: 'Well, as far as I'm concerned, most of what the BBC puts out is for looters.'

The Beeb operates in an environment where, strange to relate, its harshest critics are the people who get the most out of it. The top-notch journalist Charles Moore, a former editor of the *Daily Telegraph*, ran a public campaign against the licence fee because he objected to paying the salary of Jonathan Ross. Moore has elegant and sophisticated tastes, and I have huge respect for him. He belongs to the demographic that gets the Proms; the whole of Radio 4; the whole of Radio 3; the Chelsea Flower Show; Melvin Bragg; *Newsnight*; BBC4; even an hour on the daughter of Sir Thomas More. They receive £541 worth of programmes for £145 worth of licence fee and yet they are so angry they are spitting feathers. Meanwhile, the many millions who must be disgusted that their money is spent on documentaries about Sir Thomas More's daughter never seem to emerge.

The anger levelled at the BBC is something you accept as a fact of working there, a sort of reverse perk. Citizens pay a tax to get our programmes, a tax triggered by their first purchase of a telly. Try explaining what a TV detector van is to an American and you will see them start groping for a firearm. Our customers literally have a licence to mind, and we have a duty to listen.

Once I was in a black cab on my way to Television Centre. When we got to the gates, the driver started bellowing about the number of security guards in fluorescent green jackets: 'Look at these tossers in their luminous clothing. Makes me sick that I pay for this! How many of these clowns does the sodding BBC need, for crying out loud? Look at them. It's not like you've got the Queen visiting!'

When I got inside TV Centre I asked why there seemed to be a lot of security today.

'The Queen's visiting,' said a producer.

My grandmother was able to refuse a hearing aid. But the BBC cannot shut out the voices around it. On a very modest level, I could not ignore them when I started at Radio 2. Similarly, the Beeb feels it has to listen. And five factors have now converged, with dramatic consequences:

- If you have 61 million people on a small island and you ask them to pay a tax before they switch on a television, you're going to drive them potty no matter how good your programmes are.
- Citizens (I include myself) seem generally more angry and more assertive about their anger than they used to be.
- Technology has given us the means to publish our fury and politicians encourage us to feel it – something they call 'empowerment'.
- The BBC has decided it needs to be more accountable, so it has bought the £700 hearing aid. It urges licence fee-payers to get in touch and say what's made us angry.
- People have to resign for bad stuff now.

The result of all this is a dizzying sense of the precipice when you work at the Beeb these days. Years ago, when I was on *Today* and *Newsnight*, there were no audience emails. The closest you got to feedback was a letter in the post (by the way, I never saw a single one in green ink) or a comment left by phone on the so-called 'audience log', a list of remarks transcribed by a team manning the official complaint line. In those days if you rang the switchboard and asked to speak direct to a newsroom, they would want an assurance that you actually worked there before they patched the call through – an interesting approach to newsgathering! The log was the main way for the audience to reach us, and I occasionally copied down comments that were worth saving:

July 2005

Dermot Murnaghan stated that the only way to deal with an electrical fault was to 'hit' the piece of equipment and he often does the same to Natasha Kaplinsky to keep her in order. This was most offensive and to promote domestic violence on national TV was totally unacceptable.

When I was working on *Newsnight* a decade ago, after any single edition there might be thirty comments on the duty log and half a dozen letters: all very civilized. Now there are thousands – thousands of tweets, texts, emails, and blog references. Hashtags proliferate. High-profile polemicists can run 24-hour, 365-day campaigns without buying a single postage stamp. Whole companies can be hunted by individuals. In parallel the BBC has thrown the windows open, urging audiences to engage with its increasingly elaborate mechanisms for recording and assessing their dissatisfactions.

On Radio 2 we had a call from the Complaints Unit. The sort that sends a shiver down your spine. 'It's a problem with your coverage of the Middle East,' said the austere voice at the other end.

The stakes could not be higher. It turned out the complainant was a prominent Israeli writer who had been an invited guest on the show.

'Right,' said Phil Jones, his career flashing before him, grabbing a pen and a sheet of A4. 'Fire away.'

'He says he was not offered sweeteners for the coffee you gave him. He says you only had sugar.'

The frightening thing is that the person who called Phil to relay the complaint was *Not Joking*.

Combine the generalized anger ('most of what the BBC puts out is for looters') and the new policy of hard listening, and you have a situation where mistakes are punishable by annihilation. Nigel Lawson's 'I may not even need to have a Budget', followed by his exit from office, reminds us that life has been a business of highs and lows since time began. But at the Beeb the distance between the high and the low has been stretched, and the biggest falls now make the clifftop plunge in *Monty Python and the Holy Grail* look like a picnic. The stakes are very, very high; so is the cliff.

Perhaps stockbrokers and circus workers see that kind of danger as an incentive. But creative types frighten more easily. The message, 'Take this risk – but only if it pays off', is not one they can deal with.

*

One morning in 2003 I was coming into Radio 2 while listening to the *Today* programme on earphones. The second story on the bulletin seemed more important than the first: a reporter called Andrew Gilligan saying that someone in Downing Street had 'sexed up' the case that Saddam Hussein had weapons of mass destruction.

Funnily enough, Phil Jones and I said exactly the same thing to each other when we got into the office: 'Did you *hear* that?' It was a great scoop. We booked Gilligan to come on Radio 2 live that same day. Given that the first dossier on Saddam's WMD had been proven to have been lifted from a dog-eared dissertation written by a student in California (something the foreign secretary Jack Straw had openly called 'a complete Horlicks'), the story seemed highly believable.

But we know what became of the Gilligan report – a furious Alastair Campbell took it personally and rained bullets into the weakest plank of it, namely the source of the story and what exactly they had said. The source was revealed; Dr David Kelly killed himself; an inquiry by Lord Hutton decided BBC editors were to blame for everything going right back to the destruction of the monasteries under Henry VIII. The inquiry, incidentally, took evidence from my show because Andrew Gilligan had repeated his claims on it. This was what I wrote down in the crazy week when Hutton came out with his findings:

January 2004

Suddenly being outside news (technically R2 is part of the Music Dept) feels like an alibi. Hearing Hutton's croaking tones this afternoon exploding a bomb inside the Beeb was like hearing the sound of the whole organization being wound up . . . And I had thought Gilligan was 'broadly right' . . . Now they're saying the chairman has gone. It is like one of those international domino contests, when people start resigning in an organization as complex as this one.

[Dyke resigns.] Unaware of what is coming, on Monday I did

a picture for the front cover of the *Radio Times* – photo to illustrate piece saying my secret/favourite TV programme is *The World's Worst Car Crashes*. Just my luck. This will be published as the BBC teeters. I am wearing a shirt with a ruffle thing down the buttons and standing next to Kirsty Young and Carol Vorderman. Meanwhile real car crash is going on in Beeb. Have just sent goodbye letter to Dyke – are we on receiving end of greatest government spin operation since 1700? No WMD in Iraq, so blow up the BBC and pretend they were in there?

Almost a decade on from those slightly hysterical notes, the views of any BBC person on the saga are vitally unimportant. So I will put mine in a nutshell. The Hutton Inquiry was a poor piece of work, but there were flaws in the original story that the BBC should not have put its life on the line to defend.

I had questioned Greg Dyke at a staff seminar six weeks before Hutton concluded his report. 'This inquiry could be a nightmare for you, couldn't it?' I asked. He laughed. The hundreds in the audience laughed with him (he was very popular). I laughed too. *This guy is totally at ease with himself*, I remember thinking as I sat four feet from him. Dyke replied that Hutton would all be done in a day or a week at most, and then 'the whole sorry episode will just blow over.' His bombast was awesome. His judgement was shocking. He went off that cliff I mentioned.

Two years later I very nearly went off the same precipice after an incident which, to this day, still makes my flesh creep.

On my way into work I was looking at a story about how the Labour home secretary John Reid had indicated he would bring in a new law on paedophiles after a campaign by the *News of the World*.

In response, a Welsh chief constable, Terry Grange, accused ministers of government-by-newspaper. He said they were 'trying to find out what one particular tabloid newspaper wants and then complying with their wishes.'

It struck me that we could present listeners with a fictional

bulletin saying there was now no need to have ministers; the country was just being run direct by the tabloids. The new prime minister
is the editor of the *Daily Mail*. The new business secretary is editor
of the *Star*, and so on.

We talked about it at the 8 a.m. meeting and all agreed. The show
would discuss what would happen if tabloid newspaper editors took
every seat in Cabinet. What would their policies be if they actually
had to govern?

Phil Jones said: 'Fantastic.'

So we would mock up a bulletin to illustrate the idea. The tape
would be clearly labelled as fictional because we did not want
anyone getting confused. Two guests, the journalists Polly Toynbee
and Kelvin MacKenzie, would discuss the implications of handing
the whole business of government over to the redtops.

It was just another idea in just another programme. Nothing
about it suggested the riptide we were wading towards.

After the meeting I usually head out to read the papers – of all
sizes – and have a coffee. But today I thought I knew what the item
I'd suggested should sound like, so I told Jones I would type out the
fictional bulletin myself.

It started with me saying, 'This is our idea of what might be in the
news if the Cabinet were filled with tabloid newspaper editors
instead of politicians, to cut out the middlemen.' Then the newsreader, Fran Godfrey, would read:

Here is the news – and there is a lot of it. Murderer Ian Huntley
has been killed in his prison cell. The home secretary, who is
also editor of the *Sun*, said the people who did it would be
caught then placed on the Queen's Honours List.

More than half of all Britain's Health and Safety Laws are
being scrapped . . .

The Sports Minister, who is also editor of the *News of the
World*, declared a week off work for all public sector employ-
ees for each goal England score. Also he said, 'Scotland and

Wales need to show more support for what is, effectively, the
national team ...'

And so on. The whole thing lasted just over a minute. Life in jail
would mean life. Immigration was being halted. But 'in a sign that
the tabloid editors are not finding all decisions easy, they've asked for
a study to be done on abortion and euthanasia – by the very politicians they've turfed out of office.'

Copying the script over to Phil Jones, who checked that it did not
break any BBC guidelines, I went off for my coffee. The newsreader
voiced up our bulletin. The tape was clearly announced as fictional,
several times, when we played it on the air at ten past twelve.

I did not consider – as I most certainly should have – that any
unnecessary reference to Ian Huntley only creates more static in the
lives of the families of the two girls he murdered. His name has
become shorthand for evil, which was how I had thoughtlessly
employed it. But someone, somewhere, was walking past a shop
doorway in Cambridgeshire and heard the key phrase ' ... Huntley
has been killed ...' drift in and out of earshot. They rang the
Cambridge Evening News and asked if the paper knew about it.

Events moved fast. The paper rang the local police, whose original
investigation of the murders had been heavily criticized. They said
Huntley was alive but rang the Home Office to check. The Home Office
rang us to ask what was going on. Other confused people rang them –
possibly journalists, who will feign confusion when it suits them.

The government would have to put out a statement.

Now a Home Office statement saying that 'despite what you may
have heard on Radio 2, Ian Huntley is not dead' is big news. It may
be the opposite of a story, but it is a story all the same. The statement
started to proliferate on the wires and online.

The enormity of the error was becoming clear to me. I got off the
air at 2 p.m. and was meeting our then head of marketing, Tim
Davie, for pasta. I ran him through the incident. He looked troubled.

By the time I got back to the office it was pandemonium.

Cambridgeshire Police, who perhaps felt they had something to prove after the original investigation, had put out a statement calling the item 'irresponsible' and saying it 'may have been heard only partially by any number of listeners, giving the wholly false impression that the item was real.' A source added:

'The BBC may think this is funny, but I can assure you that there are a lot of police officers who investigated the murders of Holly and Jessica who have had a serious sense of humour bypass today.'

The BBC may think this is *funny*? That was never the approach, but it was too late to explain. We had apologized. When you apologize for something, it is taken as an apology for everything. You can't retract part of the apology on the basis that it is being used as a confession to crimes of which you were not guilty.

Lesley Douglas rang Phil Jones. He told me she just kept saying, 'Why, why, why,' in a voice that got fainter and fainter. 'Why, Phil? Why you? You are one of my best editors.'

Jones defended the item. 'It gets to the root of how a government obsessed with spin is running the country.' He reminded the controller that when David Blunkett was home secretary he had 'toasted the death of Harold Shipman and then taken a job as a columnist on the *Sun*.'

Maybe, but that didn't calm the storm. Now people who had not even heard the item were being asked what they thought about the 'hoax' R2 had put out. Their furious reactions were also running as news. Even Mark Leech, a prisons campaigner who was never off the programme, condemned us from a high horse somewhere. 'It is the sickest of sick jokes,' he announced.

Welcome to journalism, I could have told myself. Why would I be surprised that news is people reacting to third-hand reports of a broadcast they had never heard? I tried to maintain it was a serious item, but then, that same afternoon, as I was hosting a tug-of-war at Westminster for Macmillan Cancer Relief in a state of total distraction, Radio 2 released an apology for what it unhelpfully called our 'spoof broadcast'.

The offending bit of tape was eleven seconds long, which should have been mitigation. In fact it only added to the confusion, because no one was sure what they had actually heard. *Eleven seconds . . .*

The executive in charge of compliance at Radio 2, a diligent individual called Dave Barber, began writing letters of apology to the families of Huntley's victims that afternoon. The police in Cambridgeshire visited the bereaved parents to explain what had happened and make sure they had not been distressed by it. Ian Huntley himself was reportedly taken from his cell to call his mother to tell her he was still alive.

I sometimes still try to convince myself that there was nothing whatsoever wrong with the broadcast. The BBC Editorial Guidelines were changed to take account of it – since the incident no one has been allowed to announce the death of a living person, no matter how well labelled the scenario is, no matter how loathed the individual involved might be.

By lights out that evening I assumed I would have to resign. I did not sleep a wink. I lay in my bed and stared at the ceiling for seven hours; I had never had that before. Apart from anything else, I felt ashamed that my report might have caused discomfort to the families who had suffered so much already. I had not considered that when I suggested the topic and dashed off the script. If the parents criticized me or the station, I decided I would quit. I felt especially responsible because it had been my idea. Phil Jones had also ruminated: 'Like doctors, editors should do no harm – especially to the innocent.' I wondered if we would be tomorrow's front page lead in the very tabloids who presumably felt the piece was designed to kick them in the shins. We were unlikely to get any breaks from them in the circumstances.

The papers were indeed horrendous the next day. I keep them all in the top drawer of my office cabinet to remind me of just how big the drop is. When I pulled them out to write this chapter, one paragraph jumped out at me, written by Macer Hall in the *Express*:

This was more than just another of the BBC's now customary lapses of taste. For it spoke volumes about the mindset of the modern BBC, encapsulating the smug contempt for mainstream sensibilities and opinion that is rife within its Byzantine management structures.

Macer knew the BBC well. He had worked as a reporter on the *Today* programme. Actually I found the lesson to be a more personal one. Journalists need to be trusted. Day by day, report by report, in the simple business of accurately relaying stuff, of gathering news in the rain, a broadcaster or writer builds trust over years and years and years. He or she cannot broadcast a single word without it. *Trust is everything.*

But building trust is such a long, slow process, you may not even realize how much you have accumulated over how long. And how much it has cost you to do so.

Then a spoof ... hoax ... prank ... maybe just a moment of casualness ... putting out something that is not true, as if it is true. Whatever. That can explode all the trust in eleven seconds flat.

At Stormont, the building where the Northern Ireland Assembly reconvened, I once stopped to look at a hefty block of granite chiselled with the two key words in politics: BUILD TRUST. What happens when trust goes? Ask Johann Hari of the *Independent* or Jayson Blair of the *New York Times*.

The controller, Lesley Douglas, said she wanted to attend our 8 a.m. meeting the following morning. She was an imposing figure – when she walked into a room, you paid attention. Obviously I assumed what she told us would be hard listening. The hairdryer was guaranteed. She would give us all a huge rollicking for what had been a massive misjudgement and tell us it must never, ever happen again.

Interestingly, she did none of that.

The meeting ended with her sitting quietly throughout. She looked around the assembled crew.

All she said was, 'I only have one thing to tell you all. It's been a difficult twenty-four hours. But I'm telling you now—' she looked us all in the eye and said it very slowly – 'don't ever, *ever* stop being creative.'

Over my twenty-five years in the Beeb, I can't think of a moment that better defined leadership.

It was the end of the matter. A day later the whole thing started to fade. A week later it was gone, a lesson learnt. Now when I remind people of it, they struggle to remember. Phil Jones took total responsibility for what his presenter had done. That is the way the system works, however unfair it may seem. The same principle would trigger producer sackings three years later.

Surprising me, when we discussed the Huntley item recently, Phil Jones said: 'There was nothing wrong with it.'

'Well—'

He was sure. 'Sometimes the difference between the greatest item and the most disastrous one is very small indeed. I think it may have been one of the strongest items we've done. The editor of the *News of the World* became the Prime Minister's press officer. When it comes to political satire we were only on the nursery slopes.'

Jones still feels very strongly about the broadcast. Like all the best editors, he believes the most important quality in broadcasting is audacity.

But because all the vitriol was aimed personally at me, I was wounded. For me it seemed to prove the old maxim: *Never pick an argument with someone who buys their ink by the gallon.* The outcome was a realization that we were not only responsible for what people heard. We were also responsible for what they misheard. And there is a lesson for managers here too. It is – if I may – that your job is to defend people when honest acts of creativity go wrong, however tempting the punishment of the innocent may be.

In many ways it is poignant for me to relate that inspirational Lesley Douglas moment to you – 'Don't ever, *ever* stop being creative' – in the light of the Ross–Brand saga, where Lesley gave two of her most valuable presenters the freedom to have fun and as a result all three of them lost their jobs.

Chapter Twenty-Three

THE MUMS' ARMY

I had lunch with the new controller, Bob Shennan. This is how great radio is: he asked me if there was anything else I wanted to do on the station, and I said I thought we should have some documentaries in the evening which included the voices of our listeners, and he said give me an idea, and I suggested: well, what about our mums?

If there is one thing that comes home powerfully to me doing a daily show on Radio 2, it is the incredible power of the mothers who listen.

They may be pensioners; they may be any age at all. Radio 2's young mums seem to listen with especial care. Many have given up jobs and possibly careers to ensure their children have them at home. I think they must be far more frightening to politicians than a professional interviewer like me. They do not stand for any evasion, double-speak, or even a bit of lightly toasted waffle. If they ran the country we would be in less of a mess.

But the point about the mums is this – they *know*. They just do. They know everything. We just need them to tell us what they know, and then we have a programme.

So, a documentary about mums? Bob and I discussed the idea.

One theme which comes up again and again on my show is the profound care and concern that is felt for the armed forces, for soldiers fighting in distant wars. Whatever you think of the reasons for the conflicts in Iraq and Afghanistan, the bravery and dedication of our troops on the ground is without question.

We sat there and discussed those two worlds: the world of Radio 2 mums, the nuclear core of my audience; and the world of the soldier. By the time the conversation was finished, we had a title. The documentary would be called *The Songs My Son Loved*. We would speak to five mothers about the sons they had lost in those wars. They could tell the story of their short lives through music, specifically the music their boys used to love. And Bob added a revolutionary thought: 'These won't go out in the evening, Jeremy. I want them to go out during the day.'

*

Richard Hunt had been in Afghanistan for three weeks. In one of his phone calls back home he had told his parents how much he loved the country. He was twenty-one and full of life, a private serving in the 2nd Battalion The Royal Welsh. The only problem, he told Mum and Dad, was the dust. It got everywhere. As did the Taliban.

Richard's dream was to be a sniper. While he waited in the hope his superiors would tell him he had made the grade, he drove Warrior armoured vehicles. This activity concerned his parents especially. They were certain that drivers faced more danger from landmines than anyone sitting in the back. An explosion under a front wheel would be closer to Richard than his passengers.

Underlining his parents' concerns, an American tanker got bogged down in sand one day. It had to be dug out. Richard's Warrior was enlisted. The Warrior had to accompany the tanker across harder terrain, past a village packed with Taliban. On its way, the tanker hit a mine. Richard's commander told him to turn his own vehicle around and head back. But the return route was more dangerous than he realized. From a distance other soldiers in his unit were waving at him to stop, knowing he could hit a mine.

The track of Richard Hunt's Warrior did go over a mine. There was a bang. But it was only the detonator going off. No full explosion. Nobody hurt.

Needless to say, Richard's parents were greatly relieved when he told them the story. And soon he had another piece of news. He had indeed been made a sniper. No more driving Warriors, no more sitting above the front wheel.

Or so he hoped. A chance event would put him back in the driving seat one last time. Another soldier had twisted his knee; that soldier was supposed to be a driver. For one more day, Richard would be at the wheel of a Warrior.

That day he was the sixteenth vehicle in a convoy of thirty heading to a forward operating base. They all went through a narrow gulley near Musa Qaleh in Helmand Province. A landmine buried at the narrowest point did not explode under the first fifteen trucks. But when the tracks of Richard's vehicle passed over the mine, it detonated.

His gunner and commander were unconscious but not seriously hurt. The explosion had lifted Richard into the ceiling of the vehicle. A broken jaw was the least of his injuries. Members of his unit pulled him from the hatch and he was airlifted to Camp Bastion, then Kandahar. They brought him back to the UK where, with his family around him, he died in Selly Oak Hospital in Birmingham two days later.

He was the 200th British soldier to be killed in Afghanistan.

*

I met Richard's mother at the family farm in Abergavenny. The place was full of life. Dogs barked; the main road just beyond the fence kept up a constant hum. Mooing at every passing stranger, young calves with freshly printed ear tags were penned along the side of the house.

We chatted in Hazel's kitchen. The room was part of an old barn, and flies still hovered by the dozen. 'I hate them more than anything,' said Hazel. She was in her forties, attractive, strong, blonde-haired. I looked around the room. There were strips of flypaper with dozens of dead flies stuck to them, and one of those neon zappers you see in restaurants, but still flies landed on our cups and plates. Grief is like that: it will not leave you alone.

Hazel made tea. She told me she had wanted her son to come back to work on the farm, just like her and his father Phillip. She had been keen to be interviewed by us about Richard's life, partly because it would help others to remember him; partly because music had been so much a feature of it.

She took me around the farm.

Here it was that she had seen the two men in uniform get out of a car.

'I thought they had come to see our holiday cottages, and then suddenly it hit me. I started screaming and felt winded, like I'd fallen off a horse. Everything drains into your feet. I was yelling: "Don't you dare tell me my son's dead! Don't you DARE!" They told me he was seriously injured and I kept telling them he shouldn't even have been driving.'

We recorded the interview. She gave us a list of Richard's favourite songs and talked about each one. 'Sex On Fire' by the Kings of Leon was a choice that stood out – Richard's band used to play it. They got back together to play it again in a local pub after his death was announced. Richard's place on the drums was taken by his music teacher. 'The atmosphere when they played that song was incredible, electrifying,' said Hazel.

She showed me his drumkit. It stood, perhaps a little too neatly arranged, in a bright attic space that Phillip and Hazel had built as a way of persuading him to choose life on the farm. The room was vast, the size of a tennis court. What an amazing place for a young man to live. But he would never see it.

Hazel and I sat down to talk in that room with a view over the undulating terrain of South Wales, the valleys and the hills, along with Radio 2 producer Jill Misson. Jill produced the series with John Hemingway – her husband Steve is a Major in the Royal Signals, and she did all the research and preparation for the five interviews.

Even arriving at the farm I had felt such a sense of privilege, coming to hear the story of Richard's life direct from his mother. But the visit to his attic room – the apartment they completed in the knowledge that he would never return to live there – was almost overpowering.

In the middle of the space, the full-size snooker table he was determined to have.

At one end, a large spiral staircase fashioned by his dad from huge hunks of timber.

The drumkit. Dozens of photos showing the same young, intense, happy face.

Another big song for Richard was 'I Gotta Feeling' by the Black Eyed Peas. An upbeat track, perfect for a party. 'Richard had mentioned to his friends that he would like it played at his funeral,' Hazel told us. 'The family wondered if it was too much of a lively party song, then we realized it showed what he was really like.' When it started playing at his funeral service, she told me, 'the older people didn't know quite what to make of it at first, but then the younger ones started dancing.'

Now his mum and dad seem to hear it on the radio all the time. Often, Phillip told me, it would be while they're discussing some aspect of Richard's life. The song comes on and he says to Hazel, 'Ah, Richard is listening.'

So we sat in Richard's room, Hazel and I, and talked and talked and talked. She had been a nurse. When she and Richard's sisters got to Selly Oak they could see there was no hope of her son recovering.

'He had stopped breathing for himself, so we were told it was just a question of time. I went to pieces, but I was glad to have the younger bunch there with us all round his bed. It made me feel helpless, as a nurse, and as a mother. One of the nicest things the doctor said, which meant such a lot to me, was: "Not for one minute since it happened has he ever been left alone."'

Then Hazel said something which will stay with me as long as I live.

Seeing her son's situation was hopeless, but knowing he would fight and fight because that is the kind of person Richard was, Hazel told me that she quietly leant forwards and whispered into his ear:

'This is one battle you're not going to win, so you're going to have to give this one up, sweetheart.'

Richard Hunt died one hour later.

'It is the hardest thing for a mother to lose a son,' said Hazel. 'We were so lucky to get him home and to be able to hold his hand before he died, not just see a coffin coming off a plane. When he passed away, the last few minutes were so peaceful. The weather had been awful and then suddenly the sun came out.'

At this point Jill spoke gently to us from the other side of the room. 'Shall we take a break from recording for a moment? Because you're both crying now.'

*

There were five mums in total in our series: Margaret's son was Mark Evison. Cheryl's was Liam Riley. Carol's was John Jones. Helena was the mother of Cyrus Thatcher and then there was Richard's mum, Hazel. Each story was different; each loss had broken their mother's heart, and yet we spoke upliftingly about how they had lived their lives and what they loved, their music especially. What came out was the power and optimism of youth – and for all five an absolute dedication to serving their country in the army.

A quarter of a century after joining the BBC, I guess I should be cynical by now. I should hate its systems and loathe its managers. I should take every possible shortcut and show up late to work. I should record interviews with an eye to the clock and want everything done and dusted as fast as possible. I should be spending sixty per cent of my time on office politics and begrudge the other forty. I should call it, as so many do, 'just another job'. But my documentary with the mothers of the soldiers – which, by the way, I only thought of and commenced recording after beginning to write this book – brought me up short and made me think all over again about what I do for a living, and how incredibly lucky I am to do it. That, surely, is a Rule: *If you can't see how fortunate you are, it's time to stop.*

I played the soldiers' music incessantly. At home, on my iPhone, in the car. Sitting in a coffee bar in the mornings at Radio 2. One particular song I played again and again: 'Turn Back The Hands Of Time' by R. Kelly had been chosen by Helena Tym, the mother of Cyrus Thatcher. Cyrus was only nineteen when he was killed by an explosion while on patrol.

I met Helena and her husband Rob at their home in Caversham. After news of Cyrus's death had come out, his friends all gathered in the garden – he had a lot of friends. His brothers Zac and Steely were there too. They put his iPod on shuffle. When the R. Kelly song was played, Helena told me, 'Everyone just froze.' If you get a chance to hear the song, I think you will understand why.

One day my daughter Martha objected to my umpteenth play of it in the car, and asked me – from her booster seat in the back – to turn the CD off.

'Sorry, darling,' I said, 'but I have to play it because it was a song that Cyrus Thatcher listened to. He was a soldier who lost his life and I'm doing a programme about him, and I have been talking to his mum about it—'

I couldn't even go on. As I say, it was overpowering.

It made me look at everything I have written in this book. Nothing I have ever done in my career meant as much to me as the conversations I had with those mothers. They were brave enough to give us that precious thing, without which there is no journalism: access. They allowed us not only into their homes, but also into their lives. Above all, they trusted us to tell the stories of their sons truthfully. I hope we did.

Cyrus Thatcher had left a letter for his parents in case of his death. Described lovingly by them as 'somewhat disorganized', he had told a friend the letter was above a kitchen cabinet. His dad, a builder, 'took the kitchen to bits to find it', his mum told me. But the letter was not there.

Later his brother Steely came across it in a small box in his bedroom. It is heart-rending to read the thoughts of a young man from beyond the grave, written in parts like an extended text message:

Hello its me, this is gonna be hard for you to read but I write this knowing every time you thinks shits got to much for you to handle (so don't cry on it MUM!!) you can read this and hopefully it will help you all get through.

For a start SHIT I got hit!! Now Iv got that out the way I can say the things Iv hopefully made clear, or if I havent this should clear it all up for me. My hole life you'v all been there for me through thick and thin bit like a wedding through good and bad. Without you I believe I wouldn't have made it as far as I have. I died doing what I was born to do I was happy and felt great about myself although the army was sadly the ending of me it was also the making of me so please don't feel any hate toward it. One thing I no I never made clear to you all was I make jokes about my life starting in the Army. That's wrong VERY wrong my life began a LONG time before that (Obviously) but you get what I mean. All the times Iv tried to neglect the family get angry when you try teach me right from wrong wot I mean to say is I only realised that you were trying to help when I joined the army and without YOUR help I would have never had the BALLS, the GRIT and the damn right determination to crack on and do it. If I could have a wish in life it would to be able to say Iv gone and done things many would never try to do. And going to Afghan has fulfilled my dream ie my goal. Yes I am young wich as a parent must brake you heart but you must all somehow find the strength that I found to do something no matter how big the challenge. As Im writing this letter I can see you all crying and mornin my death but if I could have one wish in an 'after life' it would be to stop your crying and continueing your dreams (as I did) because if I were watching only that would brake my heart. So dry your tears and put on a brave face for the rest of your friends and family who need you.

I want each and everyone of you to forfill a dream and at the end of it look at what you have done (completed) and feel the accomplishment and achievement I did only then will you understand how I felt when I passed away.

[To his brothers:] You are both amazing men and will continue to be throughout your lives you both deserve to be happy and fofill all of your dreams.

Dad – my idol, my friend, my best friend, my teacher, my coach, everything I ever succeeded in my life I owe to you and maybe a little bit of me! You are a great man and the perfect role model and the past two years of being in the army I noticed that and me and you have been on the best level we have ever been. I thank you for nothing because I no all you have given to me is not there to be thanked for its there because you did it cause you love me and that is my most proudest thing I could ever say.

Mum, where do I start with you!! For a start your perfect, your smell, your hugs, the way your life was dedicated to us boys and especially the way you cared each and every step us boys took. I love you, you were the reason I n ade it as far as I did you were the reason I was loved more than any child I no and that made me feel special.

Your all such great individuals and I hope somehow this letter will help you get through this shit time!! Just remember do NOT mourn my death as hard as this will seem, celebrate a great life that has had its ups and downs. I love you all more than you would ever no and in your own individual ways helped me get through it all. I wish you all the best with your dreams.

Remember chin up head down. With love Cyrus xxxx

I included the entire letter for you – with Helena's permission – because I couldn't bear to take even a syllable out. Every single sentence is freighted with meaning. Where does the power come from? It is powerful because it is real. Just like the funeral address from Paulina, the maid in South Africa. What she wrote was more powerful than anything I had ever written. The same goes for Cyrus.

I began the book by saying that no matter how important a journalist may think he or she is, they are not very important. The trouble is, most of us do not realize that. Sometimes you do a story and it brings it home. You understand, maybe for the first time, that you do not matter at all.

As I type this the final edits are being made on our documentary. I hope it gives some sense of who the soldiers were and what they lived for. And some sense too of the love their mums had for them. That is all it needs to do. But it taught me a lesson as well, one I think I may need to keep relearning. Fundamentally, journalism is serious. It really is about life and death sometimes. The journalist may not be important, but the story is.

*

During my visit to the home of Cyrus Thatcher I thought I would take advantage of his dad's building skills and asked him for a DIY tip. I had been trying to drill into brickwork outside my house so I could bolt a bracket to it. The bracket would be a place to padlock my bike, as my last one was stolen.

But I didn't know what drill bit to use. I had a selection at home, yet I struggled to describe them. So rather than endure a long conversation with a DIY novice, Rob went out to his van.

'Take this, Jeremy,' he said when he came back. It was a thick steel drill bit for masonry, marked with a splash of red paint on the tip. 'You can keep it.'

I resisted, Rob insisted, and in the end I took the drill bit on one condition: when I used it I would remember his son.

Back at home, it did the job perfectly. My drill went into the masonry like a hot knife into butter. The bracket was firmly bolted into place and now I padlock my bike to it.

The drill bit is not in my toolbox. I keep it on the desk in my study, the red flash at the tip reminding me of my day with Helena and Rob and Zac. And every time I see it I think of the fallen soldier they will never stop mourning: young, strong, smiling Cyrus, who was determined to get the job done.

Chapter Twenty-Four

GOOD LUCK, AND DON'T DROP THE GUN

The idea was this. Nick Clegg, leader of the Liberal Democrats, was the new kid in town. This year he would lead his party into his first set of elections after taking over from the elderly politician known as 'Ming' Campbell. What better analogy than the Wild West saloon, with Clegg swinging into town on his horse and rapidly drawing his gun to impress the locals?

The election graphics – usually termed 'the swingometer', a catch-all term for the entire box of tricks – are a key part of our news heritage. The great Bob McKenzie (Canadian; thick specs) used a wooden arrow with a nail on it and we watched, if we were born then and interested, in black and white. I thought I heard squeaking as the arrow moved.

The graphics were rested for a while. Perhaps the wooden arrow was given a ceremonial burial. Then they returned in high-tech form with Peter Snow in 1992. In 1997 came the defining suite of graphics on the dramatic night Tony Blair swept to power. The so-called 'kaboom' graphic, showing Conservative seats as skyscrapers being blasted by missiles; here's John Major 'buried by a landslide', there's poor Major 'in a hole', and so on. Wow. The impact of Peter Snow's pictorialization of the politics that night in 1997 was stupendous.

The intense, wild and brilliant Snowie left the operation after the 2005 election. I did the 2006 and 2007 local council and Scottish elections but it became clear we had an issue that was fundamental. In the nineties, it was enough to say the BBC had a computer: 'Look everyone, I'm standing in front of a graph and it's not really there! And now I've walked behind it! Take a look at John Major and whoops, there he goes, buried in a landslide!'

But now *everyone* had a computer. And, crucially, they had better graphics than we did – the virtual space on *Grand Theft Auto III*, for example, cost £30m to produce and I have just seen a copy on Amazon for £3. We had the £3 but not the £30m. It had become harder and harder to wow people with the simple fact that we knew what a gigabyte was.

Thus the newly assembled graphics team had a choice. Either use the computers to put numbers on the wall, make the process entirely functional – or create graphics that were more and more outlandish, madder and madder, to catch the attention of the viewer. Think newspaper cartoon. Think *Tron* or *Toy Story*. Think as wild as you like: think Wild West.

So there we were in 2008, planning the council election coverage, discussing the idea of having Clegg in a cowboy outfit.

Would this work? The virtual politician could wheel round suddenly, pull out his pistol and fire at tin cans on a shelf. Each tin can – here we start to get into territory that was probably too complicated – would represent a previous year in which the Lib Dems had fought elections. If he did badly on the night, we could have him drop his gun on the floor with a clunk.

Where would I come in? Could I commentate? No, we had a better idea. I would enter the saloon too. I would be given a gun and the gun would have a clicker in it, and that would fire the graphic. Every time I shot the gun, it would trigger a bang, a ricochet noise, and the sound of the bullet hitting the can. The can would fly into the air and freeze, and I would explain that this represented how well the Lib Dems had done in a previous election and would give us comparisons with tonight's figures when they eventually came in (notice how I said the last bit in a serious voice).

In the huge studio we use, everything is painted green. The presenter is the only one who sees nothing; the graphics are generated by computer. The computer recognizes our particular shade of green emulsion and swaps every bit of green with graphic. The viewers at home see presenter-plus-graphic. I don't.

We all agreed the sequence was brilliant but was missing something. How could I be the BBC guy, turning up in a saloon with Cowboy Clegg, and then, while I commentate earnestly, pull a gun and fire at the tin cans? No, it needed something more dramatic. It needed a cowboy outfit for me.

I remembered the Stetson bought while filming the George Bush profile in Texas and was sure I could dig it out from a trunk at home. The floor manager secured a whole boxful of extra kit – the leather chaps, a holster for the gun, cravat, bullet belt and one of those tasselled waistcoats.

'I will try this, and I'll go for it,' I said in rehearsal. The hat, the accent, everything.

And I did.

The election editor was Craig Oliver and his assistant was Simon Enright.

The next day Simon called me. 'We think it was all great, but you just need to do it without the hat.'

'What about the accent?'

'Without the hat and the accent.'

'Fine,' I said, thought no more of it, and continued eating my porridge.

The next day we rehearsed again. Clegg pops up in his cowboy outfit, I explain the meaning of the tin cans and draw the gun. Trigger, bang, ricochet, tin cans flying around.

David Dimbleby comes on the line. 'Hey, wait – what happened to the hat?'

'It has been ruled out,' I say.

Thence begins a huge discussion between me, the producers, Dimbleby, the director, and even the camera operators in my studio. Didn't the graphic work better with the hat? How can you do a graphic like this at half-power?

I think the spirit of my brother entered my soul during that moment, because I felt the sudden desire to play it for drama – given that this would go out once, at midnight, before any results came in, and it was no more crazy than half of the wonderful stuff they put out on the daily political shows during the week which seem to meld the wacky and the serious with unerring skill.

A classic BBC compromise was reached. It makes me roar with laughter, looking back: I would, Craig decided, enter the saloon with the hat on, but *not the rest of the cowboy outfit.* The leggings would be going too far. As for the American accent, that could stay, but only at midnight. When the graphic returned in the early hours and real results were inputted, I could keep the hat on but I should not use the Texan accent.

Bear in mind the guy who decided all this is now Communications Director at Number Ten. So if you ever see the Prime Minister stroll through that door wearing a Stetson, you know where the idea came from.

The night came.

We began with our other graphics – some were just bar charts and histograms; others displayed the madcap qualities I described us tilting towards. A comment that the prime minister Gordon Brown had gone from 'Stalin to Mr Bean' in six months, originally made by Vince Cable MP, was turned into a whole sequence. Boris Johnson, running for Mayor of London, showed up as Lord Snooty out of the *Beano* and got into a fight with the Bash Street Kids led by Ken Livingstone. And then David Dimbleby threw to me for the Lib Dem graphic.

I remember pulling the rim of the Stetson down just a touch, thinking that if it all went wrong at least there was a chance I would not be recognized. A voice in my ear said: *Good luck, and don't drop the gun.*

Plinky-plonk saloon bar piano starts.

My opening line, delivering in a Texan drawl, was:

'Hey! Dimble!'

I went through the steps. I span the gun on my finger and didn't drop it. The director, Claire Bellis, made it look technically excellent, I must say. The camera wheeled behind the virtual tin cans so, when I fired them off the shelf, I was firing my gun at the viewer. Oh, that's a Rule too:

Never fire a gun into the face of the audience.

At last it ended, my hopeless American accent showing the strain. Clegg dropped his gun. Clunk. In the studio with Dimbleby sat Charles Kennedy, George Osborne and Tessa Jowell. There was a moment for tumbleweed to blow through. Then the future Chancellor of the Exchequer laughed. The former Lib Dem leader winced. Jowell had the look of someone who had just retrieved an item from her fridge that should have been disposed of four months earlier.

It is really not an exaggeration to say that the cowboy graphic was the worst graphic in the history of BBC News. In fact a boss told me so, in a very friendly way, a few days later: 'It was the worst graphic in the history of BBC News.' I looked like a complete and utter muppet. One friendly radio producer, who loves his politics, said he had been drifting off on the sofa at around midnight, then woke suddenly to see a cowboy shooting at Nick Clegg and did that thing you always see in movies: picked up the bottle of wine he had been drinking and looked at the label.

What we hadn't factored in, partly because I am far less digital than I ought to be, was the incredible power of the blogging and tweeting fraternity, even back then in 2008. We had invited three bloggers into the studio – believing that their contacts gave them unnatural powers of perception – and of course they just blogged about the graphics. *What the hell is Vine doing in a cowboy hat explaining the performance of the Lib Dems?* was, when you think about it, quite a tricky question for the news chiefs to get to grips with the following morning.

Many pages back, I think I mentioned that great piece of Sargie wisdom: 'The only thing They will never forgive is misplaced humour.' If the Wild West debacle proved one thing, it was that forgetting advice from Mr Sergeant can be very dangerous indeed.

*

Sometimes in broadcasting you are going to end up looking like a chump. It helps if the chump moment occurs as the result of an accident, rather than deliberately. Deliberately really hurts. But there we go. As Esther used to say, that's life.

We could offer one powerful defence of the Cowboy from a previous chapter: it was *not vanilla*. But I had a total sense of humour failure over it, and only got the whole thing into perspective when I saw a piece in the *Evening Standard* a few days later. Their diary reporter had rung the BBC press office and asked, 'Has anyone been fired over the Vine graphics?'

'Er – no,' said the press officer.

'Well, has anyone been shot?'

A lot of things are deadly serious at the time and then they become funny. Whole careers can be like that. But stuff goes wrong. It always will, it always does. Sometimes, looking back at these last twenty-five years, I just see long periods of professional output punctuated by inexplicable disasters. Then I realize that is the journalist in me. Minor disasters – non-fatal errors, I prefer to call them – are consistent with the rest; in fact they are a vital part of it.

The principle was introduced to me when Justin Webb became the first of my contemporaries to get a job presenting. Fronting

Breakfast News, he too was amazed at the sheer volume of stuff that went wrong. As he introduced a panel of interviewees, he saw that one of the politicians was being given the following description in an on-screen caption:

Cllr. PETER JEFFRIES
EXTREME RIGHT

when 'extreme right' was just an instruction about where he should be seated. Profuse apologies followed.

In 1995 the news footage being played out during a headline sequence became jumbled. Watching in my bedroom at home, I saw that one story was the Queen Mother's ninety-fifth birthday; the next was the fiftieth anniversary of atom bombs being dropped on Japan. But the film started running ahead of the presenter. So the line, 'And today, the Queen Mother celebrates her birthday with a party like you've never seen before' went out over pictures of the mushroom cloud over Hiroshima.

Justin flew to South Africa the same year, to commentate on the Queen's visit to Cape Town. The monitors in his makeshift studio went blank just as the cameras zoomed in on the Royal Yacht *Britannia*.

'KEEP TALKING ABOUT THE YACHT,' the director shouted in Justin's ear, so he did.

'And there she is, nearly seven hundred royal visits, a million miles on the clock, and still no need of a refit.'

Unfortunately the line went out over a close-up of the Queen.

In a modest way, a way that is both small and beautiful, the same principle crops up with my records on Radio 2. People often ask me who chooses the music. The answer is a piece of software that is pro-grammed by a music wizard called Michael Banbrook, whom I meet for coffee once every couple of months. I declare that I love Nerina Pallot, or Lissie, or the new one by Coldplay or the old one by Peter Gabriel, or 'I'm in a Led Zeppelin phase' ... and Michael does his thing and the record list appears on the day, melded with Radio 2 playlist choices. There are not many Wurlitzers or zithers, and I never have to play a disc I don't like. Under Jim Moir, Radio 2 seemed to work out that there are five hundred records everybody loves, and we have been playing them ever since.

Getting the music to fit with the news is the problem. The famous Radio 1 example from decades ago, when 'Crawling From The Wreckage' was played after a plane crash, can be avoided with a glance at the song title. Or should be. But the computer has a genius for suggesting the one song we cannot play, and we may not even notice until it's too late.

If these examples come over as tasteless, forgive me. But there are no tasteful versions of these playlist calamities.

After a story on conspiracy theories about the death of the Princess of Wales, I hit the play button — on came 'Killer Queen'.

It gets worse. When news came of the tragic shooting of Jean Charles de Menezes, who had been mistaken for a terrorist in the police hunt after the London bombings, I played 'First Of The Gang To Die' by Morrissey because, once again, the computer had unerringly set me up with a hospital pass.

Other disasters have been avoided. An item on torture in Africa was very nearly followed by 'Ouch That Hurt', the Dionne Bromfield song, before someone spotted the problem with ten seconds to spare.

Ken Bruce, who does the show before mine, regularly mocks me for the problems caused by mixing news and music. Then one day I appeared on his programme to say what was going to be on mine (the chat we have every day at 11.30) and I talked about a non-fatal shark attack. His next record was 'I'm Mandy, Fly Me' by 10CC, which contained the words 'Oh, I saw her walking on the water/As the sharks were comin' for me', so I quietly told Ken as the record went out: 'For once, my friend, the joke is on you!'

I was wrong. We did the shark attack story on my show. We made every effort to screen out any inappropriate songs, but the computer's suggestion seemed fine. It was a love song by Damien Rice called 'Cannonball'.

Fine, that is, until we hear the opening line being played out on the air:

'There's still a little bit of your taste in my mouth ...'

And yes, people did complain, because they always do.

It stumped me for a while. How can the computer be choosing records so perfectly inappropriate that most human beings would not even be able to find them? The answer, I decided – and it is an answer born out by almost every event in this book – is that broadcasting has a tendency to go badly wrong. Badly, hilariously, wonderfully, awfully wrong. Brilliantly wrong.

When a magazine was launched in New York showing only photos of naked men, we took it as a cue to discuss why the male and female responses to pornography are so different. The guest we booked was the journalist Victoria Coren.

The moment of broadcast neared and the editor went into the green room to fetch Victoria. The woman he approached agreed that was her name.

'I'm Phil Jones from the programme,' he said. 'Have you seen the magazine?'

She said no.

'Well, you'll need to have a look.' He held it in front of her and leafed through some of the pages. 'When you're ready, Victoria, we'll tell you what we want you to do.'

The woman gazed at the assortment of male body parts being dangled in front of her, and started glancing around with a worried expression. Jones asked if there was anything wrong, and the answer came back – *it's the wrong Victoria*. This is not Victoria Coren. This is an expert on fruit-only diets who is due to appear on Steve Wright's programme.

So things do go terribly wrong. All the time. And that is the last Rule I shall trouble you with.

Yes, working for the BBC does give you fun. When I started this book I thought I would just be writing about the stuff that made me laugh out loud. Or silently. But looking back I see I have written about death and danger as well as the craziness. And more of it was serious than I thought it was going to be. Sometimes when it goes wrong it will take you a few days to get over it; sometimes, as in the case of colleagues I have mentioned on these pages, when it goes wrong it will take your life.

I think of three in particular: Kate Peyton, John Schofield, and Gareth Butler. I worked a lot with Gareth, whose knowledge of British politics was encyclopaedic. He died very suddenly from natural causes while walking down the street. Kate and John were both shot while on assignment. All four of us were born in the same year, 1965. Three great people. There is no reason whatsoever why I should still be here, and they are gone.

*

There is that line at the end of George Orwell's Nineteen Eighty-four, when, having emerged from imprisonment and torture, Winston Smith sits in the bright sunshine and realizes: *He loved Big Brother.* I feel that way about the BBC. After twenty-five years of accident and design, being paid to have adventures; of never being bored, which is the greatest thing; of the corporation's bracing combination of loyalty and faddishness ... yep, I really do love Big Brother. I know I am a fool to, so you don't have to tell me. The Beeb doesn't ever love you back. It just finds you the least worst choice for a while.

I only have one grievance. Time flies in this place. So although the calendars confirm it really was twenty-five years, it feels like three. Not many people would choose to see their life pass faster than an express train, but half of mine just did. South Africa was yesterday. Russia was last week. The woman with the gun in the reception of Broadcasting House was the week before. I can see the October Group of news trainees sitting round me now, even though John

Ryley (to name just one) has been running *Sky News* for several years.

Well, that's it. Thanks so much for reading. I would ask the Radio 2 computer to choose a record to play us out, but we know what will happen if I do.

ACKNOWLEDGEMENTS

I am very grateful to my senior colleagues Steve Mitchell and Bob Shennan for reading this book with their BBC hats on. It can't be fun when someone lands you with a 480-page manuscript on a bank holiday, and when they saw that Chapter One was (originally) called The Importance of Humiliation, they must have feared the worst. But instead of a lengthy denunciation of our mutual employer, I think they knew they were reading a rather personal appreciation, and I am very grateful for the advice they both gave and their positive reaction.

My friend and agent Alex Armitage and his right-hand person Louise, as well as Jane and Catrina and all at Noel Gay: thank you for all the support you have given me. There is no better lunch partner in the world than my agent, whose religious note-taking during some of the livelier incidents described here I have drawn on.

Parts of this book were read along the way by Richard Ayre, Guy Burch, Andrew McDonald and Margaret Schofield. I could not have done without their insightful comments on the various sections they looked over for me.

To publisher Colin Midson (who said yes after hearing my pitch), as well as Suzanne Baboneau, Carly Cook, Jo Whitford and Helen Mockridge, and all the stars at Simon & Schuster: thank you. Photographer Lucy Sewill, copy-editor Sally Partington: you too.

Brilliant BBC editors I have worked with are hard to narrow down, but there is one to whom I do want to give particular mention. Phil Jones at Radio 2, a radio genius, stops me getting myself sacked for two hours every weekday and he's a true friend.

In lots of places where I have quoted and written about people, I've asked their permission to include them. I want to thank Milton Nkosi and Paulina Mabogale in this regard especially.

Above all this is for my family, Martha, Anna and Rachel; my brother Tim and sister Sonya, and Mum and Dad.

But my wife especially, with love always.